Praise for *Film Noir*

"William Luhr is the intrepid sleuth of cin *noir* under all the aliases – classic *noir*, pre-*noir*, neo-*noir* – that its infinite variety has produced. Writing with energy, clarity, and verve, Luhr explodes narrow conceptions of *noir* as conclusively as the Great Whatsit blew up postwar innocence in *Kiss Me Deadly*. Carry a copy of this timely, spirited book in your trenchcoat. It is a boon for film scholars, general readers, and movie buffs alike."

David Sterritt, Chairman, National Society of Film Critics

"Informed by a rich body of previous scholarship, conceptually sophisticated, yet written with grace and clarity, *Film Noir* by William Luhr provides an ideal introduction for students and fans to the dark corner of American culture represented by these gloriously perverse crime films."

Jerry W. Carlson, PhD, The City College & Graduate Center, CUNY

"William Luhr, who knows all the many questions raised by *film noir*, supplies lucid, elegant, provocative answers. His knowledge is deep, his comments far-ranging. This is an essential addition to the vast literature on the genre."

Charles Affron, New York University

"Writing with broad expertise and deep sensibility, Professor Luhr heightens our nostalgic delight in *noir* films while also pointing to the lost spectatorial experience of *film noir's* once present tenseness."

Chris Straayer, New York University Department of Cinema Studies

NEW APPROACHES TO FILM GENRE

Series Editor: Barry Keith Grant

New Approaches to Film Genre provides students and teachers with original, insightful, and entertaining overviews of major film genres. Each book in the series gives an historical appreciation of its topic, from its origins to the present day, and identifies and discusses the important films, directors, trends, and cycles. Authors articulate their own critical perspective, placing the genre's development in relevant social, historical, and cultural contexts. For students, scholars, and film buffs alike, these represent the most concise and illuminating texts on the study of film genre.

From Shane *to* Kill Bill*: Rethinking the Western*, Patrick McGee
The Horror Film, Rick Worland
Hollywood and History, Robert Burgoyne
The Religious Film, Pamela Grace
The Hollywood War Film, Robert Eberwein
The Fantasy Film, Katherine A. Fowkes
The Multi-Protagonist Film, María del Mar Azcona
The Hollywood Romantic Comedy, Leger Grindon
Film Noir, William Luhr

Forthcoming:
The Hollywood Film Musical, Barry Keith Grant

FILM NOIR

William Luhr

WILEY-BLACKWELL

A John Wiley & Sons, Ltd., Publication

Blackwell Publishing was acquired by John Wiley & Sons in February 2007.
Blackwell's publishing program has been merged with Wiley's global Scientific,
Technical, and Medical business to form Wiley-Blackwell.

Registered Office
John Wiley & Sons Ltd, The Atrium, Southern Gate, Chichester, West Sussex,
PO19 8SQ, UK

Editorial Offices
350 Main Street, Malden, MA 02148-5020, USA
9600 Garsington Road, Oxford, OX4 2DQ, UK
The Atrium, Southern Gate, Chichester, West Sussex, PO19 8SQ, UK

For details of our global editorial offices, for customer services, and for information
about how to apply for permission to reuse the copyright material in this book please
see our website at www.wiley.com/wiley-blackwell.

The right of William Luhr to be identified as the author of this work has been asserted
in accordance with the UK Copyright, Designs and Patents Act 1988.

Wiley also publishes its books in a variety of electronic formats. Some content that
appears in print may not be available in electronic books.

Designations used by companies to distinguish their products are often claimed as
trademarks. All brand names and product names used in this book are trade names,
service marks, trademarks or registered trademarks of their respective owners.
The publisher is not associated with any product or vendor mentioned in this book.
This publication is designed to provide accurate and authoritative information in regard to
the subject matter covered. It is sold on the understanding that the publisher is not
engaged in rendering professional services. If professional advice or other expert
assistance is required, the services of a competent professional should be sought.

Library of Congress Cataloging-in-Publication Data

Luhr, William.
Film noir / William Luhr.
    p. cm. – (New approaches to film genre)
    Includes bibliographical references and index.
    ISBN 978-1-4051-4594-7 (hardback : alk. paper) – ISBN 978-1-4051-4595-4
    (pbk. : alk. paper) 1. Film noir–United States–History and criticism.   I. Title.
    PN1995.9.F54L84 2012
    791.43'6556–dc23   2011041410

A catalogue record for this book is available from the British Library.

This book is published in the following electronic formats: ePDFs 9781444355925;
Wiley Online Library 9781444355956; ePub 9781444355932; Kindle 9781444355949

Set in 11/13pt, Bembo by Thomson Digital, Noida, India
Printed in Malaysia by Ho Printing (M) Sdn Bhd

1   2012

For Peter Lehman,
Who knows the darkness,
But has kept the music playing

CONTENTS

LIST OF PLATES

ACKNOWLEDGMENTS

First, thanks go to my colleagues at Wiley-Blackwell. Series Editor Barry Keith Grant has been a patient and helpful editor as well as a good friend. Jayne Fargnoli has been enthusiastically supportive on this and other projects and has my gratitude and admiration. I have received extensive editorial assistance with the manuscript from Mrs Barbara Kuzminski, and indispensable help with photographic and technical matters from David Luhr. Paula Gabbard has guided me in issues of arts permissions and design. Francis M. Nevins has an encyclopedic knowledge of *film noir* and has been frequently generous.

Thanks to the New York University Faculty Resource Network and its Director, Debra Szybinski, along with Chris Straayer and Robert Sklar of the Department of Cinema Studies, who have been valuable in providing research help and facilities, as have Charles Silver and the staff of the Film Study Center of the Museum of Modern Art. Generous assistance has also come from the members of the Columbia University Seminar on Cinema and Interdisciplinary Interpretation, particularly my co-chair, Krin Gabbard, who has gone out of his way to be personally supportive and intellectually generous for years and under difficult circumstances. He is a truly remarkable friend for whom I am deeply grateful. Christopher Sharrett's knowledgeable conversations about film history and friendship are gratifying. Other generous colleagues in the Seminar include David Sterritt and Pamela

Grace. Thanks also to Robert L. Belknap and Robert Pollack, Directors of the University Seminars, and the Seminar Office's essential staff, particularly Alice Newton. I express particular appreciation to the University Seminars at Columbia University for their help in publication. The ideas presented in this book have benefited from discussions in the University Seminar on Cinema and Interdisciplinary Interpretation. At Saint Peter's College, gratitude goes to the President, Eugene Cornacchia; Vice President, Marylou Yam; Academic Dean, Velda Goldberg; Mary DiNardo; Bill Knapp and the staff of Information Technologies; Frederick Bonato, David Surrey, and the members of the Committee for the Professional Development of the Faculty; Lisa O'Neill, Director of the Honors Program; Jon Boshart, Chair of the Fine Arts Department; John M. Walsh; Thomas Kenny; and Oscar Magnan, SJ, and Leonor I. Lega for generous support, technical assistance, and research help. My ability to do this work owes a great deal to the great talents and kindness of Keith Ditkowski, Robert Glaser, and Joseph Mannion. As always, I am deeply indebted to my Father as well as to Helen and Grace; Walter and Richie; Bob, Carole, Jim, Randy, Judy, and David.

CHAPTER 1

INTRODUCTION

The ominous silhouette of a man on crutches approaching the camera that appears under the opening credits of *Double Indemnity* (1944) provides a prototypical image for *film noir* (Plate 1). Something is wrong – with the man's legs, with the man, with what will follow these credits – and the grim orchestral music accompanying the image reinforces this impression. The silhouette applies not to a single character but to three men in the film: one a murderer, one his victim, and the third an innocent man set up to take the blame for the crime. All three are drawn into this ugly vortex by the same seductive woman who exploits them and orchestrates their doom. The dark silhouette also menaces the viewer's space – it comes at us, it somehow involves us in whatever is to happen, and whatever it is won't be nice. Something is wrong.

This image appeared at the dawn of *film noir*, before the term was even coined. *Double Indemnity* establishes one, but only one, paradigm for the genre. It concerns an adulterous couple who murder the woman's husband for insurance money; in doing so, they generate their own doom. Everybody loses. The story is told mostly in flashback by the guilty man at a point just after he killed his lover and was, himself, shot by her (Plate 2). This retrospective storytelling strategy, heavily reliant on voice-over narration, was innovative at this time and shapes the viewer's response to the film's events in three significant ways. First, it presents

Film Noir, First Edition. William Luhr.
© 2012 William Luhr. Published 2012 by Blackwell Publishing Ltd.

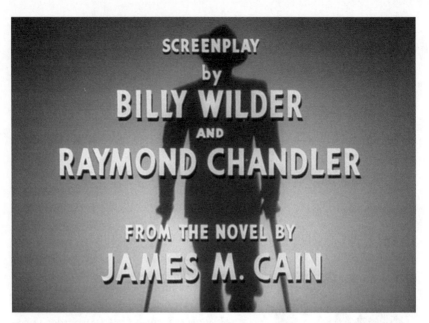

PLATE 1 *Double Indemnity* – credits: Silhouette of a man on crutches approaching the viewer. © 1944 Paramount Pictures, INC.

PLATE 2 *Double Indemnity*: Walter Neff (Fred MacMurray) speaking into a dictaphone. © 1944 Paramount Pictures, INC.

the story not from an "objective" perspective but rather from its narrator's perspective, drawing us into his anxieties, moral failures, and feelings of entrapment. It makes our main point of identification not someone who conformed to contemporary Hollywood moral codes but rather someone who violated them. This eliminated traditional viewer security in presumptively identifying with the main characters. Even if such characters in traditional movies were doomed – as when, for example, *A Tale of Two Cities* (1935) ended with Sydney Carton going to the guillotine – those movies presented that doom as heroic and uplifting. But the doom of many characters in *film noir* is neither noble nor uplifting, and viewer empathy with such characters can be destabilizing.

This leads to disorienting situations such as one in *Double Indemnity* when the couple, having just murdered the woman's husband, prepare to flee the crime scene in her car. She turns the key but the car will not start. The two look tensely at one another since this simple, unexpected problem could lead to imminent discovery. She tries again and fails again, increasing the tension between them, as well as in the viewer. The scene is shot and edited in such a way as to draw us into their anxiety, to encourage us to want the car to start. Consequently, after having just witnessed the couple murder the woman's husband and then drag his body onto railway tracks to be mangled, we are suddenly maneuvered into fearing that these cold-blooded murderers might not succeed with their grisly crime. The investment of much *film noir* in an individual rather than "objective" point of view shifts the viewer away from the position of moral security that earlier Hollywood films tended to offer and disconcertingly toward sympathy for the devil.

A second effect of the retrospective narration is to undermine suspense concerning the story's outcome. As the film progresses, we watch not to see what will happen but rather to see what has already happened. We know from the outset that the couple's scheme (which comprises most of the film's storyline) is doomed because the guilty narrator reveals that it has already failed. However high the couple's hopes rise during the flashback story, we know all along that those hopes are fruitless (Plate 3). Traditional crime/mystery films had centered upon the solver of the crime, the one who acts to rectify the wrong done to society; they had not centered upon the person who committed that wrong. Such films generally moved their narrative in a forward direction, starting with the crime or its discovery and progressing to the detective's solution of the case, with the viewer uncertain as to the outcome until the conclusion; this film, to the contrary, moves us backwards, over what has already happened. This strategy does not seek to engage us either with the puzzle of figuring out "whodunit" (as with traditional murder mysteries) or with wondering whether or not

PLATE 3 *Double Indemnity*: Phyllis Dietrichson (Barbara Stanwyck) enticing Walter into murder. © 1944 Paramount Pictures, INC.

the criminal will succeed (as with "caper" films); we already know the answers to those questions. Instead, the film entices us into voyeuristically dwelling upon the ugly specifics of the way in which these two people ruin their lives and those of others. We are watching what has already gone wrong.

A useful analogue to the viewer's position in such films is that of a reader of a tabloid newspaper. A cliché about "whodunit" mysteries is that the ending should not be revealed lest the reader lose all interest in the story. After all, why read on if you know the outcome? *Double Indemnity* and much of *film noir* operate on different premises. In a tabloid the headline and the opening sentence serve to grab the reader's attention but, at the same time, eliminate suspense. "Man Murders Lover and Her Husband, Confesses and Loses All!" And yet tabloid readers avidly read on, not to see how the story turns out, which they already know, but rather to voyeuristically learn more about the sordid details of the case.

A third effect of the narrational strategy is to infuse the narrator's dark mood into all that we see. He is in physical and psychological pain, grimly aware that he is probably dying and certainly ruined because of the failed activities he describes, and we are largely confined within his point of view. His voice-over narration runs throughout the film and becomes particularly disturbing during scenes that depict his younger self preparing for and committing his crimes. His somber, present-tense, narrating self provides a stark contrast to his earlier, optimistic self, and that contrast destabilizes everything we see and hear. Further darkening his perspective is the fact that he is confessing his crimes to his mentor and boss, a friend he respects and has betrayed. He exists in an almost post-mortem zone, without hope or a viable future.

This narrative strategy underscores the centrality of point of view structures to *film noir*. Film after film concentrates upon the doomed plight of an individual as presented from that individual's perspective, so we get not *the* story but, rather, that person's perception of the story. This shift away from presumptions of pure objectivity was not unique to *film noir*; it was widespread and part of the cultural ferment of the times. It appears in presumptively factually based biographical films like *Yankee Doodle Dandy* (1942), which presents George M. Cohan's life primarily through his retrospective description of it, and even documentaries. Frank Capra's seven *Why We Fight* films (1942–5), for example, while constructed primarily of documentary-style footage, made no attempt to conceal their propagandistic agendas. Although they present their images as having the status of "reality," those images are clearly organized to support the films' points of view. The increase in flashback sequences in Hollywood films of this time underscores the growing interest in exploring individual points of view. A wartime drama like *Passage to Marseilles* (1944) is famous for having flashbacks within flashbacks, something virtually unthinkable in Hollywood film a decade earlier. Furthermore, this shift away from presumptions of objectivity appears in many modernist art forms, from fiction and poetry to painting and sculpture, and modernism provided the dominant cultural context for *film noir*.

Much of *film noir* invites us to experience its stories from the inside out. Many films underscore their narrator's subjectivity with the soundtrack presence of that person's voice interwoven with scenes dramatizing events in that story; the subjectivity is further underscored by Expressionistic visuals evoking the narrator's nightmares, feelings of entrapment, and hallucinations. This focus upon interiority, particularly upon that of doomed people struggling to contain their own escalating panic, often foregrounds distortions of perception as well as states of paralyzing despair. This accounts for the preponderance of nightmares and of hallucinations in *film noir* and for the particular value that Freudian theory had not only in the conceptualizing of many of the films but also for the ongoing study of the genre.

In the *Double Indemnity* credits, the silhouette ominously approaching the camera resembles something from a nightmare. Its relentless movement toward the camera suggests that it will overwhelm us; it will draw us into it or itself into us. This is immediately followed by the appearance of the main character, who begins his confessional narrative. As one of the three men symbolized by the silhouette, he is bringing us into his darkness.

Much of the appeal of *film noir* involves its masochistic erotics of doom, its ability to draw viewers into nightmare-like, paranoid narratives of degeneration and failure. Where many genres, such as the Western, romantic comedy, or coming-of-age films, explore the prospect of a successful future for sympathetic characters, *film noir* tends to present flawed characters without a future and show how their past went wrong. It bucks the cliché that Hollywood films must end happily; *film noir* cued its audiences in multiple ways to expect these films to end badly, very badly.

Film noir's allure resembles that of tragedy or the horror film, forms which invite their audiences to watch worst-case scenarios unfold. For their initial audiences, *films noirs* resembled nightmares in contemporary life. They were set in and about "today." Although they evoked the audience's deepest fears about all going wrong, they did not engage the supernatural as did horror films. *Film noir* invoked dark forces, from within individuals or from criminal conspiracies or social injustices, but rooted those forces in the everyday contemporary world of domestic or business antagonisms, psychic disturbances, criminal schemes, and political machinations. Within the growing hysteria of many characters, such forces often assumed mythic dimensions, and those fears infused the films with an atmosphere of unseen but malevolent presences. This environment of doom, evil, and failure paralleled the troubled subjectivity of many of the films. It generated the sense that the characters' deepest fears were becoming palpable. Even *films noirs* without a retrospective narrational structure, like *Scarlet Street* (1945) or *The Big Sleep* (1946), often establish an atmosphere of generic doom. Many of the movies, like *Mildred Pierce* (1945) or *Crossfire* (1947), resemble traditional mysteries in that they begin abruptly with an unexplained murder which the viewer can only partially see. The remainders of the films involve the unraveling of the mystery of who committed the crime. However, where the atmosphere of doom would dissolve in traditional mysteries (such as those featuring Sherlock Holmes, Lord Peter Wimsey, or Hercule Poirot) when the crime was solved, in *film noir* it lingers on, suggesting a world pervaded with ongoing, ineradicable forces.

Although this book concludes with detailed analyses of six exemplary *films noirs*, it also uses *Double Indemnity* throughout as a reference point for multiple perspectives upon *film noir*. For example, it is one of many films dominated by the point of view of a doomed character. These characters exist on the penumbra between life and death; although most of them are alive, they have resigned themselves to imminent death. Following this logic to an extreme, *Sunset Boulevard* (1950), directed by Billy Wilder six years after he directed *Double Indemnity*, is bizarrely narrated by a character who is already dead when the film begins (Plate 4). Although this strategy clearly violated realist conventions, the movie does not invoke any other fantastic, supernatural, or science fiction strategies. With this one glaring exception, it remains resolutely realist and the exception simply reinforces its grim, post-mortem tone.

Not far removed is *D.O.A.* (1950), which opens with its central character reporting a murder. Asked who was murdered, he replies, "I was" (Plate 5). He has been poisoned, has only hours to live, and spends the remainder of the movie desperately trying to discover how and why it all happened. He becomes a surrogate detective investigating his own murder, making this film one in which the detective and the victim are the same person. *The Postman Always Rings Twice* (1946) is narrated by a character about to be executed for murder. All of these characters have led morally compromised

PLATE 4 *Sunset Boulevard*: The film is narrated by the corpse of Joe Gillis (William Holden) as it floats face down in a swimming pool. © 1950 Paramount Pictures Corporation.

PLATE 5 *D.O.A.*: Frank Bigelow (Edmund O'Brien) opens the movie by reporting his own murder. © 1949 Cardinal Pictures, INC.

lives that end badly, and that end is inevitable from the outset. *Film noir* frequently focuses upon central characters who, by traditional criteria, would have been villains and, at its inception, it deviated from Hollywood norms of narration, content, character construction, tone, representation, cinematography, and moral accountability. Its very break with/inversion of conventional practice has been cited as one of its generic hallmarks.

Such deviations contributed to the aura of transgression that surrounded the films when they initially appeared and that continues to be associated with the genre. Some were based upon source material (such as James M. Cain's "hard-boiled" fiction *The Postman Always Rings Twice* and *Double Indemnity*) that studios had earlier considered too racy, depraved, or downbeat to adapt; many of the films violated generic conventions and challenged contemporary censorship codes; some prominent actors such as George Raft declined parts for fear of tarnishing their star images with unsavory roles; reviewers commented upon heightened levels of immorality and brutality. Audiences could expect to see morally compromised characters doing the wrong thing; the underbelly of contemporary life.

Contemporary critics frequently acknowledged the transgressive appeal of the films, the pleasure of the wrong. While many registered their distaste for the films' moral transgressions, they simultaneously acknowledged how entertaining they were. *Time* magazine's unsigned review of *Double Indemnity* describes it as "the season's nattiest, nastiest, most satisfying melodrama. James M. Cain's novelette was carnal and criminal well beyond screen convention. Director Billy Wilder's casting is just as unconventional. . . . Scripter Raymond Chandler . . . is himself no mean writer of hard-boiled melodrama. With his help Director Wilder and his players manage admirably to translate into hard-boiled cinema James Cain's hard-boiled talents" (*Time*, 1944). Bosley Crowther's *New York Times* review of that film opened: "The cooling-system in the Paramount Theatre was supplemented yesterday by a screen attraction designed plainly to freeze the marrow in an audience's bones" (Crowther, 1944)

Two years later, Crowther reiterated similar presumptions in his *New York Times* review of *The Blue Dahlia*.

> To the present expanding cycle of hard-boiled and cynical films, Paramount has contributed a honey of a rough-'em-up romance which goes by the name of "The Blue Dahlia." . . . And in this floral fracas it has starred its leading tough guy, Alan Ladd, and its equally dangerous and dynamic lady V-bomb, Veronica Lake. What with that combination in this Raymond Chandler tale, it won't be simply blasting that you will hear in Times Square for weeks to come.
>
> For bones are being crushed with cold abandon, teeth are being callously kicked in and shocks are being blandly detonated at close and regular intervals. . . . Also an air of deepening mystery overhangs this tempestuous tale which shall render it none the less intriguing to those lovers of the brutal and bizarre. (Crowther, 1946a)

In closing, the review acknowledges the film's transgressive appeal: "The tact of all this may be severely questioned, but it does make for a brisk, exciting show."

The Longevity of Film Noir

Film noir is perhaps the most influential American film form as well as one particularly evocative of the socio-political fabric of the 1940s and 1950s. It emerged in the early 1940s and, with the collapse of the Hollywood studio system and the supplanting of black and white by color cinematography, among other things, died out as a commercially viable form around 1960. It reemerged by 1970 in a nostalgic mode, called neo-*noir* or retro-*noir*, and has remained potent ever since. Why? Most of the people making neo-*noir* films now were not even alive when the form they are memorializing appeared; they are invoking nostalgia for a form they never experienced first hand. But what is that nostalgia for? Is it for the American 1940s and 1950s, for Hollywood filmmaking practices of the classical era (1930s through the 1950s), for black and white cinematography, for a lost style of masculinity and femininity, for the possibly simpler evils of a bygone age?

Why is there, in the twenty-first century, a *film noir* lipstick of a deep, rich red? Most of *film noir* was photographed in black and white so, with few exceptions, color did not exist in *film noir*. On one level, the idea of a richly colored lipstick evoking a form without color is preposterous; on another, however, if we consider not the actual films themselves but rather the ways in which those films and their era have been filtered through collective memory and historical association, there is a symbolic logic behind this, presumably seductive, lipstick color. The color is meant to resemble that worn by glamorous seductresses in *films noirs* and, by this indirect, symbolic path, recalls *film noir*'s exotic, transgressive aura. Considered from the vantage point of the twenty-first century, memory and its distortions are important components of *film noir* as we have come to know it.

This informs the diverse and contested canons of *film noir*. Frank Krutnik has observed:

> Many crime-films produced from the 1950s to the present day have become incorporated within the "genre" of *film noir*. In this regard I would advise a certain degree of caution, for such films need to be considered not only in regard to the *films noirs* of the 1940s but also in regard to the cinematic and cultural-ideological contexts in which and for which they were produced. For the conditions which "germinated" the *films noirs* of the 1940s were . . . specific to the 1940s. To generalize beyond this risks destroying the credibility of both the *films noirs* and the crime films *après noir*. (Krutnik, 1989, p. 329, cited in Butler, 2002, p. xv)

Approaching this problem from another direction, David Butler begins his book *Jazz Noir: Listening to Music from Phantom Lady to The Last Seduction* by observing that his interest in the topic originated in his sharing of "a widespread belief that jazz and film noir were entwined during the 1940s and 1950s, that the shadows cast by one were inescapably echoed in the sounds of the other" (Butler, 2002, p. 3). He soon discovered, however, that this belief was not supported by research into the actual music of *films noirs*; in fact, most *films noirs* primarily used not jazz but orchestral music in the symphonic tradition (p. 3). "The association of jazz with film noir can be found in all manner of media today, but is curiously not so prevalent in the actual original artifacts – the films noir of American cinema from the 1940s and 1950s. Despite this fact, the belief that jazz flourished in these films is commonly held and perpetuated" (p. 2).

James Naremore addresses the widespread acceptance of historically inaccurate conclusions about the nature of *film noir* in his updated and expanded *More Than Night: Film Noir in its Contexts*. Partially acknowledging his resignation to the situation, he cites a newspaper reporter's famous line from *The Man Who Shot Liberty Valance* (1962), "When the legend becomes fact, print the legend" (Naremore, 2008, p. 279). Furthermore, since the *noir* tradition is ongoing, such legends have become incorporated into newer works in that tradition by younger filmmakers, and those more recent films can influence the ways in which the older ones are remembered. Shifts in cultural memory can affect the object remembered, incorrectly remembered, or desired.

Questions about precisely what it is that neo-*noir* filmmakers are attempting to evoke from the past are complicated by the permutations within *film noir*, by the fact that the term is commonly used as if it referred to a single, widely agreed-upon entity rather than a cluster of intersecting but often diverse styles, themes, ideologies, and practices. When it was coined in 1946, the term referred to films made largely on studio sound stages with dark, chiaroscuro lighting that dealt with doomed, often sexually tormented characters. By the late 1940s, however, some movies now called *noir* operated on different imperatives. Some even appear conspicuously anti-*noir* in their visual strategies and themes, employing a brightly lit, semi-documentary look and depicting "slice of life" social issues rather than individual psychological torment. Instead of voice-over narration by tormented characters, such films employed an oratorical "Voice of God" narration identified with governmental agencies like the FBI. Some addressed contemporary political issues, like anti-Communism, disease control, or nuclear anxiety. And yet these films have also been categorized as *noir*.

Nearly all *films noirs* of the canonical era were set during that era. Their initial audiences would have noticed little difference between the look, dress, and behavior of the characters on the screen and those of people on the street when they exited the theater. The movies were about their "today."

This is not the case with many neo-*noir* films. Some are "period" films like *Chinatown* (1974) set in a time noticeably earlier than that in which they were produced; neo-*noir* films that are set contemporaneously with the time of their production, like *Body Heat* (1981), evoke an earlier era, or filmmaking practices of an earlier era. Both *Murder, My Sweet* (1944) and *Farewell, My Lovely* (1975) are based upon Raymond Chandler's 1940 novel, *Farewell, My Lovely*; both are set in Los Angeles in the early 1940s; and both have roughly similar characters and plotlines. But where *Murder, My Sweet* was set in the time in which it was made, *Farewell, My Lovely* is a "period" picture. By 1975, the early 1940s was a past era. Unlike *Murder, My Sweet*, which was about the "today" of 1944, *Farewell, My Lovely* was about "yesterday." Its costumes, hairstyles, and automobiles looked nothing like what 1975 audiences would have seen when they exited the theater. Neo-*noir* films are nostalgic in ways that films of the canonical era never were and have very different agendas. They employ technologies and representational strategies largely alien to canonical *films noirs*, such as color cinematography, graphic violence, profanity, nudity, explicit sexuality, and, perhaps most extreme, nostalgia. They also have different ideological stances toward gender, race, and nation.

Reinforcing the fact that neo-*noir* films are less about the time in which they were made than about the tension between their own "present" and other times, they are more temporally diverse than their predecessors. Some, like *Body Heat*, are set in their "present" (the 1980s); some, like *Chinatown*, in eras (the 1930s) prior to the time (the 1970s) in which they were produced; and some are futuristic science fiction films, like *Blade Runner* (1982) and *Minority Report* (2002).

Consider the pre-credit sequence from the neo-*noir* film *Sin City* (2005). On an apartment terrace, a young woman in an evening gown looks out at a city at night. We hear a man's voice-over: "She shivers in the wind like the last leaf on a dying tree . . . ." A reverse angle shot shows the man suavely approach from behind and offer her a cigarette. The scene has a dreamlike quality. Its cinematography is primarily in black and white, with the exception of the woman's bright red dress and lips and, briefly, her green eyes. The smoke from her cigarette drifts languidly in the air. The slow, reflective tone of the man's voice-over gives the impression that, although he speaks in the present tense, he is describing events from long ago and far away, filtered through mists of memory as well as psychic tensions within the speaker. Although the couple seem to meet for the first time, they have an instant rapport. She appears inexplicably expectant as she looks in his eyes. He tells her she is everything a man could ever want. They embrace and we suddenly see them in a dramatic long shot as stark, white-on-black silhouettes (Plate 6). Rain has begun and soon falls heavily. As the couple kisses and the man's voice-over says, "I tell her I love her," we hear a muffled shot; he has shot her. An overhead shot then shows him gently holding her limp body, her red dress spread out like a

PLATE 6 *Sin City*: White-on-black silhouette of a young couple kissing in the rain. © 2005 Miramax Film Corp.

pool of blood. His voice-over says that he holds her close until she's gone, that he'll never know what she was running from, and that "I'll cash her check in the morning." Suddenly we hear pounding music and the camera rapidly flies up and whirls around the city. Blood-red letters form and announce the film's title, *Sin City*.

We never learn more about the woman. We can infer that she had somehow paid the man to kill her, and he did so with an unexplained compassion. But what is most apparent in the sequence is its aggressive stylization – its use of black and white cinematography with bold slashes of color, its moody voice-over narration and dialogue, its erotic tension, its shift from representational figures to stark silhouettes, its atmospheric use of cigarette smoke as well as falling rain, its ominous sense of mystery, of danger, of abrupt betrayal as well as of unexplained complicity. It should be apparent that, from the outset, *Sin City* is not only telling its own story but is also inviting us to recall films of the past, particularly the 1940s and 1950s – *film noir*.

This sequence is not unique. Comparable segments have appeared in hundreds of films since the 1970s and are not confined to American film. *Film noir* influenced and was influenced by many national film traditions, such as the French New Wave, the New German Cinema, Italian neorealist and *Giallo* films, Latin American *noir*, and the Hong Kong action cinema. The influence extends beyond movies. It appears in television series since the 1950s (such as *Peter Gunn*, the *CSI* series, *Crossing Jordan*, or *Dexter*), narrative radio since the 1940s (such as *Philip*

Marlowe or *Richard Diamond, Private Detective*), fiction such as the novels of Walter Mosley or James Ellroy, and the dystopian science fiction novels of Richard K. Morgan, video games, graphic novels, theater, ballet, advertising strategies, graphic design, and music.

Consequently, a central issue for a study of *film noir* is that of how to reconcile the facts that, on the one hand, it has become almost bewildering diverse since its inception while, on the other hand, it has, particularly since the 1970s, grown enormously as a field of critical interest and as a filmmaking tradition. A useful way to begin is with the realization that it can be divided into three separate periods since its inception and that, during each of those periods, it has meant very different things to contemporary culture. The first era came in the mid-1940s when the French critics who coined the term *film noir* were describing a new, unexpected maturity in Hollywood films. For those critics, the term indicated a promising future. When, during the second era in the 1950s, the term became widely known in Europe, it referred not to an emerging but rather to an established form in American film. By the third era, from the late 1960s to the present, *film noir* has come to mean an historical trend. It is associated neither with a promising future for American film, as in the first phase, nor with a vital, contemporaneous genre, as in the 1950s, but rather with a past, nostalgic form.

The Structure of This Book

Before we delve further into this rich and complex subject, an outline of this book's structure should provide a helpful context for the material that will follow. This Introduction has discussed major strategies of *film noir* as well as the transgressive nature of its appeal. It has explored the difficulties in defining a genre with such diverse manifestations, differentiated *film noir* from film trends that preceded it, and investigated reasons for its extraordinary longevity.

Chapter 2, the historical overview, discusses the emergence of *film noir* in the 1940s with reference to contemporaneous changes in both American society and the Hollywood film industry. The social shifts include the aftereffects of the Great Depression, the national trauma of World War II, which also thrust the United States abruptly onto the international stage, and the resultant redefinition of American identity. Some of the shifts in the American film industry included challenges to the power of industry censorship, which, since the early 1930s, had imposed a whitewashed template – detailed criteria for what could and could not be shown – upon representations of American life. That template excluded many aspects of human experience from films and required story imperatives such as the obligatory punishment of crimes and misdeeds to be made evident in the films. *Film noir* not only challenged the template but, in its use of strategies such as ambiguity, alternate narratives, and sub-textual insinuation, often made the repression of those things a near-palpable, disturbing presence in the films.

Initially, *film noir* was identified by foreign critics who observed a new sensibility appearing in American films. However, the filmmakers who first made *films noirs* – unlike those who would make films about, say, World War II or the Iraq War, or films engaging popular new trends, like horror in the 1930s or psychedelic experiences in the 1970s – were not consciously aware that they were doing so. The form had not yet been defined. Those filmmakers felt that they were making many different types of films, but they were responding to potent imperatives of their times and their films have only subsequently been categorized as *film noir*.

By 1946, some critics recognized it as a coherent form. Such recognition also came from another direction, the fact that by 1947 the tropes of *film noir* had become so widely recognized that they were parodied in mass market films. Demonstrably, filmmakers and audiences were aware of *film noir* even before they had a term to define it. Further complicating the task of defining *film noir* is the fact that, almost as soon as it appeared, it began to mutate. From the mid-1940s, the genre continually adapted to new social anxieties, stylistic practices, and changes in Hollywood itself. During the late 1940s and 1950s, many *films noirs* assumed a social dimension and embraced semi-documentary styles, foreign aesthetic practices like those of Italian neorealism, and contemporary socio-political concerns. By 1960 its initial, canonical phase was dying out as a result of, among other things, the collapse of the Hollywood studio system from which it had emerged. *Film noir* was considered passé and no longer commercially viable. By 1970, however, a neo-*noir* era appeared that has remained potent for the past four decades.

Film noir in its many forms centers on postwar culture, and its revival as neo-*noir* is, in effect, a revival of anxieties and styles of the postwar era. In neo-*noir*, *film noir* has come to represent not the present but the past as it lives on in the present. A dominating cultural context for *film noir* is dystopian modernism. Many of the grand utopian hopes for modernism of the early twentieth century were failing by mid-century, and a major social posture pervading *film noir* and neo-*noir* is the sense of what Raymond Chandler called "a world gone wrong." This provides one explanation for the blending of science fiction into some neo-*noir* films. Sam Spade in

The Maltese Falcon (1941), Philip Marlowe in *The Big Sleep*, Deckert in *Blade Runner*, and Chief John Anderton in *Minority Report* all see their societies as having failed. In this, it doesn't matter that some live in the World War II era and others in the future. All are coming to terms with a social structure that once held great promise but that has now betrayed that promise. Some films, like *Seven* (1995), *The Terminator* (1984), or *End of Days* (1999), present this theme within an apocalyptic context.

Chapter 3, the critical overview, traces major critical responses to *film noir* as well as the many approaches to assessing its development and influence. These approaches proliferated after the 1950s with the spread of film culture through journals, cine-clubs, and festivals as well as the institutionalization of formal film study in universities. During this expansion of film culture, *film noir* repeatedly provided fertile ground for developing aesthetic, ideological, and formal approaches. In the 1940s, critics laid groundwork for the acknowledgment of its very existence as a genre. By the 1960s, some critics began to develop formal, thematic, and generic analyses of the films, and histories of the film industry began to recognize its place within Hollywood's narrative. By the 1970s, many theoretically based approaches – including Marxist, structuralist, psychoanalytic, auteurist – made important contributions to its analysis. Soon after, in the post-structuralist era, various identity-based and/or empowerment fields – including those based on race, nation, gender, class, sexual orientation, and post-colonial identity – contributed new insights into the genre.

Chapters 4 to 9 are devoted to detailed analyses of six films, each of which exemplifies important trends of *film noir*. These analyses illustrate components of the genre in its formative stage and ways in which, over time, those components have been re-imagined, supplemented, and even discarded in response to new influences upon the film industry and upon American culture. *Film noir* has proven to be sufficiently elastic to incorporate an almost bewildering diversity of changes. Together, these six analyses provide a detailed overview of the topic.

In Chapter 4, the first film to be examined is *Murder, My Sweet* which, appearing in the same year as *Double Indemnity*, is one of the earliest, undisputed, and most influential *films noirs*. It employs major *noir* narrative strategies such as its retrospective, voice-over narration; major themes like sexual betrayal and manipulation; and foundational character types, like the hard-boiled private detective, the "black widow" or *femme fatale*, and the emasculated men she destroys. *Murder, My Sweet* was the second of three movies based upon Raymond Chandler's 1940 hard-boiled novel, *Farewell, My Lovely*. A parallel look at the three films illustrates major historical shifts in the genre. The first adaptation, *The Falcon Takes Over* (1942), appeared two years earlier but before *film noir* had fully emerged. It employs radically different visual and thematic strategies, and draws upon Hollywood traditions that have little to do with *film noir*. *Murder, My Sweet*, appearing only two years later, embodies full-blown *film noir* stylistics and thematics. It shows how quickly and how fully the genre developed. The third adaptation, *Farewell, My Lovely* (1975), was made three decades later as a neo-*noir*. These films, based upon the same literary source, provide revealing examples of differences among a pre-*noir* film, a major *film noir*, and a neo-*noir* film.

The next film, *Out of the Past* (1947), has often been called the paradigmatic *film noir* and Chapter 5 will show why so many critics hold it in such high regard. It will also look at how Robert Mitchum, decades later used as a *noir* icon in *Farewell, My Lovely*, began to develop that image in this film, which came near the beginning of his career. In addition, this chapter will compare *Out of the Past* to *L.A. Confidential*, made half a century later, to show how representations of race, nation, and gender in the *noir* tradition had changed radically during that period.

Many have seen *Kiss Me Deadly* (1955) as signaling the end of the initial *film noir* era as well as one of the genre's crowning achievements. Chapter 6 shows how it engages themes such as apocalyptic Cold War nuclear anxiety that were not significant to earlier *films noirs*. *Films noirs* had always been known for their brutal, often savage view of humanity and their challenging of current censorship codes, but this film pushed that envelope. Like a number of *films noirs* in the 1950s, such as *Touch of Evil* (1958), it exhibits baroque stylistic tendencies in the genre as its initial era was ending.

Where late-era *films noirs* often reveal an aesthetic of excess, many neo-*noirs* demonstrate an aesthetic of nostalgia. Chapter 7 shows how *The Long Goodbye* (1973), which appeared early in the neo-*noir* era, aggressively rejects the nostalgia – for old Hollywood, for postwar masculinity and femininity, for isolationist America, among other things – that is widespread in neo-*noir*. Made during the convulsions of the Watergate era, its anti-nostalgic posture went against the grain of the newly forming neo-*noir* films and accounted for much of its initial poor reception. Its screenwriter, Leigh Brackett, one of the screenwriters of the 1946 *The Big Sleep*, commented perceptively upon the challenges of adapting two Raymond Chandler novels thirty years apart. She was acutely aware of the changes in American culture and film genres during those thirty years and of the importance of addressing those changes in the newer film. Robert Altman cast Elliot Gould against type as Marlowe (not Robert Mitchum, an earlier possibility, whose postwar, rugged masculinity was more in line with the nostalgic approach). A central theme of the film was the danger of misplaced nostalgia for the worlds of Chandler's fiction and *film noir* that did not take cultural change into account. On the set, Altman mockingly referred to the character as "Rip van Marlowe," indicating that he was a lost soul who had simply slept through rather than adapted to the cultural changes of the previous quarter-century (*Long Goodbye* DVD, 2002).

Chapter 8 shows how *Chinatown* handled its material in a more nostalgic manner but complicated this with new approaches to racial, national, and gender themes in a *noir* context. The movie is a "period" picture, set not at the time of its production but four decades earlier. Its cynical, compromised but ultimately sympathetic detective confronts disturbing public (large-scale municipal water fraud) and personal (pedophilia and incest) perversity that he can barely comprehend. The case involves an attractive and seductive woman who initially appears to resemble the evil, manipulative *femmes fatales* widespread in *film noir*. Her resemblance to that stereotype makes the movie's ultimate revelation of her sexual victimization and brutal death a shocking inversion of genre expectations. In its characterization of a powerful white patriarch as the center of its evil, the film brings new perspectives to racial, national, and sexual injustices of the *noir* era. It shows the all-white Los Angeles Police Department largely ignoring the troubles of non-white residents of Los Angeles. When the main detective is outraged after witnessing a grotesque killing in Los Angeles's Chinatown, a white character dismissively advises him to "Forget it. ... It's Chinatown."

Chapter 9 discusses the ways in which *Seven* (aka *Se7en*) sums up and interrogates many traditions of *film noir*. Explicitly dystopian in theme and look, it is primarily set in a depressing, filthy city where it is constantly raining. The film depicts an exhausted society on the verge of collapse, without hope of renewal. The movie presents parallel approaches to crime: one using modern, rational detection methods and the other involving medieval Christian views of good versus evil in a cosmic battle. A team of detectives hunts for a serial killer of people whom the killer considers exemplary of the Christian notion of the Seven Deadly Sins. Hence, he murders a glutton by forcing the man to eat himself to death, and so on. The younger detective approaches the crimes using modern, logical investigative methods and in this the movie resembles a police procedural like many *films noirs* from the late 1940s on. The older detective, however, approaches the crimes from a philosophical and religious perspective. He feels that, since the crimes are manifestations of an eternal evil, solving them will make little difference.

In keeping with the rooting of much of *film noir* in the everyday world of the "normal," the villain is not a fire-breathing biblical monster but "John Doe." He is "one of us," someone indistinguishable from "normal" humankind. In its contrasting of modern with medieval perceptions of evil, *Seven* presents evil as pervasive and eternal. No matter how it is defined and coped with, it always was and always will exist. Apocalyptic themes existed in canonical *film noir*, but often implicitly in the doomed trajectory of individual lives, or in an atmospheric sense of a failed society. Some films, however, like *White Heat* (1949) and *Kiss Me Deadly*, climax with images of apocalyptic explosions, giving them broader social implications. But not until neo-*noir* does apocalyptic imagery become a major pattern. *Seven* draws upon many conventions of *film noir* without being nostalgic and underscores their constant reinventions and recontextualizations.

CHAPTER 2

HISTORICAL OVERVIEW

 The history of *film noir* begins in the mid-1940s with international criticism, with essays written in postwar France assessing recent developments in American film and coining a new term – *film noir* – to categorize those developments. The context and historical moment are important. New Hollywood films had not been available in France since the Nazi occupation in 1940. When, in 1946, those films began to appear in Paris, some critics, such as Nino Frank, were fascinated by a new sensibility in them, one he termed *film noir*, which translates as "black film" and refers to the darkness of the themes as well as the visuals of the films. American critics had also recognized a change in tone in these films but largely saw it as a trend for "dark" or "tough" movies. The French framed this change within a grander philosophical context. This difference in approach may have been amplified by the fact that the French critics, after having been unable to see new American films for half a decade, saw what they had missed all at once whereas American critics, who saw the films as they appeared, were less disposed to notice a major shift.

In the US, these new movies were often categorized as revealing a "European" or decadent sensibility – no surprise since many European émigrés, such as Billy Wilder, Otto Preminger, Robert Siodmak, Fritz Lang, and Alfred Hitchcock, had begun directing American films during or just prior to the war years. Furthermore, the use of "hard-boiled"

Film Noir, First Edition. William Luhr.
© 2012 William Luhr. Published 2012 by Blackwell Publishing Ltd.

source material in many of the films was consonant with French championing of American "hard-boiled" fiction in the 1930s. Such fiction was still held in questionable repute by the English-language literary establishment and, to an extent, French sympathy for the films implicitly validated French literary tastes, reinforcing the belief of some French observers that they were more attuned to the merits of American culture than were Americans themselves.

French critics identified the new sensibility in American film by connecting the dots among numerous coalescing trends, which included new representations of human psychology, gender relations, and social dynamics. These trends indicated a profound erosion of the traditional American optimism that had presumed that personal and social problems were both identifiable and solvable. Many of these new films presented ongoing troubles like crime and human dysfunction as hopelessly intractable and their origins as largely unknowable. The films also destabilized traditional gender dynamics by depicting women as more powerful and men as weaker and more easily manipulated, often in a highly charged erotic context.

In addition, the films revealed changes in moral presumptions about social organization. The postwar image of the city as the "great bad place" not only influenced the widely publicized middle-class flight from urban to suburban areas but it was also one indication of the failure of modernist aspirations for urban life as the locus for civilization's "progress" into a technologically advanced future. Although much of *film noir* is set in sinister, decaying cities, the genre generated the sense that, even beyond the boundaries of the city, such corruption never really disappeared. Where pre-World War I culture had often posited a strong opposition between urban and country life, with corruption residing in cities and the wholesome, "natural" life residing in the country, faith in such a rejuvenating, innocent place had largely disappeared by the post-World War II era. Those who continued to believe in it were considered corny, out-of-date, or simply deluded. Revitalizing rural safe havens no longer existed. Sterling Hayden's doomed hoodlum in *The Asphalt Jungle* (1950) longs for the idyllic purity of life on his farm, but when he returns there he dies. Although much of *White Heat* is set in rural areas that provide a contrast to the industrial complex in which the movie's apocalyptic climax is set, the rural environment does not ameliorate the savage robberies, mutilations, and murders committed by the Jarrett gang. James Cagney's psychotic gang leader, Cody Jarrett, carries his evil with him. Even before the canonical *film noir* period, Humphrey Bogart's John Dillinger-like gangster yearns for a peaceful retirement in the mountains in

High Sierra (1941) but finds only disappointment, failure, and death. The postwar demonization of the city extended far beyond the city limits. In *film noir*, it often reflects a loss of faith in society itself.

This sense of a world with no secure haven appears in the Val Lewton-produced RKO horror films of the 1940s (O'Brien, 2006), in postwar anxieties about malignant Communism infesting small-town America, and in many films about World War II combat veterans returning to a homeland that feels alien to them. Horror no longer resided "somewhere else" like Transylvania; it could be anywhere. Comparably, the "enemy" need not be Nazis in Germany or Japanese soldiers in the Pacific; it could be Soviet Communists who have infiltrated your workplace, your neighborhood, your own home. *The Stranger* (1946) depicts a Nazi war criminal living as a respected citizen in a stereotypical American small town, and even his wife has no idea about his murderous past. In *Shadow of a Doubt* (1943), the small-town family's beloved "Uncle Charlie" turns out to be a demented serial killer.

Most *films noirs* were initially made and perceived as belonging to traditional genres, like detective films, murder mysteries, domestic melodramas, or social problem films. However, they partook of the emerging sensibility and revealed a "something else" that differentiated them from earlier films of their type. The sensibility pervading *film noir* also appears outside of the crime and hard-boiled detective films with which it is most associated. It is evident in tormented Westerns like *Pursued* (1947), *Blood on the Moon* (1948), *The Searchers* (1956), and *Man of the West* (1958); historical dramas like *Reign of Terror* (1948); rural melodramas like *The Night of the Hunter* (1955); and social problem films like *Crossfire*.

Crossfire is significant because, on one level, it is a crime film, a murder mystery. It begins as Joseph Samuels (Sam Levine) is beaten to death and its plot follows police attempts to discover his killer. However, it does not function like traditional crime films in that Detective Finley (Robert Young), in charge of the case, can find no logical motive for the killing. All of the suspects had just met Samuels. Then Finley realizes that the killer had no traditional motive, like jealousy or robbery.

> It had to be something else. The motive had to be inside the killer himself. Something he brought with him. Something he'd been nursing for a long time, something that had been waiting. The killer had to be someone who could hate Samuels without knowing him, who could hate him enough to kill him, under the right circumstances. Not for any real reason but mistakenly and ignorantly. The rest wasn't too hard.

Although the trigger for the murder lies in the killer's rabid anti-Semitism, the movie establishes his seething rage as symptomatic of a profound psychic imbalance. Instead of a film that seeks a traditionally logical answer to "whodunit," *Crossfire* finds its answer in the unpredictable and often irrational psychology of its characters.

Double Indemnity

Double Indemnity provides an ideal springboard for tracing a history of *film noir*. Although cogent arguments can be made for earlier movies as initiating *film noir*, few films with as many major markers of the genre were so immediately recognized as heralding a new sensibility, were as widely influential, or continue to be cited as classics.

A vortex for *film noir*, *Double Indemnity* is significant in its source in hard-boiled fiction, its "European" sensibility, its involvement of creative figures important to the development of the genre (such as Billy Wilder, James M. Cain, Raymond Chandler, Edward G. Robinson, and Barbara Stanwyck), its challenging of studio censorship, its establishment of numerous narrative, thematic, character, and stylistic paradigms, and its influence upon later films.

The movie was based upon a hard-boiled novella by James M. Cain (first appearing in serial form in *Liberty* magazine in 1936, then as a novella in 1940). Hard-boiled fiction, emerging from semi-reputable "pulp" magazines of the 1920s and 1930s, often used harsh, proletarian vernacular to deal with topics like manipulative sexuality, violence, corruption, and depravity, in what were contemporaneously considered sensationalist ways. As noted above, Nino Frank discussed *film noir* and hard-boiled fiction as part of a single, ground-breaking intellectual tradition; American critics, like Bosley Crowther in the above-cited *New York Times* review, also referred to the novella in their reviews of *Double Indemnity*. Both novella and film deal with amoral, unsavory people committing adultery and murder in an atmosphere of all-consuming eroticism and greed. They depict successful businessmen as profoundly insecure, reveal "respectable" middle-class family life to be festering with resentment and betrayal, and, from the outset, establish a deterministic mood of inevitable oblivion for central characters.

The movie's director, Billy Wilder, was a German émigré who brought his experience with German Expressionism to the film, not only in giving it a pervasive sense of doom but also in the "look" he had cinematographer John Seitz design for it.. He set much of it at night and often renders scenes eerie with deep shadows or intermittent light filtered through venetian blinds. Many images resemble nightmares.

Wilder knew that adapting the Cain novella was a risky venture. Although Hollywood had optioned the rights to some of Cain's work in the 1930s, studio heads, wary of censorship, had not put the film adaptations into production because they feared that the hard-boiled content was too scandalous and depraved to be acceptable to industry censors. In 1943, Wilder sensed that the censors were becoming less rigid and took a chance on the project. He had originally planned to hire Cain to co-write the screenplay with him, but when Cain proved unavailable, he chose another hard-boiled novelist, Raymond Chandler. Chandler's style is evident in the dialogue and in the film's retrospective, voice-over narration; it has become one of the most widespread influences upon *film noir*.

Wilder's casting of Edward G. Robinson was significant in that Robinson, known in the early 1930s for brutal gangster roles and, later, for expanding his range, would appear in many significant *films noirs*, including important ones released almost simultaneously with *Double Indemnity* like *The Woman in the Window* (1944) and *Scarlet Street* (both directed by another German émigré, Fritz Lang). Short, thick-featured, and never a leading-man type, Robinson often played characters conscious of, and compensating for, their lack of classical good looks, whether savage gangsters, browbeaten or tortured losers, hard-driving professional men, or unnoticed nice guys. Such roles, combined with his potent screen presence, made him ideal for many *films noirs*.

An anecdote told by Wilder about his difficulties in casting *Double Indemnity* illustrates anxieties within the studio about the potentially censorable nature of the material. While Barbara Stanwyck agreed to play the female lead early on, the leading actors at Paramount, fearing that associating themselves with the movie would degrade their star images, turned the male lead down. Wilder finally approached George Raft, who asked him to summarize the story. As Wilder did so, Raft interrupted him, asking, "And when do we have the lapel?" Wilder did not understand what he meant, so Raft told him to continue but would periodically ask, "Where's the lapel?" When Wilder finished, Raft said, "Oh, no lapel." Wilder said, "What is a lapel?" Raft said, "You know, at a certain moment you turn the hero's lapel and it turns out that he's an FBI man or a policeman or someone who works for the government – a good guy really." When Raft learned that there was no lapel, that the main character really was bad, he declined the role. Fred MacMurray, whose career playing happy-go-lucky saxophone players in light comedy was on the decline, was finally convinced by Wilder to take the role (Gross, 1977: 48–9).

The notion of "no lapel" defines much of *film noir*. Hollywood films at the time were produced under strict censorship of their moral content, codified in the "Production Code," which was adopted by the powerful Motion Picture Producers and Distributors Association in 1930 and strictly enforced after 1934. Any studio production hoping for a successful release needed a PCA (Production Code Administration) Seal of Approval. In effect, one might say that the PCA demanded a "lapel" for all films, a clear assertion that they stood with the "proper" side of conventional morality. Much of *film noir* would challenge or violate PCA rules. Central characters engaged in anti-social, self-destructive, or criminal behavior; the films often explored the dark side of life without a safety net, without a "lapel."

Beginnings

Films that appeared almost simultaneously with or soon after *Double Indemnity*, including *Laura* (1944), *Murder, My Sweet, Phantom Lady* (1944), *The Woman in the Window, Detour* (1945), and *Scarlet Street*, quickly enabled a profile for *films noirs* to emerge. Their tone was noticeably darker than that evident in earlier Hollywood films. They concentrated upon human depravity, failure, and despair, and went against the cliché that Hollywood movies must end happily. Many shared a cinematic style – a way of lighting, of positioning and moving the camera, the use of a retrospective voice-over narration, often heavily reliant on flashbacks – and a choice of setting, generally a seedy, urban landscape, a world gone wrong. Stylistic and thematic antecedents of *film noir* include German Expressionist painting and films of the 1920s, American horror films and radio dramas of the 1930s and 1940s, American "tabloid" journalism and photojournalism from the 1920s on, French "poetic realist" films of the 1930s, and American hard-boiled fiction of the 1920s and 1930s.

Substantial foundations for *film noir* had been laid in 1941 with movies such as *The Maltese Falcon*, with its themes of widespread evil and deviant as well as manipulative sexuality, and *Citizen Kane*, with its dark, Expressionist look and fragmented narration. Even earlier, in 1940, *Stranger on the Third Floor*, with its sinister look, nightmare sequence, and atmosphere of perverse and unstable masculinity, provided a precedent.

Indeed, 1940 and 1941 were banner years in the pre-history of *film noir* since they marked the Hollywood debuts of three directors who would make significant contributions to the genre. Alfred Hitchcock made *Rebecca* (1940), Orson Welles made *Citizen Kane*, and John Huston made *The Maltese Falcon*. Presciently, each film has a dark mood and is organized around an obsessive search for something that, while promising to be important, turns out to be false or even non-existent. The deceased title character of *Rebecca* turns out not to have been a woman her husband idolized, as his new wife fears, but rather someone he hated; the reporter's search for the meaning of Kane's last utterance, "*Rosebud*," fails; and the desperately sought Maltese Falcon turns out to be a fake.

By the mid-1940s, critics began to comment upon an emerging trend in the movies. Some American critics called it "dark," "hard-boiled," or "European"; the French, as we have seen, called it *film noir*.

The genre hit its stride in the mid- to late 1940s with films like *The Blue Dahlia, Cornered* (1945), *Crossfire, Black Angel* (1946); *The Dark Mirror* (1946), *Detour, Gilda* (1946), *The Killers* (1946), *Brute Force* (1947), *T- Men* (1947), *Dark Passage* (1947), *Kiss of Death* (1947), *The Lady from Shanghai* (1948), *Out of the Past, Pitfall* (1948), *Raw Deal* (1948), *Ride the Pink Horse* (1947), *Secret beyond the Door* (1948), *Sorry, Wrong Number* (1948), *Criss Cross* (1949), *They Live by Night* (1949), *Border Incident* (1949), *Gun Crazy* (1950), and *D.O.A.*

Popularity and Parody

As these movies appeared, the hard-boiled fiction that had earlier been considered too unsavory for film adaptation suddenly provided fashionable sources for big studio productions, like *Mildred Pierce, The Postman Always Rings Twice, The Big Sleep* (Plate 7), and *Lady in the Lake* (1947). These and other productions indicate how quickly *film noir* had caught on since, by 1945, major studios like Metro-Goldwyn-Mayer, Paramount, and Warner Brothers felt sufficiently secure to invest in highly publicized movie in the genre with major stars.

Another indication of the popularity of *film noir* lies in the fact that by 1946 it had become so recognizable that its style and themes were parodied in "The Great Piggy Bank Robbery," a Daffy Duck cartoon, and a year later by Bob Hope in Paramount's *My Favorite Brunette*. The parodies are significant because they reflect the presumption of *film noir* as a unified, commercially viable, and popular genre. It would have made no business sense for a major studio like Paramount to feature one of its biggest stars in a parody of *film noir* unless it could presume widespread familiarity with what was being parodied in order that the audience would "get" the joke.

PLATE 7 *The Big Sleep:* Humphrey Bogart and Lauren Bacall, a popular *noir* couple. © 1946 Warner Bros. Pictures, INC.

My Favorite Brunette opens with ominous, exterior shots of San Quentin prison underscored by grim orchestral music. These shots are indistinguishable from the opening prison shots in *Brute Force*, a brutal *film noir* about prison injustice appearing that same year. After the opening shots of *My Favorite Brunette*, we see a prison warden solemnly enter a cellblock to escort a condemned prisoner to the gas chamber. Everything about the scene recalls "death row" films of the era. However, when we arrive at the prisoner's cell, we see that he is played by Bob Hope using the goofball, smart-aleck film persona for which he was widely known in 1947 (Plate 8). The film's mood abruptly changes. Although its story is still about a prisoner awaiting execution, Hope's persona undercuts everything about the situation. This is a comedy. Soon he is interviewed by reporters in a cell outside the execution chamber. His prison clothes, his imminent execution, images of him through prison bars, all recall dark films of the era. And as in so many *films noirs*, he recounts his story in flashback. However, the comic tone makes the cinematography, the voice-over narration, and the grim images simultaneously recall and parody many *films noirs*.

In his flashback, Hope's character reveals that he had unhappily worked as a baby photographer while yearning for the "manly" life of

PLATE 8 *My Favorite Brunette*: Bob Hope in the opening scene on death row. © 1947 Hope Enterprises, INC.

a hard-boiled detective. He idolized such a detective in a nearby office, played by Alan Ladd, an actor then known for tough-guy roles. Ladd carries a gun, drinks hard liquor at his desk, and speaks seductively over the telephone to a girlfriend. Hope's character has purchased his own pistol but clumsily fumbles when he attempts to draw it and drops it on the floor; he chokes when drinking liquor; and he has no success with women.

My Favorite Brunette parodies many tropes of *film noir* – an apparently doomed central character, his retrospective voice-over narration, a *femme fatale*, sinister plots in a malevolent environment, shadowy visual strategies, and anxieties about masculinity and femininity.

Gender Destabilization: Broken Men and Empowered Women

Although *My Favorite Brunette* is played for laughs, its parody underscores the centrality of failed masculinity and delusional desire to *film noir*. The destabilization of traditional gender securities is a major trope of the genre – the result of the era's redefinition of masculinity, femininity, and their power balance. The genre's broken men went hand-in-hand with its newly empowered and threatening women.

Film noir abuts many genres, none more so than horror. It can be described as a genre about how everyday, contemporary life, without supernatural intervention, can become as terrifying as any monster movie. A major theme of *film noir*, the sense that it's all over, appears in its trope of post-mortem men (and some women). These lost souls, having abandoned hope for a viable future for themselves, lead zombie-like existences. Many of the films begin where earlier ones might have concluded – with the central characters facing doom. Their retrospective narrations recount the failures of a past that is already unchangeable. This narrative strategy infuses everything it presents with the aura of inevitable extinction or irrelevance, like cautionary tales on tombstones. Drained of potency, these characters know it is all ending badly, or is already over. They often devote their remaining time to recounting their stories or to trying to understand why it all happened. The narrator of *Double Indemnity* tells his tale while fully aware of his own failure and imminent death. The narrator of *Sunset Boulevard* is literally dead when the film begins. The central character of *Detour* assumes the identity of a corpse and describes himself as walking around in the body of a dead man. He eventually becomes literally unable to reassume his own identity. The main character in *Sorry, Wrong Number* overhears plans for a murder and gradually realizes that she will be the victim. The *femme fatale* of *Decoy* (1946), mortally shot by one of her victims, spends the body of the film recounting the sordid activities that led her to this end. "The Swede" in *The Killers* quietly and inexplicably submits to his own murder at the beginning of the film (Plate 9). Jeff in *Out of the Past* resigns himself to his doom and orchestrates his own death. In *Crossfire*, Captain Finlay, when asked if the villain is dead, matter-of-factly replies, "He was dead for a long time; he just didn't know it."

These walking corpses inhabit a half-world between life and death, with neither hope nor purpose. Such characters often feel doomed even when, simultaneously, they appear to be succeeding in their endeavors. This is clear in a scene in *Double Indemnity* occurring just after Walter Neff has murdered his lover's husband and everything in his plan seems to have gone off perfectly. In a final move to establish his alibi, he leaves his apartment and we hear his voice-over:

> That was all there was to it. Nothing had slipped, nothing had been overlooked, there was nothing to give us away. And yet . . . as I was walking down the street to the drugstore, suddenly it came over me that everything would go wrong. It sounds crazy . . . but it's true, so help me. I couldn't hear my own footsteps. It was the walk of a dead man.

PLATE 9 *The Killers*: "The Swede" (Burt Lancaster) inexplicably awaiting his own murder. © 1946 Universal Pictures Company, INC.

The men in these films experience a profound sense of emasculation; they feel that they are losing their power over women and over their own destinies, a power that they had once considered their birthright. This is inseparable from contemporary shifts in the status of women. The long struggle for women's suffrage so important to twentieth-century social history had climaxed with the passage of the Nineteenth Amendment to the US Constitution in August 1920. This social realignment came after great resistance and, even when accomplished, produced ongoing re-sentment in many men. *Film noir* reflects the erosion of the traditional power balance between the sexes and often constructs women as more powerful and men as weak and threatened. An important character type is the *femme fatale* or "black widow," a woman who seduces, exploits, and then destroys her sexual partners. These were women who, according to widespread presumptions about gender roles, did not "know their place," meaning subservience to men. Their potency also testifies to the inability of men to "control" them. Black widows like Brigid O'Shaughnessy in *The Maltese Falcon*, Phyllis Dietrichson in *Double Indemnity*, Helen Grayle in *Murder, My Sweet*, Kitty in *The Killers* and Kathie Moffat in *Out of the Past* were presented as evil and homicidal, but they were also smart and ambitious. More importantly, they were largely self-determining, not so much adjuncts of their men as their competitors. As discussed in the next chapter, this was unusual with traditional representations of women. These characters did not need the support or approval of men to define themselves. Although contemporary social norms required that they be punished by the ends of the films, some influential feminist scholars such as E. Ann Kaplan (1998) have characterized their emergence as a progressive step in introducing complex representations of women into film. Granted, the films depicted such women as emasculating, manipulative, and immoral but, in a back-door manner, the films also made them the intellectual equals, if not superiors, of the men, perhaps for the first time in film history. The flip side of this new empowerment of female characters was the emasculation of many of the male ones, an aspect of the genre that plays itself out repeatedly. The black widow, appearing at a time when social gender roles were in flux, has been seen as an embodiment of male paranoia toward women. An alternate title for *Gun Crazy*, *Deadly is the Female*, encapsulates this perception.

Out of the Past provides a useful instance. Jeff (Robert Mitchum) is a private detective hired by a gangster, Whit (Kirk Douglas), to locate his girlfriend, Kathie (Jane Greer), who has both shot him and stolen $40,000 from him. Jeff finds her but she seduces him and they run off together. He thereby reneges on his professional responsibility to Whit. When Jeff's partner tracks them down, Kathie kills the partner and returns to Whit. Later, they conspire to frame Jeff for murder. In the end, Kathie kills Whit and, when Jeff tries to turn her in to police, she kills him by shooting him in the groin, making his emasculation literal.

Kathie exploits and betrays the men. Although they are intelligent, strong, and resourceful, she repeatedly degrades them, and they come back for more. She shoots and robs Whit, yet he wants her back; she entices Jeff to betray his employer, his partner, and his hopes for a new life, yet he also returns to her. Both men die at her hands after repeatedly demonstrating their inability, while fully aware of her treachery, to resist her spell.

Although the black widow character caught on quickly and soon became a stereotype, it was so new to films when it appeared that some critics hardly knew what to do with it. Otis Ferguson's review of *The Maltese Falcon* in *The New Republic* reveals such confusion in discussing Mary Astor's character.

> The story is one of the few cases where they have their cake and eat it too, for the detective *is* in love with the mystery woman, and she *might* turn out in the end to be another case of (a) innocence wronged, (b) the most trusted agent of the United States Government. But she doesn't, and he sends her

up for twenty years. There is . . . confusion in this, for an audience likes to know where it stands, and . . . Mary Astor's [role can't] . . . quite get over the difficulty of seeming black and then seeming white, and being both all along. (Ferguson, 1941)

Astor's character deviated from traditional representations and, for many, this new type of screen woman was disorienting.

Such disorientation existed within the larger context of gender power reorganization in the United States. During World War II, the federal government, badly in need of defense industry labor to replace men serving in the armed forces, encouraged women to abandon traditional presumptions about their being too physically weak, unreliable, and intellectually inferior to undertake such work. Governmentally sponsored images of women successfully performing "men's work" while remaining "feminine" supported this agenda. "Rosie the Riveter," for example, became a popular icon representing the roughly six million women who replaced men serving in the armed forces during the war by working in defense industries (Rockwell, 1943). Many women considered their success in the workplace to be proof that their prewar anxieties about their inferiority had been misplaced, and felt liberated by their new empowerment. But it ended abruptly when, at the war's conclusion, the government reversed course and urged these women to leave their jobs and return to their traditional, subordinate roles in order to make room for returning veterans in the workplace. This led to gender anxiety on both sides – resentment on the part of recently empowered women and anxiety on the part of men threatened by those women's incursions into their traditionally privileged domains. Furthermore, the very fact that many women had performed "men's work" as successfully as the men eroded male presumptions about their "natural" superiority and fueled paranoia. Such discontent found resonant chords in the images of dominating women and emasculated men common to *film noir*.

Social Context

Film noir reveals not only American wartime and postwar anxieties but also diverse intellectual influences of the time, such as Freudian theory, naturalist and modernist literature and film, and the emerging existentialist philosophical tradition.

Film noir presents an image of America that differs radically not only from the jaunty optimism of many wartime films but also from more recent categorizations of that era as productive of America's "Greatest Generation." Tom Brokaw (1998) depicts the World War II generation in heroic terms as one that, responding to the global menace posed by the Axis powers, selflessly united in common cause to triumphantly win the war and pave the way for a wholesome future. *Film noir*, however, depicts precisely that same generation in a wholly different light. Its characters are not united in common cause, they are isolated; they are not engaged in productive social activity but are self-destructive and dysfunctional; they are a doomed generation without a viable future. At precisely the same historical moment, the ideology of the "Greatest Generation" celebrated the ascendant and utopian American Dream while that of *film noir* lamented that dream's failure. *Film noir* depicted the contrarian underbelly of American popular culture's heroic image of itself.

Film noir appeared as the US was emerging from two national convulsions: the Great Depression and World War II. The postwar world, however, brought not a return to the idealized "normality" of prewar years but rather a defamiliarized society that had changed in profound ways. As postwar French critics "returned" after a significant absence to American film and found that it had changed fundamentally, many Hollywood films dealt with failed attempts to recapture a lost, prewar way of life. Many of these even focus upon an overwhelming mood of despair while characters simultaneously experience great success. While many movies celebrated the Allied victory in World War II, many others reflected a sense of emptiness, dislocation, and loss. This appears in numerous films about returning veterans, such as the one that swept the 1946 Academy Awards (winning seven), *The Best Years of Our Lives*. It depicts the homecomings of three veterans, one of whom has lost his hands. All feel deep anxiety about returning to the land for which they fought and sacrificed. They fear that, during their absence, their homeland had gone on without them, that they will be irrelevant to the postwar world, and that their home and loved ones will no longer be "the same."

A more bitter film from the same year is *The Blue Dahlia*, a *film noir* which begins as three wounded naval veterans of the war in the Pacific return home to Los Angeles. No parades are there to welcome them; no one even notices them or seems to value their sacrifice. When they enter a bar for a farewell drink, their leader, Johnny (Alan Ladd), gives a melancholic toast, "Well, here's to what was" (Plate 10). He then returns to his home to find that his wife has been having an affair with a criminal who hadn't served in the armed forces and who had grown rich during wartime. Soon after this, she is found murdered, Johnny is blamed, and he becomes a fugitive. His long-anticipated homecoming, the fruit of

PLATE 10 *The Blue Dahlia*: Homecoming World War II GIs in a bar – "Well, here's to what was." © 1945 Paramount Pictures, INC.

victory, then, has become a nightmare. Comparably, *Act of Violence* (1948) concerns the postwar lives of two veterans who had been incarcerated in a German prisoner of war camp. Frank (Van Heflin) has become a successful businessman and seems to have left his wartime experience behind him; Joe (Robert Ryan) limps badly and is profoundly embittered by his wartime experience, including his belief that Frank betrayed him to their Nazi captors. Their troubled encounter reveals that the war had irrevocably damaged both men, whether or not that damage is evident in their surface behavior. They have carried their demons home with them.

Crossfire, cited above, is also about a veteran's disorientation. Set soon after the end of the war, it deals primarily with returning soldiers. It begins with a sequence showing a man being brutally beaten to death that is shot in such a way that we cannot identify the participants. We soon learn that the victim is Joseph Samuels (Sam Levine), who had recently been medically discharged from the military after having been wounded in combat. Suspicion for his murder initially falls on Corporal Mitchell, a soldier Samuels befriended in a bar.

Through flashbacks we see that Mitchell was disoriented and confused, not drinking but appearing drunk. Samuels empathized with Mitchell's disorientation and discussed it with him as a symptom of postwar confusion, of the profound difficulty that returning soldiers experience in adapting to a peacetime life where they have lost the focus that wartime combat gave them. He tells Mitchell,

> I think maybe it's suddenly not having a lot of enemies to hate anymore. Maybe it's because, for four years now, we've been focusing our mind on, on one little peanut – the "win the war" peanut – that was all. Get it over with, eat that peanut. All at once, no peanut. Now we start looking at each other again. We don't know what we are supposed to do. We don't know what's supposed to happen. We're too used to fighting. We just don't know what to fight. You can feel the tension in the air, a whole lot of fight and hate that doesn't know where to go. A guy like you maybe starts hating himself. Well, one of these days, maybe we'll all learn to shift gears. Maybe we'll stop hating and start liking things again, huh?

Ironically, later that evening, Samuels is murdered and Mitchell, although innocent, is even more confused.

The pervasive destabilization in *film noir* extends far beyond reassimilation problems of returning veterans. Victory in World War II had placed the US irrevocably on a global stage. Prewar isolationism became increasingly untenable and the new world order meant relinquishing traditional assumptions about, for example, the presumed superiority of US white males over women and peoples of other colors and nations. This perceived erosion of gender, racial, and national privilege became compounded domestically with growing demands for social empowerment by women and peoples of color, with labor unrest, and with international business competition, among other things. These broad social changes were particularly unsettling for those who had enjoyed privilege under the old social order, who had anticipated that wartime victory would reward them with greater empowerment, but who now felt their privilege disappearing and the ground shifting under their feet. That previously privileged class had provided the dominant point of view for much of classical Hollywood cinema, and their destabilization, their anxiety, pervades *film noir*.

The Late 1940s: New Influences and Changes in Film Noir

By the late 1940s, *film noir* was not only thriving but also moving in diverse directions, partly influenced by new trends in cinematic "realism" as well as by technological innovations and cultural developments. Where the earlier films tended to focus upon psychological problems of individuals, some later ones foregrounded social concerns. Where many of the earlier films had a highly controlled, expressionistic, "studio" look (never lost but maintained in films like *Secret Beyond the Door, Sunset Boulevard,* and *Touch of Evil* –1958), later films like *Call Northside 777* (1948), *White Heat, Act of Violence, The Naked City* (1950), *Side Street* (1950), and *Panic in the Streets* (1950) employed a semi-documentary look influenced by American newsreels (such as the *March of Time* newsreel series produced by Louis de Rochemont, who also produced *Call Northside 777,* among others) as well as Italian neorealism. Voice-over narration continued to be widely used but, instead of a despairing narrating voice, some of the new films used authoritative and oratorical "Voice of God" narration. The later films used substantially more location shooting with apparently "natural" lighting than their predecessors and often presented their characters and stories as emblematic of the modern urban environment ("There are eight million stories in the naked city…"). The earlier films focused upon individual crimes and private detectives; the later ones often dealt with organized crime and the procedures of law-enforcement agencies. Where the earlier films might be seen as seeking "psychological realism," the later ones appeared more interested in "sociological realism."

Movies like *The Naked City* presented themselves as semi-documentaries about the daily life of the city, at times making the city itself resemble a dominating character. Mark Hellinger, producer and narrator of *The Naked City* (as well as producer of *Brute Force* and *The Killers*) had been a popular newspaper columnist who had chronicled New York City life from the 1920s and was drawn to gritty films about contemporary life. In his narration for *The Naked City,* he asserts that no scene in it was shot in a studio; it was all shot on actual New York City locations. He characterizes the lives of the characters as reflecting the life of the city itself and his story opens as diverse residents awaken to a new day and prepare to pursue their diverse lives. It then focuses in on one of the eight million stories in the naked city, that of a murder investigation, but implies that the movie could have as readily focused on many other stories. It uses multiple locations around the city and climaxes with the entrapment of a murderer on top of the Williamsburg Bridge, with the city itself providing a picturesque background (Plate 11). Many of these semi-documentary films emphasized state-of-the-art surveillance technologies used by law-enforcement agencies, like the FBI and the Treasury Department, while at the same time shifting the image of law-enforcement agents from one of two-fisted individual heroism (as in 1935 with James Cagney's FBI agent in *"G" Men*) into one of corporate or organizational heroism which subordinates the individual to the unified efforts of largely faceless professionals.

PLATE 11 *Naked City*: Out-of-studio, documentary-like cinematography in the climax atop New York City's Williamsburg Bridge. © 1948 Universal Pictures Company, INC.

Implicitly, such a shift moves beyond narratives of individual success or failure to the notion of progress in society at large.

A major difference between detectives in the new police procedurals and those in either the British detective tale as typified by Sherlock Holmes or the American "hard-boiled" detective tales lies in the procedural's implicit rejection of individual agency. Detectives in the earlier traditions often solved crimes that baffled the police, and police were often represented as inept or corrupt. The "private" detectives often worked in isolation, relying on their intelligence, intuition, and sheer nerve. Detective figures in police procedurals tend, to the contrary, to be team players and, as such, interchangeable. If one is killed or given another assignment, another agent can step in to handle the case as effectively.

In the postwar era, the FBI and other federal law-enforcement agencies appropriated heroic images of the World War II military to characterize themselves as peacetime armies. The agencies often cooperated in the making of the films, allowing some of their activities to be photographed and permitting reference to their case files. Some of the films resemble recruitment advertisements. They present agents as regimented in service of the greater good. However, the flip side of these images of regimentation tapped into a major postwar anxiety, that of the erosion of individual identity in an increasingly corporate culture.

During the war, Hollywood and government propaganda had characterized fascist governments as destructive of individual freedoms. The German and Japanese military, for example, were often represented as inhuman martinets and automatons, with their defeat promising a liberated world. For many, however, that liberation never came; instead, they saw new modes of social oppression emerging in the postwar era, whether the totalitarian regimes in the Soviet Union and Eastern bloc countries, the National Security state in the US, or a generalized anxiety about governmental intrusions upon individual freedoms, even identity. The 1940s produced both the alienated urban landscapes of *film noir,* reflective of contemporary experience, and George Orwell's *Nineteen Eighty-Four* (1949), which projected postwar anxieties onto the (then) future. Orwell's futuristic novel introduced to the popular consciousness the notion of an after-modern, technologically advanced society that has degenerated into a dystopia. A central emblem of the society's advanced technology as well as its dehumanization lies in its state-sponsored surveillance – "Big Brother is watching You!" That omnipresent surveillance works to ensure that everyone rigidly conforms to state policy by eroding the freedoms and compromising the very identities of those subject to it. Such compulsion to conformity drains individual identity and leads to human interchangeability.

Simultaneously, however, the police procedural presented state-sponsored surveillance in a radically different light. These films (the procedural also appeared at this time in radio and television series, like *Dragnet* and *The Lineup*, and detective fiction) dealt like *film noir* with the world of crime but focused less on the plights of individual criminals (as in *Double Indemnity* or *The Postman Always Rings Twice*) or on private investigators (as in *The Big Sleep*) and concentrated instead on the procedures by which governmental agents (whether members of municipal police forces or national agencies) acted in coordinated groups to solve crime. These movies implied an alternative to dystopian works like *Nineteen Eighty-Four* because they posited a benign and not a malignant state. Although the detectives or agents in such films are functionaries of the state, they work to ensure and not repress individual liberty.

Police procedurals were often curious combinations of both utopian and dystopian modernist strains: utopian in that they showed benign state organizations using advanced technology to root out criminals, but dystopian in their acknowledgment of the pervasive and ongoing nature of contemporary crime. These contradictory tensions often extended to the stylistics of the films. *T-Men*, for example, depicts the US Treasury Department's pursuit of a murderous national gang of counterfeiters. The movie's frame story resembles a utopian documentary. In its prologue, a "Voice of God" narrator describes the duties and advanced technology of Treasury agents and we see well-lit, documentary footage of the monumental US Treasury Building in Washington, DC and work being done in its sophisticated, state-of-the-art crime laboratories. An actual Treasury Department official, Elmer Lincoln Irey (who was also known at the time as the director of the Internal Revenue Service's lead investigation unit during the successful federal tax evasion prosecution of the notorious gangster Al Capone), directly addresses the viewer to provide the historical context for the film's events (Plates 12 and 13). The film employs an entirely different style to portray the world of the counterfeiting gang. Images of that world, in severe contrast to those depicting the Treasury Department, conform to those of classical *film noir*: darkly lit rooms and corridors, and sinister exteriors like nighttime shipyards. The film presents the furtive and sleazy environments of underworld activity – pool halls, steam baths (Plate 14), back-room gambling emporiums, filthy boarding

PLATE 12 *T-Men* – opening: Documentary images of the US Treasury Department Building. © 1947 Pathé Productions, INC.

PLATE 13 *T-Men*: US Treasury Department official Elmer Lincoln Irey directly addressing the viewer in the movie's prologue. © 1947 Pathé Productions, INC.

houses – in direct contrast to the well-lit, out-in-the-open world of governmental law enforcement. The Treasury Department images imply a brightly lit world efficiently progressing toward a better future; the underworld images imply a dark vortex of exploitation and doom.

A fascinating gloss on the identity tensions of the era appeared in the popular television series *I Led Three Lives* (1953–6). The main character was an undercover FBI agent who posed to the public as an insurance agent. His "third" life was as a spy who had infiltrated the Communist Party. He did not disguise himself for his different roles – he looked exactly the same in all three. And all three were roles that could be taken by anyone else in the group: insurance agents, FBI agents, Communists. Implicitly, in defending the US against identity-eroding Communists, he was becoming exactly like them. In Cold War thinking, the opposing political forces competing for the modern world shared a common element: devotion to corporate ideology. The title of John Le Carré's 1965 Cold War novel *The Looking Glass War* implies this – in looking at our enemies we are looking at ourselves.

PLATE 14 *T-Men*: A trapped man is murdered in a steam room as his sadistic killer watches through glass. © 1947 Pathé Productions, INC.

From the late 1940s on, films like *I Married a Communist* (1949), *Pickup on South Street* (1953), *Panic in the Streets*, *Shack Out on 101* (1955), and *Kiss Me Deadly* incorporated anxieties about the threat of Soviet Communism, nuclear annihilation, and the spread of infectious disease into *film noir*. In the 1950s, some late *films noirs*, like *Kiss Me Deadly*, *Touch of Evil*, and *Psycho* (1960), became noticeably baroque. Whether employing visual strategies that were dark, cluttered, and disorienting, even by *noir* standards, or ratcheting up levels of sadistic violence, or exploring sexually deviant themes, they pushed the borders of censorship and at times appeared like *film noir* on steroids. *Psycho*, for example, was marketed as a thriller that bordered on horror. It infused "normality" with a gothic sensibility and graphic violence that was unusual for mainstream cinema. It not only came at the end of the *film noir* era but it has also been considered a precursor to the "slasher" movies of the 1970s and 1980s such as *The Texas Chainsaw Massacre* (1974) and *The Hills Have Eyes* (1977). These films reveled in graphic gore but, like *film noir*, situated horror not in the exotic or supernatural but rather in the "normal," particularly in the once-idealized American nuclear family.

When did *film noir* end? One popular candidate for the final film in the first phase of *film noir* is Orson Welles's last Hollywood film, *Touch of Evil*, although *The Wrong Man* (1956), *Underworld USA* (1961), *Experiment in Terror* (1962), *Psycho* and others would serve as well. Whichever endpoint one chooses, by the 1960s *film noir* seemed like an exhausted form, associated with the perceived obsolescence of black and white film stock and the dated, tough-guy cynicism of a past generation. The cinematographic norm had shifted to color and black and white films suddenly looked old fashioned. The crime and detective dramas so important to *film noir* that had pervaded movies in the 1940s and 1950s had also, by the 1950s, become commonplace in radio and television series such as *Peter Gunn, Richard Diamond, Private Detective, Dragnet, Sam Spade, Philip Marlowe, The Lineup, T-Man,* and *Martin Kane, Private Eye,* among many others. By the 1960s, films in this mode sometimes looked like they were imitating television. And, by the mid-1960s, television itself had upgraded to color. All of this occurred within the larger context of the collapse of Hollywood's studio system with its established patterns of production, distribution, and exhibition. Because many *films noirs* were set contemporaneously and did not use major stars, they could be inexpensively produced and distributed as "B" movies. When the studio system with its assured distribution for studio products disappeared, so did the traditional "B" film. By the mid-1960s, both narrative radio and black and white films had largely disappeared owing to changing industrial circumstances. *Film noir* appeared dead.

The 1960s: Transition in Hollywood and Revival of Film Noir

The 1960s produced a sea change in American culture, one in which the younger generation became known as the "counterculture" and aggressively rejected the values of their parents, the World War II generation. This rejection fueled major social shifts and attacks on embedded patriarchal structures, highly visible in the student revolutions of 1968 and, later, the worldwide reaction to the Vietnam War, Watergate, and the rise of various empowerment movements for marginalized groups such as women, peoples of color, various national and ethnic groups, and gays and lesbians. Classical Hollywood was at times perceived and attacked as one of those embedded structures. Figures like John Wayne, widely respected in earlier decades, were denounced as embodying what was wrong with the World War II generation.

During these convulsive times, *film noir* at first seemed forgotten, but then it came back, with a vengeance. Its revival, however, like its initial emergence, occurred within an historical and industrial context far broader than the genre. For complex reasons, at precisely the same time that classical Hollywood was dying out, numerous Hollywood genres were revived not only in the US but also in different national cinemas. These revivals often had a highly nostalgic tone. The late 1950s and 1960s British Hammer Studio's revival and remakes of 1930s American horror films, such as *The Curse of Frankenstein* (1957) and *The Horror of Dracula* (1958), provide one example; "Spaghetti" Westerns made in Italy and Spain in the 1960s and 1970s, such as *A Fistful of Dollars* (1967) and *Once Upon a Time in the West* (1968), provide another; attempts to revive the aesthetic of silent slapstick comedy by directors such as Stanley Kramer (*It's a Mad Mad Mad Mad World*, 1963), Blake Edwards (*The Party*, 1968), Mel Brooks (*Silent Movie*, 1976), and Jerry Lewis (*The Bellboy*, 1960), provide yet another.

The tropes of *film noir* appeared in many national cinemas at this time, perhaps most famously in films of the influential French *Nouvelle Vague*, whether François Truffaut's *Shoot the Piano Player* (1962) or *The Bride Wore Black* (1968), or Jean-Luc Godard's *Breathless* (1959) or his futuristic *Alphaville* (1965). The tropes appear in works by major figures in the New German Cinema like Rainer Werner Fassbinder (*Veronika Voss*, 1982) and Wim Wenders (*The American Friend*, 1977, and *Hammett*, 1982, a fictionalized account of the life of Dashiell Hammett). In Japan, the decayed urban environment in Akira Kurosawa's *High and Low* (1963) showed the influence of *film noir*, as did Seijun Suzuki's *Branded to Kill* (1967).

The Revival of Classical Hollywood and the Rise of Neo-Noir

These revivals of old Hollywood genres occurred during a time of a growing internationalization and academicization of film discourse. The general public had greater access to film history than at any earlier time owing to the availability of both old and recent films on television. Furthermore, from the 1950s, film culture had proliferated in cine-clubs, film journals, and festivals, and this led to the intellectual cache of the international art cinema (of directors like Federico Fellini, Ingmar Bergman, Michelangelo Antonioni, Jean-Luc Godard, and Akira Kurosawa). By the 1960s, film study was entering universities as an academic discipline. The 1970s produced the first generation of directors (such as Francis Ford Coppola, Martin Scorsese, Steven Spielberg, and George Lucas) who did not learn their craft in the traditional way by working their way up from within the industry but, rather, had been trained in film schools. These directors actively reengaged old genres in inventive and/or heavily nostalgic ways. Some made large-budget films in genres long dismissed as of "B" status. Examples include science fiction (the *Star Wars* series), the gangster film (the *Godfather* films as well as *Goodfellas*, 1990), and the exotic jungle adventure movie (the *Indiana Jones* movies). They also remade some old films and made sequels and series films.

Film noir benefited in many ways from this climate. The attention, from the 1950s on, of the influential French critics of *Cahiers du Cinéma* and other journals like *Positif* to American auteurs of the studio system provided *film noir* with a critical boost. In denouncing their own cinematic "tradition of quality" of directors such as Jean Delannoy whom they considered lacking in individuality and too subservient to their screenplays, in favor of visually dynamic Hollywood genre films that had been previously dismissed as mere entertainment by studio hacks (like Howard Hawks, John Ford, and Frank Tashlin), the *Cahiers* critics empowered a reverse snobbery for previously despised genres like the Western and *film noir*. It didn't hurt that auteurist heroes like Howard Hawks, Orson Welles, Samuel Fuller, and Fritz Lang had produced major and largely forgotten works in *film noir*. The low esteem in which much of *film noir* had traditionally been held provided an impetus for the aggressive *Cahiers* critics to show how stupid the older critical establishment had been. Furthermore, many of these critics, such as Claude Chabrol, Godard, and Truffaut, went on to make films in which *noir* tropes were highly visible.

Some critics of the 1960s and 1970s embraced *film noir* as an historical alternative to the dominant Hollywood style of the classical age, a notion particularly attractive to the counterculture in its reassessment of American film. Where many films in the *noir* tradition had been considered at the time of their release to be degenerate entertainment or "B" films at best, the tradition now assumed the aura of a major and subversive style. And not only a major style but, at the very time that the Hollywood studio system was crumbling, it became associated with undervalued work of Hollywood's "Golden Age." These critics were more likely to praise *Detour* or *Pickup on South Street*, which had been largely ignored at the times of their release, than Hollywood blockbusters like *Gone with the Wind* (1939) or *Ben-Hur* (1959).

Changes in Film Censorship, Self-Referentiality, and Genre Blending

Many films noirs had engaged potentially "forbidden" material in muted, suggestive ways in order to qualify for the Production Code Seal of Approval necessary for mainstream exhibition. However, by 1966 the Production Code had been repeatedly and successfully defied and major studios were ignoring it; it had become irrelevant. In 1968 the Motion Picture Association of America (MPAA) replaced it with various modifications of CARA (Classification and Rating Administration) which no longer prohibited film content. CARA instituted classifications like SMA or X or NC-17 that did not prevent films from including material considered morally questionable but instead restricted access by age to some films to conform with presumed community standards. Furthermore, American culture had changed so much since the 1940s that many things that had then been considered shocking were no longer so.

Many of the new films were able to explicitly present material that previously could only be suggested. *Gunn* (1967) deals with transvestism and *Chinatown* with pedophilia and incest; both show graphic, mutilating violence in ways unthinkable during the canonical era of *film noir*. Such material is still considered of questionable morality, however, and its use, while permitted, can categorize a film as shocking or of borderline morality. Such borderline morality also remains associated with hard-boiled film sources: witness the advertising campaign for the 1981 remake of *The Postman Always Rings Twice* presenting it as a film showing uncontrolled, animalistic sexuality – a "daring" film. Such movies could draw from their source material in different ways than their 1940s counterparts could; they could show what, in the 1940s, films could only obliquely suggest. By the late 1960s, graphic violence, profanity, and nudity became commonplace on film. What had once been "daring" had become mainstream and, hence, not nearly as transgressive.

From the late 1960s on, films made in the *noir* tradition evoked a past era. *Films noirs* of the 1940s and 1950s had reflected a contemporary sensibility; they were about the "today" of their era. After the 1960s, films in this tradition, even when set contemporaneously at the time of their release, tended to evoke the past. Private detectives in films of the 1940s and 1950s appeared to their initial audiences as contemporary men on the street; in later films they evoked both an out-of-date mode of masculinity and an earlier era of filmmaking. By the 1960s the very notion of a "private eye" recalled figures of an older generation, like the recently deceased Humphrey Bogart, in old black and white films. At times, as in *The Long Goodbye*, he is a pathetic anachronism; at others, as in *Gunn* or *Marlowe* (1969), he is a noble remnant of a better age in a debased society. But in all three cases, the world has clearly passed him by.

The effect of changing times is also evident in movements between television and film. The *Peter Gunn* television series of 1958–60 featured the eponymous private eye as a hip, tough man attuned to his times. When, in 1967, that character was revived in the contemporaneously set movie *Gunn*, he was presented as out of step with the times, as a relic from a bygone era now adrift in the "swinging sixties." And when the character was again revived in *Peter Gunn*, a 1989 made-for-television movie, the movie itself was set in the early 1960s, the time of the original television series, making it no longer about "the present," as with the series, but rather about "the past." Clearly, the character's creator, Blake Edwards, realized that traditional genres carried value and cultural systems with them, and that those genres meant different things to different eras.

These social shifts inflect similarities and differences between films of the canonical *noir* era and neo-*noir*. Movies of both eras tend to have downbeat thematics and an investment in dystopian notions of society and of destabilized masculinity and femininity that are rooted in postwar culture. However, where canonical *film noir* often subverted contemporary Hollywood filmmaking conventions, neo-*noir* draws upon the older *film noir* practices *as* its conventions and, in this, is retrospective, nostalgic, and conservative. The time gap between the two forms rendered practices that were once considered deviant not only familiar but, in fact, the new norm. Neo-*noir* films do not generally reject or subvert traditional styles; they are in direct continuity with, and evoke nostalgia for, them. Hence, where *film noir* was destabilizing to its contemporaries by subverting securities of existing conventions, neo-*noir* provides comfort in the now-established conventions of *film noir*.

Films noirs of the 1940s and 1950s were unselfconscious of their tradition in ways that post-1960s films are not. In fact, most post-1960s films conspicuously place themselves within the *noir* tradition. While there is some continuity between films of the two eras, a great deal is radically, perhaps unconsciously, different. Much of canonical *film noir* is presented from the point of view of white American males in peril, and that peril often resulted from the new empowerment of women, peoples of color, and peoples of other nationalities and ethnicities. Movies of the time often depict such peoples as exotic and/or evil, as in *The Maltese Falcon*, *The Postman Always Rings Twice*, and *Out of the Past*. Neo-*noir*, however, generally takes the opposite perspective. Instead of women or peoples of color or foreigners, they frequently place white American males at the center of evil (as in *Chinatown*, *L.A. Confidential*, 1997, *Mulholland Falls*, 1996, and *Devil in a Blue Dress*, 1995).

Some neo-*noir* films used stylized color to approximate the aesthetic distance the older black and white ones now produced; instead of the murky darkness and sinister shadows of the 1940s films, they used sinister, too-bright, color surfaces, or dense sepia and amber tones to evoke old color photographs. It must be remembered, however, that such stylization spoke to how black and white photography appeared to 1970s audiences, not necessarily how it had appeared to audiences in the 1940s. Some of the films using stylized color, like *Chinatown* or *Farewell, My Lovely*, were set in the earlier era and used amber filters or saturated neon lighting to approximate the color tonalities of 1930s–40s magazine advertisements and photography. They sought to replicate ways in which people of the 1970s remembered the recent past. Often, as with the frequent use of jazz in neo-*noir*, this reveals much more about perceptions and distorted memories of filmmakers of the 1970s than about the actuality of the earlier films. Other movies, like *Point Blank* (1967), *Marlowe, Dirty Harry* (1971), *The Driver* (1972), *Hustle* (1975), and *Taxi Driver* (1976), were set in contemporary times but evoked *noir* themes or stylistics in various ways, such as story patterns, dialogue, and atmosphere.

In the 1980s, numerous films, such as *Blood Simple* (1981), *Blue Velvet* (1986), *Body Heat*, and *Angel Heart* (1987), either explicitly evoked *noir* traditions or blended recognizable *noir* elements with those of other genres, such as science fiction. Science fiction films using *noir* tropes, such as *Blade Runner, Radioactive Dreams* (1986), the three *RoboCop* films (1987, 1990, 1993), the four *Terminator* films (1984, 1991, 2003, 2009, and their spinoffs), and *Minority Report*, have even been categorized as a sub-genre – *tech noir*. Such films generally present the future, or the techno-logically enhanced present, as a failed past and link *noir's* trope of the decline of the modern with dystopian fiction's and science fiction's trope of the degeneration of the future. They conflate *film noir* and science fiction within a nexus of dystopian modernism and are centrally con-cerned with abuses of state power that lead to erosions and fragmentations of individual identity. In this they place themselves within the Orwellian tradition. Many are also police procedurals because they feature agents of the state dealing with crime. Intriguingly, this blending of *film noir* and science fiction had its beginnings in the classical *noir* era. *Kiss Me Deadly* demonstrates a strong interest in surveillance techniques. Its detective, Mike Hammer, played by Ralph Meeker, famously has what is probably the first telephone answering machine in Hollywood film. But more importantly, its object of desire, "the Great Whatsit," is some sort of explosive nuclear material, which, in 1955, was considered the terrifying power of the future.

Unlike many earlier science fiction films, like *The Tunnel* (1935) or *Things to Come* (1936), that depicted the future as a potentially utopian time and space of advanced technology with wondrous possibilities, these films, taking their cue from Orwell's *Nineteen Eighty-Four*, present the future as a time in which hopes for a technologically advanced, utopian world have failed. They depict future cities as collapsing or prison-like. Some evoke the figure of the cynical private eye from *film noir* because many hard-boiled private detectives considered their own world a failure. The aspirations of early twentieth-century modernism for cities as enabling centers of human development had degenerated into frightening images of pervasive urban waste and corruption, and the city of the private detective was a dark jungle of cruelty, betrayal, and failed dreams. Films like *Blade Runner* invoke the cynicism of 1940s detectives for their futuristic central character. Such characters, whether in the past or the future, share a sad sense of their own world in irrevocable decline (Plate 15).

Further testifying to ongoing interest in the genre, many remakes of classic *films noirs* also appeared during this period, and continue unabated. Examples include *The Postman Always Rings Twice* (1946–1981), *The Big Sleep* (1946–1978), *D.O.A.* (1950–1988), *The Narrow Margin* (1951–1988), *Detour* (1945–1993), *Kiss of Death* (1947–1995), and *I, the Jury* (1953, perhaps the only *film noir* filmed in 3D, –1982).

As with films like *My Favorite Brunette* during the canonical era, numerous parodies of *film noir* appeared in the neo-*noir* era, including *Play it Again, Sam* (1972), *The Black Bird* (1975), *Dead Men Don't Wear Plaid* (1982), the partially animated *Who Framed Roger Rabbit?* (1988), and *Fatal Instinct* (1992). These parodies share the nostalgia for the older films that pervades neo-*noir*. However, the nostalgia for the newly formed genre that appears in the earlier parodies provides a comfort level that places those films in marked contrast to the disorienting, vigorously anti-nostalgic tone of the canonical *films noirs* that were contemporaneously appearing. Furthermore, *Fatal Instinct* is intriguing in that it does not so

PLATE 15 *Blade Runner.* Harrison Ford's cynical, detective-like character in a futuristic, dystopian city. © 1982 Blade Runner Partnership

much parody canonical *film noir* as much as it parodies the erotic thriller, a branch of neo-*noir* that emerged in the 1980s and included films like *Body Heat, Fatal Attraction* (1987), *Sea of Love* (1989), *Basic Instinct* (1992), and *Sliver* (1993). These films offered graphic sexuality in an atmosphere of smoldering erotic compulsion and betrayal.

More recent films such as *Devil in a Blue Dress, Mulholland Falls, L.A. Confidential, Hollywoodland* (2006), and *The Black Dahlia* (2006) are set in the historical period associated with *film noir*. Others such as *The Grifters* (1990), *After Dark, My Sweet* (1990), *Reservoir Dogs* (1992), *Natural Born Killers* (1994), *Seven, Fallen* (1998), *Heat* (1995), *The Usual Suspects* (1995), *This World, Then the Fireworks* (1997), *Out of Time* (2003), *Twisted* (2004), *Derailed* (2005), *Kiss Kiss Bang Bang* (2005), and *Sin City* are set at the time of their release, but evoke *noir* codes. All engage the tradition in complex ways and testify to its plasticity and longevity.

CHAPTER 3

CRITICAL OVERVIEW

Emergence of a New Sensibility in American Film

The formative discourse about *film noir*, which provided the bedrock for future criticism, appeared in postwar France. It drew upon issues important to the French intellectual climate of the era, particularly upon Existentialist thought (emerging in the 1940s and going full blast in the 1950s and 1960s), upon Surrealism of the 1920s and 1930s, and upon French fascination with "tough" American literary and cinematic culture – with Hemingway and other writers of the 1920s and 1930s, and hard-boiled writers of that era.

Paris had been a center for the influential "Lost Generation" of the 1920s, where, for the first time, American writers using the American vernacular and American subject matter (like Hemingway, F. Scott Fitzgerald, Robert Frost, John Dos Passos, Gertrude Stein, and even including the less "American" and more "Continental" T.S. Eliot and Ezra Pound) were considered the new wave of Western literature. The French at times adopted a proprietary attitude towards this flowering of American culture, feeling that they were championing the expatriate work of artists not yet appreciated in the US, artists who had to come to Europe to be appreciated.

The term *film noir* (meaning black film) as applied to American films was introduced in France by Nino Frank in two review essays that appeared in

Film Noir, First Edition. William Luhr.
© 2012 William Luhr. Published 2012 by Blackwell Publishing Ltd.

August 1946 and, almost simultaneously, in writings of Jean-Pierre Chartier (1946; see Luhr, 1991). Recent Hollywood films had been unavailable in France during the Nazi occupation, which began in 1940, and when they appeared in Paris after the war, Frank was struck by a new, darker quality in some of them that he called *film noir*. He particularly noticed this quality in five movies that appeared in Paris between mid-July and late August of 1946. They were *The Maltese Falcon, Laura, Murder, My Sweet, Double Indemnity*, and *The Woman in the Window*. Together, the films gave him the sense that something fundamental had changed in American cinema and that a new and important movement was beginning. Frank's use of the term *film noir* carried with it associations of "black" French films of the 1930s (such as Marcel Carné's *Hotel du Nord*, 1938, or *Le Jour se lève*, 1939) as well as Marcel Duhamel's *Serie Noire* books, which were largely translations of British and American crime novels that Gallimard began publishing in 1945.

In his most influential essay on the topic, "A New Type of Detective Story" (1946; see Frank, 1995), Frank contrasted films embodying this new sensibility with the work of Hollywood's older generation, specifically referring to films appearing at the same time by established directors like John Ford (*How Green Was My Valley*, 1941) and William Wyler (*The Little Foxes*, 1941). Although he respected the Ford and Wyler films, Frank felt that, artistically, they signified the end of a line, as having achieved a kind of perfection, but also an ossification. In contrast, Frank felt that the work of novice filmmakers like Billy Wilder (*Double Indemnity*), Otto Preminger (*Laura*) and John Huston (*The Maltese Falcon*) promised fertile new directions for American film, a virtual sea change.

Frank's critical approach had a strong literary component, and he viewed many of the developments in the films as direct extensions of their literary sources. Many of the provocative new movies were crime or detective films, and Frank compared the recent shift in Hollywood film with the shift two decades earlier in detective fiction from what he described as the sterile perfection of the British tradition evident in stories by Agatha Christie or Sir Arthur Conan Doyle to the newer and more protean American "hard-boiled" tradition of Dashiell Hammett and Raymond Chandler. He describes the detective character in the older tradition as little more than a "thinking machine" whose sole purpose was to solve complicated but lifeless narrative puzzles. In the newer works the narrative puzzles are much less important than their ability to attune audiences to complex psychological issues and to an "impression of life as it is lived, and to certain atrocities that actually exist and that no good purpose is served in hiding" (Frank, 1995, p. 133). Frank's observations are not only thematic; he also points to the significance of the formal strategies of the new films, particularly in their employment of retrospective, voice-over narration: "Parallel to this internal revolution, one ought to notice another, purely formal one, in the treatment of the story: A narrator or commentator is introduced and that permits the fragmentation of the story, the rapid gliding over the various transitional elements. This permits the emphasis on life as it is lived" (pp. 133–4). In addition, he cites the importance to these movies of their dwelling on "faces" and "behavior" rather than the meaningless unraveling of glib puzzles. Of the older tradition in both fiction and film, he proclaims, "We are witness to the death of this formula" (p. 132). He is so enthusiastic about these new developments, about the dawning of a new epoch in cinema, that he poses the rhetorical question, "Has Hollywood definitively outclassed Paris?" (p. 134).

Intriguingly, when he first attempts to classify these films, he shifts among different terms, revealing a tendency to link them with existing genres that is complicated by his awareness that, however much they may resemble older genres, they also represent something new. "They belong to what one used to call the detective genre, but it would be better to use the term criminal adventure or, better yet, criminal psychology" (p. 132). This instability in terminology indicates that the ongoing difficulties in defining *film noir* were present at the very beginning of attempts to grapple with the form.

Frank contrasts *film noir* with the Western.

> It is one of the great cinematographic genres that have replaced the Western; and there would be an amusing conclusion to draw from this displacement of the dynamism of the chase and the stirring idyll by the dynamism of violent death and the enigma to be clarified. And don't forget the replacement of the décor of vast and romantic nature by the décor of the "contemporary fantastic." (p. 132)

The dynamism attributed to "violent death and the enigma to be clarified" is particularly significant since *film noir* is so centrally concerned with death as well as enigmas, many of which are, ultimately, never clarified. Furthermore, Frank's notion of the "contemporary fantastic" is compelling since it roots the nightmare-like images and sensibility of *film noir* in the everyday world of "the normal."

He closes his essay by jokingly soliciting the reader to restrain his (Frank's) enthusiasm about the dawn of a new age in cinema: "Above all, don't make me say that the future belongs only to detective films told in the first person" (p. 135).

A jubilation in the discovery of a new form that is similar to Frank's remains visible nearly a decade later in Raymond Borde and Etienne Chaumeton's *Panorama du film noir américain*, the first book-length study, which appeared in Paris in 1955. Borde and Chaumeton attempted to define *film noir* as a "series," meaning "a group of nationally identifiable films sharing certain common features (style, atmosphere, subject), features sufficiently strong to mark them unequivocally and to give them, over time, an inimitable quality" (Borde and Chaumeton, 2002, p. 1). At other places, however, they call it a genre, a mood, and a zeitgeist. But unlike the earlier essays by Frank and others, this book treated *film noir* as an established film cycle, not an emerging one. It sought to codify and define it, and provided a baseline for much subsequent work on the form.

It is significant that Borde and Chaumeton take great care to situate *film noir* within its historical moment, as a form that arose in response to a cultural climate specific to the postwar era and one that held unique meanings for audiences of that era. They acknowledge that subsequent eras might very well respond differently to the film: "Film noir is noir *for us*, that's to say, for Western and American audiences of the 1950s. It responds to a certain kind of emotional resonance as singular in time as it is in space. It's on the basis of a response to possibly ephemeral reactions that the roots of this 'style' must be sought" (p. 5).

Borde and Chaumeton cite Nino Frank in declaring that the most constant characteristic of the form is "the dynamism of violent death" and also make note of the misogyny widespread in the genre. They differentiate between what they consider *film noir* and the newer trend of police procedurals like *The Naked City* that began in the mid-1940s, which they consider something altogether different. Borde and Chaumeton describe *film noir* as crime presented from within and from the point of view of the criminals, whereas the police procedurals present crime from without, from the point of view of the police investigating it. They cite the differences in narration – the procedurals do not have a troubled narrator but rather an authoritative agent of a benign state; differences in the hero – the hero in the procedurals is not a tormented sinner but rather a morally righteous government agent; and differences in style – the procedurals are not dominated by dark, studio-bound images but rather have a semi-documentary look. The distinction is certainly useful, although most subsequent critics tend to enfold the two together as different strains of *film noir* rather than as separate entities.

Regardless of their strong differentiation between those entities, Borde and Chaumeton make a singularly perceptive observation about the ways in which their notion of pure *film noir* functions. They comment that, although the individual shots in the films have a contemporary, semi-documentary quality to them, their cumulative effect is that of a nightmare. They feel that this resulted from a shift in film conventions during World War II, leading to the abandonment of the primary reference point of earlier films, a moral center. Furthermore, the loss of this formerly stable point of reference accounts for the form's destabilizing effect on the viewer, propelling him or her into the disorienting chaos of a nightmare and ultimately generating a profound sense of anxiety and alienation:

> The action is confused, the motives uncertain. This is a far cry from classic dramas or the moral tale of the realistic era. . . . The film takes on the quality of a dream, and the audience searches in vain for the good old logic of yore.
>
> In the end, the violence "oversteps the mark." This gratuitous cruelty and this one-upmanship in murder add to the strangeness. The sense of dread is dissipated only in the last images.
>
> It is easy to come to a conclusion: the moral ambivalence, criminal violence, and contradictory complexity of the situations and motives all combine to give the public a shared feeling of anguish or insecurity, which is the identifying sign of film noir at this time. All the works in this series exhibit a consistency of an emotional sort: *namely, the state of tension created in the spectators by the disappearance of their psychological bearings.* The vocation of film noir has been to create *a specific sense of malaise.* (pp. 12–13)

When Borde and Chaumeton's book appeared, however, the commercial viability of *film noir* was declining, and its commercial obsolescence in the 1960s would position all future critics differently. They were no longer able to discuss a vital current form, like romantic comedy or the then-thriving historical epic, but rather had to examine retrospectively the legacy of one from the past.

Early English-Language Discourse on Film Noir

The expansion and academicization of cinema culture in the US and the UK in the 1960s gave *film noir* its first widespread English-language attention. One component of this ferment was the galvanizing influence of French auteur theory, first championed in Paris by *Cahiers du Cinéma* and later, in the US, by Andrew Sarris. Auteurism, however, with its primary focus upon careers of individual artists, had shown little interest in transdirectorial phenomena like *film noir*. English-language discussions of the topic, while acknowledging French intellectual discourse upon it, did not substantially engage *film noir* until the 1970s.

Important essays like Raymond Durgnat's "Paint It Black: The Family Tree of the Film Noir" in 1970 (Durgnat, 1998), Paul Schrader's "Notes on *Film Noir*" in 1972 (Schrader, 1998), and Janey Place and Lowell Peterson's "Some Visual Motifs of *Film Noir*" in 1974 (Place and Peterson, 1998) popularized the notion of *film noir* in the English-speaking world. They laid groundwork for exploring it (posing major questions such as how to define it and whether it is a genre or a visual style) within the growing academic and journalistic film culture in Europe and the United States. Some commentators initially used the translation "black film" instead of *film noir*, only to have it changed to *film noir* in republications of their work when it became obvious how embedded the term had become. These early articles tended to be typological and structuralist in approach, and to employ socio-historical contexts and existential thought as a guide to the world of the films.

The left-wing British critic Raymond Durgnat begins his ambitious essay "Paint It Black" with the French classification of *film noir* in 1946 and, responding to some critical castigation of it as "Hollywood Decadence," situates the form within grand contexts such as three earlier "black cycles" – Greek tragedy, Jacobean drama, and Romantic Agony – which he cites as "earlier responses to epochs of disillusionment and alienation" (Durgnat, 1998, p. 37). Distinguishing *film noir* from these cultural cycles, he states that the "American *film noir* paraphrases its social undertones by the melodramatics of crime" (p. 37). He explores the ways in which American films have used the world of crime as a site for social criticism and, in particular, a critique of capitalism. Durgnat reveals presumptions important to later discourse on the form. He asserts early on that he does not consider *film noir* a genre, like the Western and gangster film, but that, instead, it should be classified by motif and tone (p. 38). Furthermore, like Nino Frank as well as Borde and Chaumeton before him, he discusses it as primarily an American form. However, while doing so, he also con-textualizes it among examples of *film noir* traditions in France (citing instances of French *noir*-ish films of the 1930s as well as the 1950s gangster cycle, particularly the films starring Eddie Constantine, later homaged by Godard in *Alphaville*), Italy, Germany, and Britain. He devotes the dominant portion of the essay to cycles, motifs, subcategories, and crossovers in the American crime film from the 1920s to the late 1960s. In tracing out these numerous categories, he makes no distinction between *film noir* of its canonical era and neo-*noir*. He discusses *Bonnie and Clyde* (1967), *In the Heat of the Night* (1967), *Point Blank*, and *The Boston Strangler* (1968) within the tradition of the canonical films rather than as part of a revival of the form. This is quite understandable given the initial

1970 publication date of the essay, a time when notions of neo-*noir* were just forming.

Paul Schrader's "Notes on *Film Noir*" was a fountainhead essay introducing *film noir* in the United States. Schrader, like Peter Bogdanovich before him, not only wrote critical and historical essays about film but also became a practicing filmmaker. Like Bogdanovich also, both his critical and filmmaking activities were informed by a deep affection for classical Hollywood cinema. Many of the films on which he worked, whether as a writer (*Taxi Driver*, 1976) or director (*Hardcore*, 1979), reveal profound affinities with *film noir*.

Unlike Durgnat, Schrader discusses *film noir* as a past form and displays nostalgia for old Hollywood. Furthermore, much of his essay is concerned with the critical discourse on *film noir*. He asks why the form had been neglected during the revival of critical interest in classical Hollywood cinema during the 1960s, implicitly attributing it to auteurist focus on patterns of individual careers rather than on transdirectorial movements, and proposes that a new, non-auteurist sensibility is needed to understand its value. In describing *film noir*, he places himself in continuity with Durgnat's approach by beginning with French critics in 1946, speaking of *film noir* as an American form, and declaring that it is not a genre but rather a group of films defined by tone and mood. He also categorizes it in temporal terms as "a specific period of film history, like German Expressionism or the French New Wave" (Schrader, 1998, p. 53). He defers to Durgnat as having already categorized its themes, with the caveat that Durgnat missed an important one – "the over-riding noir theme: a passion for the past and present, but also a fear of the future" (p. 58). He calls *film noir* one of Hollywood's best but least known periods and says it "gives auteur-weary critics an opportunity to apply themselves to the newer questions of classification and transdirectorial style" (p. 53).

He avoids the issue of why *film noir* is not a genre, saying that, rather than haggling over definitions, he "would attempt to reduce *film noir* to its primary colors (all shades of black), those cultural and stylistic elements to which any definition must return" (p. 54). He lists four "catalytic elements" – wartime and postwar disillusionment, postwar realism, the German influence, and the Hard-Boiled Tradition – but then moves on to what seems to interest him most – stylistics. He acknowledges that a study of *film noir* stylistics does not yet exist but presents his "notes" about its recurring techniques such as lighting, composition, contrast, narration, and chronology. He closes by returning to the question of why critics have neglected *film noir*, particularly amid the revival of critical attention to Hollywood film. He feels that a significant reason for this is that the 1960s revival was largely auteurist and that auteurism concentrates upon what makes directors different whereas *film noir* criticism concentrates upon what they have in common (p. 62). He also describes American critics as having always been less interested in visual style than theme, and argues that *film noir* depends more on choreography than sociology, condescendingly calling critics sociologists first and scientists second. He feels that "*film noir* operates on opposite principles: the theme is hidden in the style, and bogus themes are often flaunted . . . which contradict the style" (p. 63).

He closes with the observation: "Because *film noir* was first of all a style, because it worked out its conflicts visually rather than themat-ically, because it was aware of its own identity, it was able to create artistic solutions to sociological problems" (p. 63). He feels that, since 1930s gangster movies were often thematically transparent about addressing causes of social problems, the more stylistically dense 1940s gangster films are artistic in ways that the more famous 1930s ones are not.

To an extent, Schrader's essay put out a call that Janey Place and Lowell Peterson's "Some Visual Motifs of *Film Noir*" picked up in 1974. Their essay largely ignores the issue of defining the genre and, instead, takes its cue from their assertion that virtually all attempts to define *film noir* have agreed that visual style is the consistent thread connecting the diverse films. Starting from this presumption, they raise the question of how critics might usefully assess visual style. The essay appeared at a time when film studies was struggling to move beyond vaguely symbolic or subjective critical statements ("You could feel the rage in his eyes" or "She appeared against a sunset of indescribably beauty" or "The camera is a character in the film") and develop an aesthetic vocabulary with which to productively discuss the specificity of film style. In their attempt to do this, Place and Peterson drew upon the technical terminology of Hollywood directors, cinematographers, and technicians. They begin with a primer on film lighting and camerawork and establish *film noir* practices as deviating from the normative in pursuit of destabilization.

Place and Peterson, who wrote this essay during a pre-VHS/DVD era when access to films for detailed analysis was far more restricted than it later became, have been criticized for basing their conclusions upon too limited a selection of films. Nevertheless, this piece is important in basing its observations upon the textual specificity of the films under discussion rather than upon broad thematic and impressionistic assertions. It was an early effort in formal analysis of film, part of the 1970s movement to differentiate academic film study from other fields like literary study by concentrating less on thematic and narrative issues, which many fields share in common, and focusing more upon the formally specific workings of movies.

In 1978 John G. Cawelti published his milestone essay, "*Chinatown* and Generic Transformation in Recent American Films," which laid important groundwork for discussing *film noir* within the larger context of genre theory as well as for understanding the shift from canonical *film noir* to neo-*noir*. The essay contextualizes the film *Chinatown* within mythic, literary, and cinematic traditions, and makes a strong case for genres as not fixed but, rather, constantly evolving entities. It is prophetic about much in the subsequent development of neo-*noir*.

Cawelti begins by categorizing the hard-boiled detective story as an important American myth, "if a myth can be defined as a pattern of narrative known throughout the culture and presented in many different versions by many different tellers" (Cawelti, 1985, p. 506). After describing the literary origins of the hard-boiled detective story, he proceeds to discuss the films in which it appears and conflates those films with *film noir*. *Chinatown* provides evidence of a paradigm shift in the genre. First, it was photographed in color, not black and white, which was somewhat disorienting to 1970s audiences, who then associated such films with black and white cinematography. Next, its director, Roman Polanski, both invokes and works fundamental variations upon the established hard-boiled paradigm – in narrative patterns, in social critique, and in character development. Cawelti notes that early viewers experienced a generic confusion resulting from the collision of established with newly developing generic conventions in the film and places this within the larger context of the 1970s transformation of generic conventions in literature, drama, and film. Many 1970s films employed the conventions of popular genres but within altered contexts. Four major modes emerged in the relationships of the new films with traditional generic structures: the use of burlesque, parody, and nostalgia; destabilizing intrusions of reality into generic conventions; the demythologization of generic tropes; and the affirmation of myth for its own sake. Cawelti describes genres as having lives of their own, ones that evolve from the establishment of their conventions to widespread audience familiarity with those conventions, then to eventual overfamiliarity, and, ultimately, to cultural exhaustion. Such exhaustion can result in collisions with newly formed generic tropes and, ultimately, generic transformation. This model provided sophisticated insights into the shift from canonical *film noir* to neo-*noir*.

The Proliferation of Film Noir Studies

By the 1980s, interest in *film noir* had gathered considerable momentum and numerous book-length studies appeared, a trend which continues unabated. In 1981, Foster Hirsch's lavishly illustrated and lucidly written *Film Noir: The Dark Side of the Screen* outlined historical influences, important visual and narrative styles, and major directors, actors, and settings in the form. Three years later, Spencer Selby took a virtually opposed approach in *Dark City: The Film Noir*. Lamenting what he considered to be the contemporary tendency to fit the films into grand categories, Selby provided detailed (primarily narrative) analyses of twenty-five individual films, along with appendices of historical and bibliographical data, to illustrate his premise of the importance of considering the films individually. In 1985, David Bordwell's *Narration in the Fiction Film* presented a sophisticated analysis of theories of cinema narration as well as its practice and history. Bordwell does not consider the narrative practices of *film noir* sufficiently unique to qualify it as a genre, referring to it instead as "a set of transtextual conventions" (p. 198), but nevertheless his book provides helpful contexts and tools with which to intelligently explore narrational structures of *film noir*, and it makes perceptive comments about canonical *films noirs* like *The Killers* and *The Big Sleep*. He also discusses the form in *The Classical Hollywood Cinema* (Bordwell *et al.*, 1985), where he argues that it is incorrect to see *film noir* as challenging basic norms of classical Hollywood cinema on the grounds that its narrative and stylistic conventions are integrated into classical editing patterns.

Since the late 1970s, psychoanalysis, particularly in its Lacanian form, has become the *lingua franca* of much discourse on *film noir* and it inflects many approaches. One such approach, as evidenced in E. Ann Kaplan's collection of essays *Women in Film Noir* (1998), as well as Joan Copjec's *Shades of Noir* (1993), draws upon post-structuralist, feminist film discourse to reveal the significance of gender constructions within the films. Kaplan and others, for example, contest earlier categorizations of *film noir* as primarily reactionary in its depiction of women. They grant that the *femmes fatales* so central to many *films noirs* are presented as exploitative villains who are severely punished, often by death or imprisonment, by the conclusions of the films. Such punishments, however, involve more than the specific crimes these characters commit in the films; they reflect the ideological transgressions they make against patriarchal structures by not "knowing their place" as subservient to the men. What can be seen as progressive in the genre is that, perhaps for the first time in film history, the films present such women as intelligent competitors with the men. They do not want a comfortable dependence upon the men but rather self-determination on their own terms. They seek what the men seek – money, power, independence, social status – and often prove more savvy and more ruthless than the men in acquiring those things. Although cultural codes of the time required their punishment, these characters, in a back-door manner, demonstrated a strength and independence not previously held by women in American film.

Jans B. Wager's *Dames in the Driver's Seat: Rereading Film Noir* (2005) examines much feminist work on *film noir* with a particular sensitivity to postcolonial issues involved. It explores changing representations in both *film noir* and neo-*noir* with reference not only to cultural shifts in under-standings of gender but also to those in class and racial identity. Feminist film scholarship also influenced the field of masculinity studies in cinema, which had developed by the 1990s and employed many of the approaches of feminist scholarship. A highly influential, psychoanalytically inflected approach that contributed to this emergent field is that of Frank Krutnik in *In a Lonely Street: Film Noir, Genre, Masculinity* (1991). Krutnik challenges much previous discourse on *film noir* as impressionistic and lacking rigor, noting that, in describing *film noir* as deviating from dominant Hollywood practices, many earlier critics provided little sense of precisely what they meant by these practices. Furthermore, the diversity of works called *film noir* contributed to a widespread resistance to classifying it as a genre. Krutnik argues for a wholesale reformulation of the determinants of *film noir* using precise historical and theoretical tools. A first step is to differentiate between hard-boiled or "tough" *films noirs* of the 1940s and other modes of crime film. He makes a strong case for the employment of Freudian psychoanalysis in defining the "tough" thrillers. He finds those movies "driven by challenges to the mutually reinforcing regimes of masculine cultural authority and masculine psychic stability" (Krutnick, 1991, p. xiii). This approach has given his book its greatest influence. He describes the films as obsessed with troubled male figures who are both internally divided and alienated from the culturally permissible parameters of masculine identity. His sophisticated exploration of the representation of such figures probed the cultural construction of masculinity itself and laid groundwork for further masculinity studies.

Another approach to the genre/no genre issue is that of Tony Williams in his 1988 article "*Phantom Lady*, Cornell Woolrich, and the Masochistic Aesthetic," which applies Gaylyn Studlar's (1988) work on masochism to films related to the fiction of Cornell Woolrich in a way that attempts to shift discussion of *film noir* from tropes of content to tropes of affect.

Studlar, particularly in her work on the films of Josef von Sternberg, demonstrated the centrality of a dynamic in those films by which viewers were invited to empathize with the ongoing suffering of masochistic central characters. Williams shows how such an aesthetic is evident not only in the works of Cornell Woolrich but also, and particularly since Woolrich was highly influential upon *film noir*, in the genre itself. Arguably, much of the appeal of *film noir* lies in the attraction that its depressive, tormented milieu holds for its audience.

Vivian Sobchack's 1998 essay "Lounge Time: Post-War Crises and the Chronotope of Film Noir" examines canonical *film noir* from a phenomenological perspective. It explores the genre's recurrent physical spaces by grounding them in the specific socio-historical significances they held for the initial makers and viewers of the films. She cogently argues that the articulation of such spaces contributed to the internal logic of the movies as well as to the external logic of the culture that produced them. She finds such spaces to be historically tangible as well as emblematic presences in postwar life; they include the cocktail lounge, the dance hall, the bar, the hotel room, the boardinghouse, the diner, the motel, and the bus and train station. Each held a meaning in the postwar world that might have been quite different a generation earlier or later. Cocktail lounges, nightclubs, and hotels, for example, tended to be spaces of glamour and sophistication in movies of the 1930s. A decade later in *film noir*, however, they tend to be impersonal, decadent, and dangerous.

Sobchack takes the notion of a chronotope from literary theories of Mikhail Bakhtin and argues for the significance of the temporal and spatial specificity upon which cultural productions draw. She claims that the spaces of *film noir* redundantly emphasize the absence in the films of traditionally valued American home and family life. It is a structured absence, indicative of a deeply felt loss. Supportive nuclear families are rare in *film noir*, as are happy homes and children. In their place we find imperfect substitutes such as lonely hotel rooms, cocktail lounge sexual encounters, impersonal meals in diners or nightclubs, and social interactions with unreliable and often manipulative strangers. Sobchack associates these with the widespread sense of anxiety, loss, and disconnection in *film noir*.

In addition to gender approaches, more recent articles dealing with racial and national representation in *film noir* have opened up an important new field of exploration. They include Manthia Diawara's "*Noir* by *Noirs*: Towards a New Realism in Black Cinema" (1993b), Eric Lott's "The Whiteness of *Noir*" (1997), and Julian Murphet's "Film Noir and the Racial Unconscious" (1998), and raise issues such as the erasure or marginalization of peoples of color in many *films noirs* and the use in those films of highly coded racial imagery. Jazz, for example, was often coded as African American music and, within social codes of dominant cinema in the postwar era, presented as signifying savage or evil behavior. These films generally do not directly attribute evil to African American characters or environments but rather symbolically associate anti-social behavior with them. This occurs in movies like *Phantom Lady* with the representation of a frenzied jazz drummer. Even though the character is played by Elisha Cook, Jr, a white actor, his behavior symbolically associates him with racist images of blackness. An African American band drives the white nightclub audience in *D.O.A.* into a similar, animalistic frenzy, and in that club the murder of the main character is concealed.

By the late 1980s, a number of works appeared that engaged not only the form, but also the history of discourse upon the form, and indicated an awareness of *film noir* as a cultural tradition. J.P. Telotte's *Voices in the Dark: The Narrative Patterns of Film Noir* (1989) focuses upon the cultural significance of the form's narrative mechanisms, particularly with relation to those of the classical Hollywood cinema. In the 1990s, numerous collections of essays, many of which had been previously published in relatively obscure journals, testified to the academic institutionalization of *film noir*. These collections gathered diverse approaches to the genre in one place and enabled students to readily gain a sense of the history of the discourse upon it as well as major points of debate about its identity and cultural significance. R. Barton Palmer, for example, collected historically influential essays and reviews about *film noir* as well as commentary on major social and cultural trends of the 1940s in *Perspectives on Film Noir* (1996). Alain Silver and James Ursini took on an ambitious, long-term project of gathering useful materials in their volumes *Film Noir Reader* (1996), *Film Noir Reader 2* (1999), *Film Noir Reader 3: Interviews with Filmmakers of the Classic Noir Period* (co-edited with Robert Porfirio, 2002), and *Film Noir Reader 4: The Crucial Films and Themes* (2004).

Some significant work has appeared that does not fall under the dominant categories of recent approaches. One example is John Belton's "*Film Noir*'s Knights of the Road" (1994), which discusses *film noir* in relation to the road movie and in particular to the figure of the tramp, arguing that the romanticized tramp associated with Charlie Chaplin from the 1910s on had, in the *noir* era, become a misanthropic and even sinister figure. The article includes an insightful survey of important issues related to *film noir*.

James Naremore's *More than Night: Film Noir and Its Contexts* (2008) provides an elegant and comprehensive overview of much of the discourse surrounding the form as well as its contradictions. On page 5 of the first chapter, he writes, "I contend that *film noir* has no essential characteristics and that it is not a specifically American form." He follows this apparent dismissal of the genre with more than three hundred pages on *film noir*. This is neither a contradiction nor an indication of poor scholarship but, rather, an honest acknowledgment of the at times bewildering complexities of his topic in what is probably the best book upon *film noir* for a long time to come. Building upon Naremore's approach, a central concern of this book engages this complexity and places *film noir* alongside terms like "tragedy" or "James Bond" (see below) which have had multiple and contradictory meanings over time, and yet persevere in common usage with the presumption of their having a single, universally apparent, meaning.

In 2004, Edward Dimendberg's *Film Noir and the Spaces of Modernity* presented original insights into the genre by demonstrating its profound engagement with the concerns and influence of modernism, most particularly in the shaping and significance of the modern urban landscape, with that landscape's redefinition, and with the social influences of urban spaces. The book uses tools of film history, urban history, architecture, and philosophy to show how the anxiety associated with *film noir* reflects an urban landscape in a moment of convulsive transition. It is a landscape in decay, revealing the collapse of utopian hopes for the modern city and inspiring anxiety about what will follow. Dimendberg discusses ways in which these depictions of urban life created new ways of seeing. One instance appears in the blank, unseeing stares of people in crowded public spaces like the New York City subway in *Pickup on South Street*, which allow a pickpocket to rob people in full view of a crowd whose eyes are open but who are conscientiously not seeing. Another instance is in the aerial photography of urban spaces in films like *The Naked City*, a new way of photographing cities that, because of its associations with wartime bombsight photography, implies human irrelevance as well as human vulnerability. *The Naked City* was based upon a book of Weegee photographs, which presented cold, unromanticized, black and white flashbulb images of the seamy side of urban life. All glamour and any nostalgia for the things depicted in the images are absent. Such films invoke anxieties about surveillance, dehumanization, and state control. The appearance in the late 1940s of the police procedural film made particular use of such patterns of seeing as well as the impersonal "Voice of God" narration. They promoted science as a tool not only for fighting crime but also for unemotionally examining humanity itself. Another insightful and original book about the cultural significances of urban space is David L. Pike's *Metropolis on the Styx: The Underworlds of Modern Urban Culture,*

1800–2001 (2007). Pike explores the historical ways in which underground spaces in the modern city have been conceptualized and perceived over the past two centuries. This is not a book about *film noir* but rather one about the environments, historical or mythic, from which *film noir* emerged and which appear repeatedly and significantly in the genre.

In 2007, *"Un-American" Hollywood: Politics and Film in the Blacklist Era*, edited by Frank Krutnik, Steve Neale, Brian Neve, and Peter Stanfield, gave a number of sophisticated approaches to ongoing debates about the socio-political contexts from which many important *films noirs* emerged. Although the book's main focus is upon Hollywood in the Blacklist era, its essays present substantial material on *films noirs*, their filmmakers, and their production and distribution history. Charles Affron and Mirella Jona Affron's *Best Years: Going to the Movies, 1945–1946* (2009) provides helpful reception contexts for *film noir* in its formative years.

Perspectives on the Generic Status of Film Noir

Barbara Klinger, in *Melodrama and Meaning: History, Culture, and the Films of Douglas Sirk* (1994), employs a useful term, "mass camp," to indicate historical ways in which later generations have employed outdated conventions, such as those of *film noir*, for chic, aren't-we-superior-to-it-all referentiality in newer works. Hence, the very dialogue, postures, and situations that were disturbing in canonical *film noir* have later been used for comic effect.

One example appears in an August 9, 2007 *New York Times* review by Jonathan Kalb of Ian W. Hill's play *Necropolis #1&2*. The review's very title, "To Sleep the Big Sleep: Call it Murder, My Sweet," cites titles of two classic *films noirs*. It begins:

> Among the many pleasures of classic noir films from the 1940s and '50s is their chiseled dialogue. Goons, floozies and stoolies talk in aphorisms and one-liners, usually at machine-gun tempo. A hard-boiled dame playing coy won't just say, "Go away," when she can say, "That's between me and the lamppost, and you ain't no lamppost." A gumshoe on the hunt always has a wisecrack in his back pocket, like, "It's funny, but practically all the people I know were strangers when I met them."
>
> This pleasure in language, as much as the erotic allure of the crime stories and the Expressionist visual style, explains why noir has been so frequently mined for material by theater people. Theater is our most venerable showcase for language. For the noir-besotted writer and director Ian W. Hill, however, it's more an animate postmodern notebook.

Kalb goes on to describe the play as composed of dozens of recorded lines from canonical *films noirs*, which are played and performed by lip-synching actors who strike *noir*-like poses against projected images of vintage photographs of urban scenes. This is a theater, not a film, review, and yet the playwright and the reviewer clearly use *film noir* not only to refer to individual films but also as an extra-filmic cultural referent invoking character types, iconic situations, images, and language use. Here, the legacy of *film noir* no longer evokes anxiety and fear but rather a sense of ridiculously outdated tropes, or what Klinger terms mass camp.

In this instance, the camp sensibility drains *film noir* of any substantive meaning. But it touches upon the enduring question of what, exactly, is meant by *film noir*? The respected critic Dave Kehr (2008) has written, "*Film noir* is a notoriously difficult concept to define, and after years of futile attempts I've come to rely on the time-honored method of the Supreme Court Justice Potter Stewart: I know it when I see it, as he so succinctly observed in regard to pornography." This also echoes Louis Armstrong's famous description of jazz, another form comparably difficult to define. Such observations do not really solve the problem of definition as much as they point to it, while at the same time indicating that the speakers believe that the form they are discussing, whether *film noir*, pornography, or jazz, has its own integrity. Grappling with a functional definition of it, however, is complicated.

One useful model in approaching this notion of continuity amid diversity is that used by Tony Bennett and Janet Woollacott in their *Bond and Beyond: The Political Career of a Popular Hero* (1987). The book demonstrates how a specific character, James Bond, with a specific role, British secret agent, who appears in novels and films with similar narrative trajectories has not one meaning but many. Everyone knows James Bond. The character is widely presumed to be a single entity, unchanged over time (even when the actors playing him in films have changed) from the early 1950s to the present. Bennett and Woollacott demonstrate, however, that the various manifestations of Bond present us with a bundle of contradictions that collectively show how the meaning of Bond has changed radically over time, again and again. In some instances he is an anti-Soviet, British Cold War secret agent; in others a secret agent who supports *Glasnost*-era British–Soviet cooperation; in others simply a secret agent foiling an apolitical, multinational criminal conspiracy. Sometimes he is a cocky sexual predator who seduces many women; at others he appears virtually monogamous. The book demonstrates how an ongoing popular image can contain an almost preposterous and virtually incoherent bundle of contradictions while continuing to be widely perceived as having a single, unchanging meaning. *Film noir* is a much more diffuse entity than James Bond, but the way in which the term is used and perceived works in a similar fashion.

Another helpful model appears in Terry Eagleton's *Sweet Violence: The Idea of the Tragic* (2003), which analyzes what tragedy has meant through history. Although the term "tragic" is commonly cited as if it had a single, widely understood meaning, it has been and continues to be used in diverse and contradictory ways. Should its meaning by confined to fifth-Century BC Greek drama as categorized by Aristotle, or should it be expanded to include Shakespearean plays such as *Antony and Cleopatra* that do not conform to Aristotle's definition? Should it include twentieth-century American plays like *Death of a Salesman*, novels like *Anna Karenina*, historical disasters like the sinking of the RMS *Titanic* in 1912, or the personal loss of a loved one? The term has certainly been used to describe all of these. Eagleton finds little more commonality in its many meanings than the idea of something that is "very sad." At first, such a definition might seem reductive, but its very simplicity might explain tragedy's multi-cultural, multi-millennial potency, utility, and continuity. Similarly, the most useful and elastic definition of *film noir* may have been established at its inception in 1946 – "black film," or "dark film," or film about the "dark side."

Chris Straayer provides a third model with her discussion of subject formation in "Transgender Mirrors: Queering Sexual Difference" (2008). Commenting upon the work of Elizabeth Grosz in her book *Volatile Bodies: Toward a Corporeal Feminism* (1994), which asserts that the experience of one's body contributes to the formation of subjectivity, Straayer speculates on subject formation as not a fixed but as an ongoing process that responds to bodily changes, such as sex change or menopause. Straayer describes gender in such a light and argues that "an interplay of representation, perception, and experience with regard to subject formation allows that the (changing) body can influence subjectivity without discounting contrary gender identifications" (p. 31). Hence, it is continuity not of a single thing but rather of a bundle of things, with some dominant at certain times and others virtually disappearing.

A related model appears in Leonard Leff's (2008) discussion of David Halperin's delineation of expanding postwar models for homosexuality. In the post-Kinsey era, homosexuality was no longer "a notion of orientation, a notion of object choice, [or] a notion of behavior alone" but rather an "unstable conjunction of all three." Both Straayer's notion of gender as not a fixed entity but rather an "interplay" of components, and Halperin's notion of homosexuality as not a fixed entity but rather an "unstable conjunction" of different components, are useful as categorizations of entities traditionally perceived as unitary and fixed in their nature but that are better understood as constantly evolving sites demonstrating diverse and shifting influences.

Such transformational models for gender and sexuality are pertinent to genre (particularly as Cawelti has described it), which can usefully be perceived not as a fixed entity but rather as one that is constantly evolving in response to multiple influences, such as industrial practice, critical evaluation, a growing and diversified canon, and socio-cultural shifts. Even the film genres generally perceived as the most stable have in fact undergone continual change during the short history of film. The Western had once been considered a sexually puritanical genre set in a specific place, the western United States, and time, the latter third of the nineteenth century, and supporting a specific agenda, the conquest of the American West by white people using righteous violence. However, particularly since the 1960s, virtually all of that has changed. Films like *The Searchers* (1956), *Cheyenne Autumn* (1964), *The Wild Bunch* (1969), *Little Big Man* (1970), *McCabe & Mrs Miller* (1971), *Doc* (1971), and *Brokeback Mountain* (2005) have infused the Western with violence that is not righteous but meaningless, hetero- and homosexuality, and geno-cidal white racism. The Western hero is no longer sexually pure, his agenda no longer righteous, and his place in history no longer progres-sive. Genres come and go, but those that live on commonly change in numerous ways.

Film noir is best understood as a bundle of generic characteristics, rather than as a single paradigm, as can arguably define the Western, the detective film, the coming of age film, or the biblical epic. Characteristics central to some films do not appear in others at all. Classical *femmes fatales* appear in *Double Indemnity*, *Out of the Past*, *Decoy*, *The Killers*, and *Scarlet Street*, but not at all in *T-Men*, *Brute Force*, or *Kiss of Death* (1947). Hard-boiled private detectives appear in *Murder, My Sweet*, *The Big Sleep*, *Out of the Past*, and *Kiss Me Deadly*, but not at all in *The Woman in the Window*, *The Postman Always Rings Twice*, *Crossfire*, and *The Killers*. Many of the films have unhappy endings but not *Crossfire*, *Lady in the Lake*, *The Big Sleep*, or *Gilda*. *Murder, My Sweet*, *Double Indemnity*, and *Out of the Past* employ voice-over narrations but not *The Maltese Falcon*, *The Big Sleep*, or *Scarlet Street*. *Scarlet Street*, *Out of the Past*, *Crossfire*, and *Kiss Me Deadly* use Expressionistic, chiaroscuro lighting but not (primarily) *The Maltese Falcon* or *The Big Sleep*. The list can go on, but the point is that numerous characteristics seen by many as defining *film noir* do not apply to all of the films commonly understood as belonging to the genre.

One reason for the utility of this "bundle of generic characteristics" approach is the importance to *film noir* of mood and affect, of an anxiety-producing disorientation experienced not only by the characters in the films but also by the viewer, what Raymond Chandler (referring to hard-boiled fiction) called

> the smell of fear which these stories managed to generate. Their characters lived in a world gone wrong, a world in which, long before the atom bomb, civilization had created the machinery for its own destruction, and was learning to use it with all the moronic delight of a gangster trying out his first machine gun. The law was something to be manipulated for profit and power. The streets were dark with something more than night. (Chandler, 1995, p. 1016)

Many of the films reverberate with a post-traumatic sensibility of which characters may not even be consciously aware. Titles like *Out of the Past* and *The Dark Past* (1948) point to the lurking ability of experience from the almost forgotten past to emerge and menace ostensibly happy lives. Other titles like *Cornered* and *No Way Out* (1950) evoke the sense of despair-inducing entrapment in a deterministic world that is widespread among the movies. Many films center upon threats to or erosions of identity, whether through paranoia, amnesia, or clinical insanity (as in *Spellbound*, 1945, *High Wall*, 1947, and *The Snake Pit*, 1948), and some use nightmares or drug hallucinations to signify psychic instability.

Unlike genres with clearly defined and widely acknowledged conventions, *film noir* is a moving target, hard to nail down. In this, it resembles comedy, another genre notoriously difficult to define. Affect is also important to film comedy. One might call a film a comedy if it makes its audiences laugh. This would be the case whether the film is set in contemporary times or the Middle Ages, whether in Chicago or Mumbai; whether the narrative trajectory is upbeat or downbeat, classically linear or episodic, or concerns crime, romance, or gold prospecting; whether its comedy results from sophisticated verbal interplay or baggy-pants slapstick pratfalls; and whether it adheres to codes of realism or discards them in favor of those of fantasy. Comedy has the cultural advantage over *film noir* of a long pedigree, stretching at least as far back as Aristophanes and Menander and appearing in virtually every genre, from theater, poetry, fiction, opera, and film, among others. As Terry Eagleton in his study could find little commonality among things termed tragic than that they are "very sad," comedies may have little more in common than that they are "very funny," a description that covers a bizarre diversity. *Film noir* is similar. All *films noirs* are "very dark," but beyond that are difficult to define collectively'

The Reception Context of Film Noir

Why did these films appear when they did? Why do they enjoy the reputation they have developed? Why, today, have they, more than contemporaneous films of other genres, come to represent their era to us? What chords do they strike? How do people remember them and how have the films changed in the process of being remembered? How and why are they constantly being reinvented? These significant questions have many possible answers.

Why has this tradition remained so potent and pertinent today? One explanation may also account for the recent interest in the "Greatest Generation." The members of the generation of the 1940s and 1950s are now elderly and will soon be gone. This is the last time when people of that generation can be actively engaged; in the future, only the historical record will be available. Those people are the parents, grandparents, and great-grandparents of contemporary filmmakers and film scholars and an engagement with that generation gives contemporary filmmakers and scholars what may be their last opportunity to directly examine their own origins. Beyond the personal and historical connections that *film noir* affords contemporary filmmakers and writers, the films also represent for many the last era of Hollywood's "Golden Age." The end of *film noir* in the early 1960s also marked the end of the Hollywood studio system and its filmmaking practices, the end of black and white as the dominant film stock, the end of censorship codes of classical Hollywood, and the end of a certain kind of gender stylization and verbal wit, the passing of an era.

Intense nostalgia for *film noir* first became visible in the late 1950s with the French *Nouvelle Vague*, even while late *films noirs* were still being made. Jean-Luc Godard famously dedicated his first feature film, *Breathless*, to Monogram Studios (a poverty-row studio in the US that produced some *films noirs*) and had his tough-guy leading character, played by Jean-Paul Belmondo, conspicuously mimic Humphrey Bogart. His *Alphaville* and François Truffaut's *Shoot the Piano Player* (1962) comparably acknowledge *film noir*. Because the image of *film noir* is so bound up with the era of its initial production (as, for example, Westerns, romantic comedy, or musicals are not) and because neo-*noir* films so conscientiously evoke that era, it is useful to outline pertinent elements of the historical, social, and filmmaking contexts within which classical *film noir* emerged.

Furthermore, since every era has crises, traumas, and dark sides, it is important to be historically specific about the ones upon which *film noir* drew.

When the films first appeared, the US was engaged in World War II and the convulsions of global war were an everyday reality. That war had not erupted into an idyllic peacetime but had followed more than a decade of catastrophic economic depression. These two traumatic historical eras infused the national consciousness with the awareness that the kind of ebullient prosperity the country had enjoyed in the 1920s could not be relied upon, that social and economic stability were fragile. Widely circulated contemporaneous newsreel images of countries devastated by the war reinforced that sense of social fragility. Although the probability of Allied victory was strong by the time most early *films noirs* appeared, anxiety persisted about what profound damage had already been done, and what might follow, and what did follow was the Cold War. These three historical traumas – the Depression, World War II, and the Cold War – bracket the classical era of *film noir* and pervade its sensibility. Furthermore, the very abruptness of the shifts from one period to another had destabilizing effects. National fears lurched from anxieties about economic disaster to foreign enemies to an enemy within. Orientation to each new social menace required new social and ideological alignments. Enemies suddenly became friends and vice-versa. Old strategies for dealing with social convulsion became suspect if not treasonous. Destabilization appeared even in victory.

In film, this paranoia extended far beyond *film noir*. Resonant examples appeared in other genres such as horror, science fiction, and the Western. In *Invasion of the Body Snatchers* (1956), an alien force from outer space systematically takes over a small, middle-American town. We never see any space creatures at all; rather, the people of the town become hosts for alien beings. Mysterious plant-like pods appear and grow into replicas of the townspeople. When those people sleep, they are replaced by the replicas, which continue to look and behave outwardly like their hosts. The central character, a respected physician, is bewildered when people begin to tell him things like, "My uncle is not my uncle," only to find the uncle apparently unchanged. When greater numbers of people say this, he thinks he is witnessing a strange mass hysteria. He gradually learns that it is not mass hysteria at all but that the entire town actually is being taken over. Former friends even approach him and implore him to become "like us." He can trust fewer and fewer people and, eventually, the townspeople begin to hunt him. He fears the loss of his own identity as well as the civilization he knows.

The screenplay was written by Daniel Mainwaring, who, a decade earlier, had written *Out of the Past* (under the pseudonym Geoffrey Homes, the same name he used in writing the novel *Build My Gallows High* upon which the screenplay was based). In his insightful study of *Invasion of the Body Snatchers*, Barry Keith Grant (2010) describes numerous connections among Mainwaring's screenplays in different genres, many of which relate to trends in the film industry as well as in the culture at large. Both *Out of the Past* and *Invasion of the Body Snatchers* clearly embody the era's anxiety about destabilizations of identity.

Intriguingly, *Invasion of the Body Snatchers* has been cited as a parable about leftist as well as rightist politics in the 1950s. Some have seen it as reflecting rightist fears about the invisible spread of Soviet Communism, fears about its ability to turn everyone in the US into ideological automatons. Others have seen it as reflecting leftist anxieties, as commenting upon national pressures toward rightist conformity during the McCarthy era. But regardless of whether the film serves as a rightist or a leftist parable, it underscores the era's anxieties about the erosion of stable identity, its paranoia about the reliability and nurturance of society itself, and its fears about invasion by invisible forces.

High Noon (1952), a respected and popular film from an entirely different genre, the Western, shares central themes with *Invasion of the Body Snatchers*. Its genre is important since the Western, perhaps more than any other genre of the era, was based upon the celebration of heroic individualism in the historical foundation of the American identity. In *High Noon*, a respected town lawman learns on his wedding day that a vicious outlaw he had sent to prison years earlier has been released and is returning to seek revenge. Since he sent the outlaw to prison as part of his service to the town, he asks the townspeople to help him defend himself. Nearly everyone refuses. They feel that the outlaw is now the lawman's problem and they want him to simply leave town, feeling that his departure will eliminate the problem. He finally faces the outlaw and his two henchmen alone, defeats them, and disgustedly throws his badge into the dirt as he leaves the town.

This gesture of contempt for a debased society was later echoed at the end of *Gunfight at the O.K. Corral* (1956) when Wyatt Earp throws his badge away after the famous gunfight, and even later at the end of the neo-*noir Dirty Harry* (1971) when the title character does the same thing. And later still, at the end of the neo-*noir Point Break* (1991), Keanu Reeves's FBI agent tosses his badge into the ocean. Like *Invasion of the Body Snatchers*, *High Noon* has been interpreted as a parable of the right as well as of the left. Some on the right saw the disloyal townspeople as resembling Communist subversives in the US. Some on the left saw parallels with the rising tide of McCarthyism with its demands for ideological conformity rendering the average citizen terrified of opposing it, even when innocent people were being pilloried. But whether right or left, both films spoke to a nation deeply anxious about its social cohesion. The central characters in each film are honorable, heroic men who suddenly find their society changing in destabilizing ways around them. They go from enjoying the respect and admiration of their fellow citizens to being entirely isolated from and menaced by them. In both films, the role of the villain that menaces the hero is, in effect, given to society itself, a corrupted society in decline. The hero is not able to vanquish the evils of society but, in both cases, simply abandons it. It is no longer supportive or worth saving. Comparably, detectives in *film noir* often solve the film's motivating crime, but not the endemic social evil that underlies it.

It is important to understand, however, that *film noir* existed within and not outside of mainstream cinema. Many of the films were produced by major studios, many were not, but most received distribution in mainstream venues. They might have appeared on the bottom half of a double bill, have received few if any reviews in mainstream newspapers or magazines, and have received very limited distribution, but, by and large, they were physically and ideologically accessible to the average moviegoer. This differentiated them from movies produced by genuinely alternative modes of filmmaking, such as most foreign films of the era, the independent African American film industry, avant-garde and experimental film, industrial or educational films, or pornography. These alternative films were seldom reviewed in mainstream newspapers and magazines or shown in mainstream theaters. They received highly specialized and limited distribution, generally to specialized audiences who had to seek them out.

The late 1940s marked the beginning of the popularly perceived "decline" of Hollywood during which audiences declined precipitously, the industry was forced into extensive restructuring, and new competition appeared. For ten years starting with 1947, the industry experienced a ten percent decline in box office receipts. Various shifts in international tax laws made overseas production more attractive, further destabilizing the domestic industry. The rise of network television in the 1950s made home entertainment, including old movies, a new and feared competitor to the film studios. Thus, the status of *film noir* as an alternative to or underbelly of Hollywood joined with other forces to imperil popular notions of Hollywood's power and security and feed paranoia. This shifting of the sands in Hollywood occurred as part of a larger national pattern of social change.

CHAPTER 4

MURDER, MY SWEET

Murder, My Sweet (1944) is one of the earliest, full-blown *films noirs*. Major components of the genre are firmly in place in its disorienting visual and aural strategies, its complex narrative organization, and its character construction as well as its formal, thematic, and ideological structures. It is a rich, densely constructed work to which one can readily point when asked, "What is *film noir*?"

This chapter positions *Murder, My Sweet* within its historical moment and within the larger arc of the emergence, establishment, and decline of *film noir*, followed by its revival as neo-*noir*. It describes major thematic, formal, and narrative aspects of *Murder, My Sweet* as well as its relationship to its source in hard-boiled fiction, to earlier detective movies, and to changes in Hollywood at the time. It begins with the ways in which it signaled new directions for detective films, then develops its central strategies of disorientation, and moves on to delineate its themes of sexual manipulation and perversity. The second section of the chapter outlines four aspects of the film that illustrate major trends encompassing all of *film noir*, beginning with the confusion that occurs during times of genre shifts and then, once a new genre like *film noir* has been established, ways in which it is imitated, in which it continues to change, and its eventual decline and revival. The third trend involves the relationship of *film noir* with the development and restructuring of actor's star images and the fourth discusses the genre's revival as neo-*noir*. The chapter's final section examines the film's remake thirty years later, *Farewell, My Lovely*, as a neo-*noir*.

Film Noir, First Edition. William Luhr.
© 2012 William Luhr. Published 2012 by Blackwell Publishing Ltd.

A New Direction for Detective Movies

From its opening, *Murder, My Sweet* establishes itself as a bold departure from earlier detective movies. As discussed above, prior detective films of the sound era tended to mix murder and comedy. Although their crimes might have been grisly, their detectives solved them with light-hearted aplomb and wisecracks. The semi-comic, all-will-work-out-in-the-end tone of such films suppressed the grim implications of their motivating crimes. Many such movies were part of multiple-film series with which viewers were already familiar, and that very familiarity established a comfort zone for audiences which implied that nothing very bad could happen to major characters. Audiences knew those characters from earlier films and could reasonably presume that they would return for the next installment. Unlike *Murder, My Sweet* and many *films noirs*, these films do not draw the viewer into worlds in which the unsettling implications of crimes and social ruptures are not contained but rather expand disturbingly.

Murder, My Sweet, based upon Raymond Chandler's 1940 hard-boiled novel *Farewell, My Lovely*, was the first film to feature Chandler's detective, Philip Marlowe, and the first Chandler adaptation considered a *film noir*. Although Chandler's fiction had been adapted to film twice earlier, both movies had appropriated the novel's storylines but not their hard-boiled atmosphere. Those films shaped the storylines into the parameters of pre-existent semi-comic detective series. In the first instance, the plotline of *Farewell, My Lovely* was appropriated for *The Falcon Takes Over* (1942), one of RKO's "Falcon" films about a debonaire, high-society amateur detective. In the second instance, story elements of Chandler's 1942 *The High Window* were used in *Time to Kill* (1942), one of Twentieth-Century Fox's Mike Shayne films about a happy-go-lucky, wisecracking detective.

Murder, My Sweet, although based upon the same novel that *The Falcon Takes Over* had adapted only two years earlier, and produced by the same studio, was something altogether different. From its first scene, it signaled a new era for detective films, that of *film noir*.

Strategies and themes of disorientation

It begins by disorienting the viewer in multiple ways. Its credits appear over an odd, overhead shot of a table in a dark room. The camera slowly descends toward a barely recognizable jumble of what appear to be the tops of heads, hands, and a table lamp. When the credits end, the film proper opens with a confusing, unoriented shot of what we later learn is the reflection of a lamp on a desk-top. We soon hear dialogue, and it becomes evident that police detectives are aggressively interrogating Marlowe (Dick Powell). His eyes are bandaged. The lighting is uneven, with things that are directly under an overhead light lit starkly while the rest of the room is obscured in murky shadows (Plate 16). When Detective Randall (Don Douglas) enters, Marlowe asks, "The boys tell me I did a couple of murders. Anything in it?" Randall's face is grim as he quietly advises Marlowe to tell the whole story from the beginning. "With Malloy, then," replies Marlowe. "Well, it was about seven. Anyway, it was dark." As he talks, the camera moves past him toward, and then out of, a window and we see a montage sequence of Los Angeles at night.

On the soundtrack, Marlowe describes how he had been working on a petty case that he had never solved and had only accepted because he was broke. "I just found out all over again how big this city is." At the end of the city-at-night montage, we see Marlowe in flashback, alone, without the eye bandage, in his dark office. His voice-over tells us that he had been depressed, and that his "office bottle" had not helped him calm his depression. As a flashing light outside intermittently illuminates his

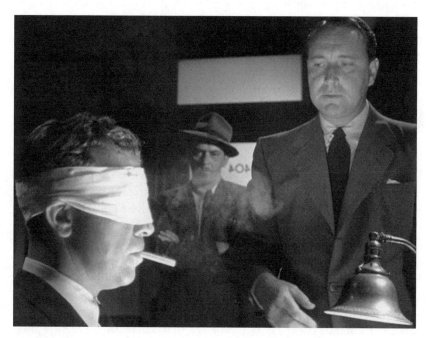

PLATE 16 *Murder, My Sweet* – opening police interrogation: Marlowe (Dick Powell) with eyes bandaged. © 1945 RKO Radio Pictures, INC.

office in an eerie, desolate way, the camera moves in on him. His voice-over tells us, "There's something about the dead silence of an office building at night – not quite real – the traffic down below was something that didn't have anything to do with me."

He sits before a large window overlooking the city. Suddenly, we see the reflection of a huge, sinister-looking man who seems to have materialized from nowhere. It is Moose Malloy (Mike Mazurki), who appears, disappears, and reappears with the flashing light. Marlowe sees him, represses his shock, and reluctantly goes off with him to search for Malloy's lost sweetheart, Velma.

The sequence establishes major patterns of formal and thematic dis-orientation for the viewer as well as for characters in the film. The very first shot, of the lamp's reflection, is impossible to situate until the camera moves back to show that the reflection is on a table in the interrogation room. But at first, the viewer literally does not know what he or she is looking at: a lamp, the reflection of a lamp, a blank wall, or an abstract space. Marlowe is confused and compromised. Most obviously, he is blinded and in police custody. Initially, he does not even know whether or not Randall is in the room. We also learn later that he does not know how the major events of the story he relates turned out, since he was blinded and knocked unconscious by gunfire at its climax. He is literally and meta-phorically "in the dark." When he refers to the inceptive moment of the events he is describing by saying, "Anyway, it was dark," his dialogue underlines the fact that the darkness extends far beyond the interrogation room in which the film opens. It refers to the police station, to Marlowe's office, to Los Angeles, and, most importantly, to Marlowe's state of mind.

Marlowe's state of mind is developed largely through his retrospective, voice-over narration, which drives the film's narrative. As with *Double Indemnity*, *Out of the Past*, and many *films noirs*, the narrator is under profound psychological pressure. His narration is not neutral and "objective"; its texture reflects his depressed, destabilized point of view.

Nothing in the opening sequence has any narrative parallel in Chandler's source novel. The novel does not have an unresolved retrospective narration begun *in medias res*; its Marlowe is never blinded, and its Malloy never comes mysteriously to Marlowe's office. These things are under-stood not with reference to the novel but rather to the then-developing strategies of *film noir*. Many *films noirs*, such as *Detour*, *The Big Clock* (1948), *Sunset Boulevard*, and *D.O.A.*, open with retrospective narrations by or about profoundly confused or doomed central characters, frequently place them literally or metaphorically "in the dark," and commonly introduce the spectator, both visually and thematically, to a disturbing world.

Later in *Murder, My Sweet,* Marlowe's ongoing confusion is encapsulated when he stumbles into Ann Grayle's house for refuge after having been beaten and drugged. Ann (Ann Shirley) tells him: "You go barging around without a very clear idea of what you're doing. Everybody bats you down – smacks you over the head and fills you full of stuff, and you keep right on hitting between tackle and end. I don't think you even know which side you're on!" Expanding upon her football metaphor of wholesale confusion, Marlowe replies, "I don't know which side anybody's on. I don't even know who's playing today."

This disorientation extends to other characters as well as to the viewer. When Marlowe begins to recount his story and the camera moves out of the window for a montage of shots of the city at night, the film gives us no clear marker as to the temporality of those images. At first, it seems that these shots occur at the same time as Marlowe's interrogation. When the montage ends, however, we see Marlowe's flashback of himself at an earlier time in his office, but the point of transition is uncertain. We do not know which of the images of the city show it at the time of Marlowe's interrogation and which ones show it at the time that his retrospective story began. Are we meant to link them to the timing of specific scenes, or are we meant to view them as establishing a non-specific, quasi-symbolic temporality? Marlowe's observation, "I just found out all over again how big this city is," points to how easily one can lose one's bearings in it, as the viewer just has.

On one level, *Murder, My Sweet* is a murder mystery, and such films traditionally confuse the viewer. Part of the appeal of the genre lies in its challenge to the viewer to figure out "whodunit." This film, however, moves beyond a sequence of puzzling events for the detective to cleverly decipher; it draws the detective and the viewer into the confusion. At times we even see Marlowe's drug-induced hallucinations, removing those scenes from any pretense at "objective" reality. The movie is less about an aberrant mystery briefly erupting into a stable, comprehensible world before being solved and more about a mystery that is indicative of an unstable world. In the many mystery films featuring Sherlock Holmes and Nick Charles, for example, those detectives might become frightened or puzzled for a time but never for very long, and never existentially so. The world they inhabit is inherently stable and benign. Marlowe's plight is fundamentally different.

Murder, My Sweet's storyline begins as the ex-convict Malloy hires Marlowe to find his lost sweetheart, Velma, whom he has not seen since he was sent to prison eight years earlier. Marlowe has little success at this when a second, seemingly unrelated, case consumes his attention. Lindsay

Marriott (Douglas Walton) hires him for protection while he exchanges ransom money for a stolen necklace. It promises to be a simple, uncomplicated job. However, at the exchange, Marlowe is knocked unconscious and Marriott is murdered. Marlowe soon learns that the necklace belonged to the wealthy and powerful Helen Grayle (Claire Trevor) and, later, he learns that it had never been stolen at all. The two plotlines come together when Marlowe discovers that the high-toned Helen Grayle and the low-life saloon singer Velma are the same person. In order to conceal her previous identity as well as her relationship with Malloy, Helen Grayle had lied about the theft, then set up the false ransom exchange and murdered Marriott and others. She and most of the other characters, except Marlowe and her stepdaughter Ann, wind up dead.

Although the plot contains numerous puzzles, the movie uses multiple strategies to weave confusion itself into its very fabric. Most significantly, it presents nearly everything to us filtered through the point of view of the main character, who is himself confused. How can we rely on anything he tells us? This central perceptual problem works hand in hand with other strategies that are evident in the film's editing, cinematography, confusing timeline, character disorientation, and even in the questionable reliability of some of its images. The film develops an atmosphere of a world gone wrong where social institutions that had traditionally existed to provide comfort and security have become perverted, whether they are healing professions like medicine or interpersonal bonds like marriage and the nuclear family. Within this atmosphere, the central dynamic linking the film's diverse characters is that of sexual manipulation.

One example of the film's disorienting editing comes soon after Marriott is murdered. Discovering the body, Marlowe looks at Marriott's driver's license. We see a shot of the license in a man's hand and presume that the hand is Marlowe's. But then the camera cuts to show that it is now Randall, and not Marlowe, who is holding the license, and that we are no longer at the murder scene but are in a different time and place altogether. We see Randall looking out of a window at night-time Los Angeles. Since it is in the same room in which the film's framing story occurred, since it is at night, since Randall is dressed similarly and speaks in the same tone of voice, we are led to believe that the narrative has jumped back from the murder scene to the initial interrogation scene from which Marlowe is narrating the film. But it has not. Randall moves across the room and the camera follows him. Suddenly we see Marlowe without bandaged eyes, and this fact places the scene not within the frame story but immediately after Marriott's death. The way in which the editing produces these two relatively minor dislocations of viewer expectations underscores the film's strategy of repeatedly disorienting the viewer and of indicating that the world of the film itself is fundamentally unstable.

A second, related disorienting strategy is evident in the movie's cinematography and lighting, especially low-key lighting, stark contrasts, and visually jarring shadows. The movie's visual textures frequently suggest a nightmare-like world. At times this is evident in the lighting, as at the beginning in Marlowe's office when Malloy's reflected and ghostlike image is visible only when the eerie outside light flashes. At times it is evident in the ways in which sets are designed and photographed, as when Marlowe and Marriott drive to what appears to be a misty, primeval-looking forest for the ransom exchange. At times, the sets themselves appear unworldly, as during Marlowe's hallucination scenes.

When Marlowe and Malloy search for Velma in Florian's bar, the place where she last worked, for example, one side of the barroom set is visually dominated by the sharp, criss-crossed shadows of stacked chairs reflected on the wall and ceiling. The shadows seem more substantial than the objects that cast them – and infinitely more sinister. Most of the film occurs at night, and its strange, at times jarring, shadows suggest a greater darkness beyond.

The meeting place to which Marlowe and Marriott go to ransom the stolen necklace resembles nothing urban but rather a prehistoric forest. It is wooded and murky, and mist rolls over the damp earth. The camera pans to follow the ghostly mist across the weird landscape. Marlowe is startled by a deer. He has no idea what lurks in the darkness and, as he looks around, is suddenly knocked unconscious. When he awakens, an un-known woman is shining a light in his face. She runs off. He then finds that Marriott had been savagely beaten to death. It all seems like a crazed nightmare. The place at first seems very different from the city at night, but like the city it also is dark, and its darkness contains unknown threats. It is more than dark; it implies an intensely subjective menace.

The uncertain border between "objective" and "subjective" is inten-sified by the fact that most of the film is presented from Marlowe's point of view. We see not so much what happens, as Marlowe's perception of what happens: things that occur only within Marlowe's mind are depicted as though they were actual events. When he hallucinates in a drugged state, we see his crazed, paranoiac nightmares. When he is knocked unconscious and describes the sensation – "a black pool opened up at my feet. I dived in. It had no bottom" – we see the frame slowly covered by spreading blackness, like an oil slick. The spectator knows that this is not an actual black pool, even though it looks like one on screen, but its tangible presence underlines the fact that we see nearly everything in the film from

Marlowe's recollected point of view. Just as that point of view does not discriminate between "objective" occurrences and hallucinatory perceptions, so there is no assurance that even the "objective" events are not highly colored by Marlowe's perception.

At times, subjectivity becomes the subject of scenes, none more so than when Marlowe is drugged and imprisoned for days in a pseudo-medical establishment at the hands of Dr Sonderborg (Ralf Harolde). Marlowe calls the surreal experience "a crazy, coked-up dream," and we see images that cannot be anything but subjective. Many of them recapitulate in distorted ways people whom we have already seen. We see Marlowe approach gigantic, menacing faces of both the psychic Jules Amthor (Otto Kruger) and Malloy, similar to images in horror films or carnival fun houses. We see Marlowe sucked into a huge whirlpool. He is then confronted by four doors that float in black space. As he stumbles through them, Malloy and Dr Sonderborg follow him (Plate 17). After the third door, Sonderborg injects him with a hypodermic needle. Again, we see Marlowe at the center of an eye-like whirlpool. Much of this is shown through a layer of heavy smoke whose immobility (unlike the floating cigarette smoke appearing throughout the film) renders it eerie.

PLATE 17 *Murder, My Sweet*: Marlowe's "crazy, coked-up dream." © 1945 RKO Radio Pictures, INC.

Suddenly, in what appears to be the sequence's first "realistic" image, rooted once again in the narrative, a sweaty Marlowe awakens in a dingy, locked room and yells. A burly attendant, followed by Malloy, enters and asks Marlowe what's wrong. Marlowe, still affected by the hallucination, says, "The doors are too small. The stairs are made of dough." The attendant mockingly says to Malloy, "I think this guy's nuts." When they leave, Marlowe, now aware that he has been drugged, paces the room to revive himself. The heavy, immobile smoke still covers the image. Marlowe's voice-over says, "I walked; I don't know how long. I didn't have a watch. They don't make watches for that kind of time anyway." Soon the smoke disappears and Marlowe escapes.

The sequence is remarkable for the extent to which it relinquishes any attempt to root itself in traditional realism. It is clearly attempting to depict Marlowe's psychic distortions as he experiences them. Only at the end do we see him distinguishing hallucination from reality. The layer of immobile smoke covering the image signifies the presence of the hallucination; when Marlowe regains psychic coherence, it disappears. This sequence not only conveys Marlowe's perception of the story's events, it also gives the ruptured breakdown of his perception that is only loosely framed by narrative events.

Murder, My Sweet not only develops patterns of disorientation by means of strange camera angles, unexpected editing, and lighting strategies, but it also repeatedly places Marlowe in situations that are exotic or perverse. The settings for these situations seem to have little in common. They vary from sleazy low-life dens – the filthy, littered house of Mrs Florian (Esther Howard) and Florian's seedy bar – to the dwellings of the ultra-rich – the high ceilings, wood paneling, and cavernous interiors of the Grayle mansion; the overlit, ultramodern apartment of the suave psychic, Jules Amthor (Otto Kruger); the shadowy sensuality of the Grayle beach house – to Marlowe's shabby apartment and office; from the bright lights of Los Angeles at night to the primeval canyon in which Marriott is murdered.

Many of the settings through which Marlowe moves convey a sense of something gone wrong or of perverse forces at play. Amthor's apartment and Dr Sondergard's house are supposed to be medical establishments. However, Amthor suavely admits that he is a "quack," and we learn that he uses his psychic consultations to blackmail his patients; Dr Sonderborg permits his house to be used to imprison the kidnapped and drugged detective. Both men clearly pervert their professions. The luxurious Grayle mansion and beach house are places of seething resentments and betrayals.

The thread connecting these diverse locales is sexual manipulation. As in many *films noirs*, the locus of the film's events is its "black widow," the wealthy Helen Grayle, who had also been Malloy's girlfriend, Velma. She initiates much of the film's evil in order to conceal her earlier life. The movie presents her as intensely attractive and deadly. She acts seductively toward Marlowe, even boldly comes to his apartment at night, comments on his good physique, and invites him to an exotic nightclub. In her beach house near the end, she disrobes before Marlowe to reveal a clinging slip, asks him to murder Amthor for her, and pleads with him to spend the night. She soon tries to kill him, and we learn that she had earlier tried to kill him before they had even met because he had been inquiring about Malloy's lost Velma (Plate 18).

Marlowe is the only major male character in the film (excepting detective Randall) to resist her allure, and live. All others die violently. Malloy had been involved with Helen Grayle/Velma eight years earlier and still loves her; her husband (Miles Mander) remains desperately in love with her, which leads to his continual humiliation and suicidal despair; Marriott

PLATE 18 *Murder, My Sweet*: Mrs Grayle (Claire Trevor) acting seductively toward Marlowe. © 1945 RKO Radio Pictures, INC.

had had an affair with her but had outlived his usefulness. All of these men, as well as Jules Amthor, who were powerfully attracted to her, die as a result of their involvement with her. The nature of Amthor's involvement with her is unclear. She claims to have gone to him for psychic consultation and to have been blackmailed by him. Whether or not they ever became sexually involved is never established, but it is not unlikely.

The film associates perversity with sexuality. All of Helen Grayle's sexual partners are unlikely choices for her: Malloy is a grotesque gorilla of a man, whose dim-wittedness and criminal background could never satisfy her social aspirations; her wealthy husband appears at least twice her age and frail; Marriott is foppish and ineffectual. Helen Grayle's association with these men is clearly manipulative. She uses her sexuality to exploit them, and then moves on to others.

The pervasive aura of sexual manipulation affects even the one traditionally normative relationship in the film – that of Marlowe and Ann Grayle. After her father nearly commits suicide in humiliation over his wife's treachery, he pleads with Marlowe to abandon the case. Marlowe falsely assures him he will but then convinces Ann to help him search the beach house for evidence, telling her that things have gone too far to be abandoned. At the beach house, they become affectionate and kiss. Abruptly, Marlowe suggests that, since her father could not buy him off the case, "you decided to be nice to me." She becomes insulted and bitter. Marlowe retracts the suggestion, but it still remains a possible motivation and taints the innocence of her sexuality. It also points to Marlowe's suspicion of all sexual motives. And he is quickly justified, since Helen Grayle has been secretly watching him and Ann together, and will soon attempt to seduce Marlowe and get him to murder Amthor.

The film develops areas of sexual perversity without parallel in the novel. The novel does have an Ann with whom Marlowe becomes romantically involved, but she is not Mr Grayle's daughter. In the film, Ann is profoundly upset by her father's sexual humiliation at the hands of her stepmother. When Ann first meets Marlowe, she takes pains to establish the fact that her father's wife is not her mother. When Marlowe comes to their mansion, she watches in agony as Helen flirts with him. Her pain comes from a dual sexual jealousy: she is developing a fondness for Marlowe, and she has an intense, possibly neurotic, desire for her father's affection. Here, she watches her stepmother flirt with Marlowe to the abject humiliation of her father.

Ann fears that she and her stepmother are rivals for the affections of both her father and Marlowe – and that she is losing. When she and Marlowe find her father preparing to commit suicide because he thinks his wife has spent the night with Marlowe, he pathetically explains: "I am an old man. You can see that. I only have two interests in life – my jade and my wife." Although he quickly adds "And, of course, my daughter," it is obviously little more than a polite afterthought and indicative of a domestic situation that has caused his daughter anguish. Then, increasing her humiliation, he desperately pleads with Marlowe to reassure him that Helen is "beautiful and desirable."

This linkage of the family with perversity (as with *Double Indemnity*, *Scarlet Street*, *The Postman Always Rings Twice*, *The Prowler*, 1951, and many *films noirs*) occurs both on the level of the movie's actual events and on that of its dark humor and wisecracks. After Ann sees her father nearly commit suicide and admit his degrading, pathetic obsession with his wife, he begs Marlowe to stop pursuing the case, to leave all alone. Marlowe agrees and leaves, but Ann finds him outside preparing to go and search the Grayle beach house for more evidence. He clearly has no intention of abandoning the case. She asks why and he replies that things have gone too far and must be dealt with sooner rather than later. He adds, referring to Marriott's murder, that "I'll stick anyway because a guy who hired me got killed, and I don't want my kids to think I had to hit a guy twenty times to kill him." This grisly image of his instilling family pride in his future children by bragging about how few times he has to hit a man to kill him is clearly meant as a sardonic joke but, joke or not, it fits in with the movie's dark image of family life.

Ann has lived in the middle of a Freudian nightmare – one without parallel in Chandler's novel – and the climax of the film makes it worse. She sees her stepmother shot dead by her father, then her father and her stepmother's former lover kill one another, and then the man she cares for blinded. She soon appears at the police station to exonerate Marlowe, whose blindness, we learn, will only be temporary, and the film closes as they romantically embrace in a taxicab.

Even this final kiss, however, is presented within a humorous context of inappropriate sexuality and murder. As the still-blinded Marlowe is led into the taxicab by Detective Nulty, Nulty departs and Ann secretly enters the cab. We see Marlowe sniffing, indicating that he smells her perfume. Marlowe then, in the film's last line, says, "Nulty, I haven't kissed anybody in a long time. Would it be all right if I kissed you, Nulty?" He and Ann then embrace and kiss. The idea of Marlowe kissing Nulty is presented as an obvious joke, but it also recalls the movie's pattern of strange and inappropriate relationships. Furthermore, as Marlowe begins to embrace Ann, he pulls back, removes a gun from his breast pocket, and resumes the embrace. It recalls a moment during the fatal night at the Grayle beach house before Helen, Mr Grayle, and Malloy were killed. After Marlowe and Helen kiss, she draws a pistol on Marlowe, taking his gun and coyly telling him that he shouldn't kiss a girl while carrying a gun. She had felt his pistol against her body while kissing him. She intends to kill him. At the film's conclusion, Marlowe's removal of his pistol prior to kissing Ann recalls this dark moment.

Its "happy ending" barely covers over *Murder, My Sweet*'s atmosphere of manipulative and deadly sexuality, with overtones of incest and prostitution, which combines with other factors in suggesting a profoundly disturbed world. That atmosphere was a major indication of the ways in which *film noir*, like hard-boiled fiction a decade earlier, first challenged and then stretched censorship codes of the time.

Four Major Trends in Film Noir

RKO premiered *Murder, My Sweet* in Minneapolis in December 1944 under its production title, *Farewell, My Lovely* (by which it is still known in the UK). The studio soon discovered, however, that the title had confused some viewers. The words "my lovely" combined with the then-dominant image of the film's star, Dick Powell, had led them to expect a light-hearted musical or a comedy, not a hard-boiled thriller. To avoid future confusion, RKO changed the title to the more sinister and hard-boiled-sounding *Murder, My Sweet* for the film's New York City opening in March of 1945.

This relatively minor incident underscores four salient trends related to the emergence as well as to the longevity of *film noir*. The first trend – genre shifts and transitional confusion – involves the disorientation experienced as the genre first appeared, or what might be termed its "growing pains." In the early 1940s, *film noir* was something new. It had no clear popular image, no "brand," and no set of widely recognized generic tropes. What was it? Studios had little sense of how to market it and audiences needed time to accustom themselves to its patterns. The second trend – imitation, continued change, decline, and revival – resulted from the way in which, like many genres over time, *film noir* did not remain a stable entity. Once it became established, it was not only widely imitated but, revealing the influence of numerous contemporary styles, it also began to change internally. After a time, it entered a period of decline and, eventually, one of revival. During that revival, *Murder, My Sweet* was remade as neo-*noir*. The third trend – *film noir* and star images – involves the influence of *film noir* upon the careers of actors associated with it and the resultant ability of studios to promote films featuring those actors in new ways. The success of *Murder, My Sweet* led to a wholesale reformulation of Dick Powell's star image from that of a young, carefree musical or comedy star to that of a cynical, middle-aged tough-guy. Many other actors had similar experiences with the genre. The fourth trend – neo-*noir*: genre revival and retro star images – parallels the shift in Powell's image during the *film noir* era with the use of Robert Mitchum's image during the neo-*noir* era, focusing upon the 1975 remake, *Farewell, My Lovely*. While neo-*noir* films draw upon *film noir* in numerous ways, they also produce a substantially different form. Where the 1944 film moved Powell's image into a new direction that would influence his subsequent career, the 1975 film, attuned to neo-*noir*'s agenda of genre revival, resurrected a past image that Mitchum had largely discarded.

Genre shifts and transitional confusion

When the emerging *film noir* introduced new themes and representational practices, the studios were initially uncertain as to how to market these films. Such uncertainty often occurs during periods of genre change or paradigm shifts, when older categories no longer apply and the emerging conventions have yet to coalesce into ones readily accepted by and marketable to the public. In 1931, for example, Universal Pictures did not initially know whether to promote *Dracula* as a dark love story or as horror film since, in the early sound era, horror was not yet an established genre. To cite other instances, the popularity of successful genres of the 1940s and 1950s that had valorized masculine power and triumphal violence, like the Western, the war film, or the "sword and sandal" biblical epic, declined precipitously during and after the Vietnam War era. In response, some works redefined their generic premises (as with *McCabe and Mrs Miller*, 1971, for the Western, or *Apocalypse Now*, 1979, for the war film) while other genres largely disappeared, as with the biblical epic. It is no surprise that the sea change in American cinema that *film noir* represented, and upon which French critics commented in 1946, disoriented initial viewers.

As discussed above, *film noir* foregrounded new and transgressive character types such as the "black widow" and "respectable," middle-class criminals in addition to downbeat, deterministic narrative trajectories for these characters; it presented heightened levels of violence and sexuality; it developed overtly Freudian character motivations, despairing sensibilities, and new visual strategies. Some of these things would have violated censorship codes only a few years earlier and were perceived by many of their initial viewers as either daring or distasteful.

RKO's title change for *Murder, My Sweet* underscored the fact that it appeared during a transitional time. The movie could not be marketed as a detective story/murder mystery in the 1930s mode because it deviated from then-standard patterns for such films; it couldn't be marketed as a "Dick Powell movie" because, in 1944, it didn't fit that perception either. It couldn't be marketed as a "Raymond Chandler" film because his name had not yet become a "brand" in Hollywood. However, just over two years later, the tropes of *film noir* would become widely recognizable and all of these popular perceptions would change. Murder mysteries would become widely associated with what was later termed *film noir* and could readily be marketed as such; Dick Powell would enjoy a revived career starring in such films, and Chandler, after two Academy Award nominations, became a high-profile and widely imitated screenwriter.

The confusion that resulted from the use of the novel's title for the film could hardly have been anticipated when Chandler named his novel or when RKO purchased the film rights to it in 1942. In naming all of his novels, Chandler resisted lurid, "pulp" titles that promised steamy sex and sadistic violence. Instead, he selected titles like *The High Window, The Little Sister,* or *The Long Goodbye* that would be appropriate for works in nearly any genre. Since RKO had initially purchased the film rights to *Farewell, My Lovely* for its "Falcon" series, it immediately replaced Chandler's title with *The Falcon Takes Over.* By the time *Murder, My Sweet* was in production, its working title was that of Chandler's novel. That might have worked had not the casting of Dick Powell, with the light romantic associations of his earlier films, confused initial audience expectations.

Imitation, continued change, decline, and revival

It is not unusual for a genre, once it has become established, to change its defining components repeatedly over time in response to industrial or cultural developments. Furthermore, genre tropes that were ground-breaking and somewhat confusing to their initial audiences have, with popularity, become accepted and eventually even considered clichéd.

By the late 1940s, *film noir*, Dick Powell, and Raymond Chandler had widely known, marketable identities. Other Marlowe films with different lead actors had appeared and hard-boiled detective films had become commonplace, so much so that they were frequently satirized. Some audiences now familiar with the once-innovative strategies of these films eventually came to regard those strategies, when appearing in new films or even in revivals of the original films, as clichéd. James Naremore (2008, p. 21) noted that Raymond Borde and Étienne Chaumeton, authors of the first full-length book on *film noir* in 1955, described the audience response at a 1953 revival of *Murder, My Sweet* presented by the Ciné-Club of Toulouse. Although the innovative film was only nine years old, people laughed whenever Philip Marlowe lost consciousness and disappeared into a black pool, and in the discussion afterward the picture was treated as a "parody of horror" (Borde and Chaumeton, 2002, p. 181).

One sign of the rapidly growing popularity of *film noir* is the fact that, even while it was becoming established, its tropes were not only appropriated by other media such as radio and television but they were also widely satirized. In 1947, CBS Radio broadcast the series *The Adventures of Philip Marlowe* as a summer replacement for the popular *Bob Hope Show*, and in the following year it became a full-fledged series of its own. This followed upon the popular success of *The Adventures of Sam Spade* radio series featuring Dashiell Hammett's hard-boiled detective, which ran from 1946 to 1951. In 1947 also, Bob Hope starred in *My Favorite Brunette,* one of the earliest feature film satires of *film noir.* The title of the November 5, 1949 episode of the popular radio series *Richard Diamond, Private Detective,* starring Dick Powell, was "Satire on Radio Detectives" (This episode is sometimes called "Richard Diamond's Singing Voice"). The appearance of such satires in different media underscores the popularity of *film noir.* It makes no sense for a mass market movie or network radio show to satirize something unless what is being satirized is widely recognizable by the general public; the audience needs to "get" the joke.

By the 1960s, *film noir* seemed exhausted as a viable commercial form and appeared to die out. However, in the 1970s it was revived as neo-*noir.*

Film noir *and star images*

Film noir had a substantial influence on the careers of numerous actors, particularly in forming or changing their "image," and the popular success of these new, darker personae indicates a shift in popular taste that found such personae compelling.

From the World War I era on, a star image was an important commodity in Hollywood, commonly used in promoting films and drawing audiences. A star image involved much more than the success or failure of individual performers; it was a major component of the ways in which studios promoted individual films as well as the Hollywood industry itself. Studio executives knew that many viewers selected films primarily on the basis of their stars, regardless of genre, and expended considerable resources shaping and maintaining star images. Major stars often earned higher salaries than any other individual connected with a movie, including producers, directors, and writers, and stars were featured prominently in advertisements and posters for the films. Once a successful star image had been formed, it was precarious to tinker with it, unless that image was losing its commercial potency, as happened with the aging of the star or a decline in popularity for various reasons.

Dick Powell's appearance in *Murder, My Sweet* was a career changer for him. He had appeared in films since 1932, mainly as a tenor in musicals or in light comedy. Concerned that he was entering his forties and getting too old for such roles, he conscientiously set about changing his image. He first lobbied unsuccessfully for the lead in *Double Indemnity*, a comparably career-changing role that went to Fred MacMurray. But Powell succeeded with *Murder, My Sweet*.

In the following year he starred in another *film noir, Cornered*, also directed by Edward Dmytryk, and he continued to play dark, troubled characters in films like *Johnny O'Clock* (1947), *Pitfall* (1948), *Cry Danger* (1951), and others. In 1954 he played Marlowe again on television in *The Long Goodbye* for the *Climax Mystery Theater*. He also starred in the *Richard Diamond, Private Detective* radio series from 1949 to 1953 and went on to become a major figure, as star and producer, in 1950s and 1960s television as well as a director of feature films in the 1950s.

Powell was not unique; *film noir* provided career renewal for many actors. Numerous established stars entering middle age found new careers in *film noir*. Other examples included Robert Montgomery, a romantic lead in the 1930s, who also played Marlowe in *Lady in the Lake*, Humphrey Bogart, who went from a second-tier actor in the 1930s to a major star in the 1940s with films like *High Sierra, The Maltese Falcon, The Big Sleep, Dead Reckoning* (1947), and others. Joan Crawford, a glamorous MGM star in the 1930s, was dropped by the studio in the early 1940s owing to her aging. Her career was revived after she received a "Best Actress" Academy Award for *Mildred Pierce*, in which she played a betrayed, middle-aged woman. Edward G. Robinson, a star of the 1930s who often played either gangsters or historical figures in prestigious films, accepted his first supporting role in *Double Indemnity* and became a mainstay in many *films noirs*, such as *The Woman in the Window, Scarlet Street*, and *Key Largo* (1948). Other established actors to whom *films noirs* brought career renewal included James Cagney, Barbara Stanwyck, and Henry Fonda. In addition to middle-aged actors changing their images, many emerging stars gained their first visibility with *film noir*, including Robert Mitchum, Robert Ryan, Alan Ladd, Veronica Lake, Richard Widmark, Burt Lancaster, Lizabeth Scott, Kirk Douglas, Lauren Bacall, and Raymond Burr.

Some established stars not generally associated with *films noirs* appeared in them hoping that such roles would give depth and range to their glamorous, more lighthearted images. These include Tyrone Power (*Nightmare Alley*, 1947), Lana Turner (*The Postman Always Rings Twice*), Robert Taylor (*High Wall*), and William Holden (*The Dark Past* and *Sunset Boulevard*).

Neo-noir: *genre revival and retro star images*

In 1975, the notion that a title like *Farewell, My Lovely* in a film featuring Robert Mitchum could confuse anyone in the way that the same title had done three decades earlier was absurd. *Film noir* was no longer an emerging form; in fact, it was one that had peaked and declined decades earlier, and by 1975 was in the process of revival. Audiences could no longer be confused about what *film noir* was.

Robert Mitchum's performance as Marlowe in *Farewell, My Lovely* is singular in that he could have played the same role three decades earlier in *Murder, My Sweet* when both he and the genre had been young. Nearly sixty in 1975, Mitchum was participating in a nostalgic revival of a virtually dead genre in which he had been a considerable presence as a young actor. His 1975 presence echoed his 1940s persona.

The fact of an aging actor playing a role that recalled his or her younger persona is not unusual in film history. Mitchum himself had earlier played such a role in *The Hunters* (1958, coincidentally directed by Dick Powell). Mitchum's character was a World War II pilot returning to service during the Korean War to fly an F-86 Sabre jet fighter. A younger pilot (Robert Wagner) at first mocks his age and background in now–obsolete, propeller plane technology until Mitchum's character proves himself a superior jet pilot. The sixty-year-old John Wayne played a similar role, though in a more comic mode, in *True Grit* (1969), proving that his "one-eyed fat man" character can still defeat younger outlaws. In *The Band Wagon* (1953), Fred Astaire plays an aging musical comedy star, like himself, who feels his career is in decline and that he is losing out to a younger generation. He successfully bridges the generation gap and stars in a hit musical.

At times such a strategy has been used to contrast different eras, generally privileging the earlier one. Newly released from prison, Humphrey Bogart's gangster in *High Sierra* displays a skill and integrity that the younger generation of gangsters cannot equal. In *I Walk Alone* (1948), Burt Lancaster plays a Prohibition Era gangster who emerges from a fourteen-year jail sentence to find that the criminal world he knew has been replaced by a colder, more corporate one in which he no longer belongs. His old partner (Kirk Douglas), now part of the corporate criminal world, balks at paying him money promised him. Three decades later, the two stars appeared in *Tough Guys* (1986) about two elderly gangsters released from a thirty-year prison term into a world that has changed. This comic film trades on the older personae of the actors as well as the contrast in historical eras. They even stage a successful train robbery, a type of crime associated with the past. In these cases the actors and the characters they play carry their own pasts with them and assert its ongoing potency.

Such contrasts of old and new do not always favor the old and, at times, have been used for horrific ends, indicating that the actor/character has not triumphed over age but rather has been rendered grotesque by it. This pattern can also reveal sexist presumptions within Hollywood about the effect of aging on women as opposed to men, Examples include movies like *Sunset Boulevard* (1950) or *Whatever Happened to Baby Jane?* (1962), which show once-glamorous actors, like Gloria Swanson, Joan Crawford, and Bette Davis, as grotesque crones.

In the late 1950s another component appeared in such films of referentiality to actors and character types that provides a direct antecedent to neo-*noir*. In this, not only were the individual pasts of the actors and characters evoked, but so also was the history of the Hollywood industry itself in which those character types and actors had been created. Many directors of the French *Nouvelle Vague* employed this strategy, partially as a way of declaring their allegiance to Hollywood genre cinema which had been denigrated by the French critical establishment in favor of the French "Cinema of Quality." These new films were less interested in affirming older actors or character types than institutions of cinema themselves. In Jean-Luc Godard's first film, *Breathless*, Jean Paul Belmondo's character mimics Humphrey Bogart's mannerisms while looking at a poster for a Bogart film. Here, Belmondo's character is not invoking himself at a younger age but rather a recently deceased Hollywood star's persona. But it involves more than an individual actor. Throughout the film, Godard references classical Hollywood filmmaking, even, as we noted in the previous chapter, dedicating the film to Monogram Pictures, a poverty-row Hollywood studio.

At this time, much of Godard's work referenced older cinemas. In *Contempt* (1965), he had the influential film director Fritz Lang play himself as a director making an epic film of Homer's *Odyssey*. Godard's satirical *Alphaville* was part dystopian science fiction set in the near future and part *film noir*, whose central character, a secret agent played by Eddie Constantine, is a parody of brutal hard-boiled detectives. These films, and others by *Nouvelle Vague* directors like François Truffaut (e.g. *Shoot the Piano Player*, 1965), evoke not only individual older films and characters but also cinematic institutions like old Hollywood genres.

Such evocations of historical eras and genres laid the groundwork for neo-*noir* and films like *Farewell, My Lovely*. But where many *Nouvelle Vague* films were satirical and distanced, even Brechtian, in their referencing of older films, neo-*noir* films tended to be nostalgic and immersive.

Farewell, My Lovely *and* Neo-Noir

While the success of *Murder, My Sweet* led to an image change and career renewal for Dick Powell, three decades later, Robert Mitchum drew upon an outdated, retro image for *Farewell, My Lovely*.

Farewell, My Lovely, the third Hollywood adaptation of Chandler's novel, reveals an adaptation strategy as well as an engagement of *film noir* as different from that of *Murder, My Sweet* as that film's strategy had differed from *The Falcon Takes Over*. Where *The Falcon Takes Over* typified 1930s Hollywood strategies for adapting detective fiction, and *Murder, My Sweet* engaged tropes of the then-emerging *film noir*, *Farewell, My Lovely*, coming three decades later, demonstrates nostalgia for *film noir* of the 1940s as well as for the long-gone, classical Hollywood era.

In the 1940s, *film noir* reflected a contemporary sensibility; the hard-boiled private detective was a man of his era. By the 1970s, however, the romanticized private eye, like the cowboy, recalled a past age. He had become associated with value structures and styles of filmmaking that were as anachronistic as the fedora or Lucky Strike Green. Even when presented as contemporary men dealing with contemporary problems, such characters could not help but recall a past age, like modern-day cowboys in pick-up trucks. Like the Western, private eye films and television series were enormously popular in the 1950s. Since then, however, they have nearly disappeared, with the private eye genre being largely replaced by the police drama.

As mentioned above, there has been considerable debate about whether or not *film noir* of the 1940s and 1950s is a genre. Factors contributing to this are that the term was used primarily in European criticism until the

1960s and that neither Hollywood filmmakers nor US critics of the era considered many of the films as part of a tradition. Many filmmakers who made *films noirs* in the postwar era, such as Edward Dmytryk (director of *Murder, My Sweet* and *Crossfire*, among others), have claimed that they never heard of *film noir* during that time. They felt that they were making films in other genres, such as detective films, crime films, social problem films, or melodramas. Although the issue of intentionality does not necessarily deny genre status to *films noirs* made prior to 1960, that issue simply does not apply to neo-*noir* films made from the late-1960s onward. Post-1970 movies like *Chinatown, Farewell, My Lovely, Body Heat, The Postman Always Rings Twice, Blood Simple, Miller's Crossing* (1990), and *This World, Then the Fireworks* (1997) clearly and intentionally position themselves within the *noir* tradition. Some, like *Farewell, My Lovely* and *The Postman Always Rings Twice*, are literal remakes of canonical *films noirs*; others, like *Chinatown* and *Mulholland Falls*, are set in the *noir* era, while still others, like *Body Heat* and *Blood Simple*, are set at the time of their production, but all use visual and narrative strategies to evoke *film noir*.

With such works, the question arises: what, exactly, are they evoking or adapting? Does one call *Farewell, My Lovely* a remake of *Murder, My Sweet*, an adaptation of Chandler's novel, or even a remake of *The Falcon Takes Over*? It gets complicated and it goes beyond the relationship of individual works. *Chinatown*, while based on an original screenplay, constantly evokes older movies. It is set in 1937 and its credits appear in black and white in an old aspect ratio and use the Paramount logo from the 1930s. Before the movie goes to a widescreen and Technicolor, it gives viewers the impression that they are literally watching an old movie. These films draw not only upon individual sources but also upon a genre and an historically specific style of filmmaking. They display intense nostalgia for classical Hollywood filmmaking practices and for postwar American culture. This nostalgia perhaps marks the most significant change in approach from canonical *films noirs* to neo-*noir*. The films of the 1940s and 1950s were set at the time of their release and spoke in disquieting ways to their contemporary audiences about issues and sensibilities of their time. As noted above, the post-1960s films do not engage the era of their release as much as they do the remembered past. Even though many events and characters within the films are disturbing and sleazy, the movies tend to associate those things with problems and sleaze of the past, not the present. Consequently, they have a tone almost unthinkable in canonical *film noir*—nostalgia. While the themes of the recent films are dark and chilling, their tone often works to establish a comfortable, not disquieting, reception climate of nostalgia for dark and chilling moments in old films. Viewers might see murders and betrayals, but they often respond to them as to murders and betrayals in "good old Humphrey Bogart or Alfred Hitchcock movies" of the 1940s. The films provide less a disturbing view of the present and more of a trip down memory lane.

Just as an examination of the circumstances surrounding the making and reception of *Murder, My Sweet* provides a useful prism into the early development of *film noir*, a look at *Farewell, My Lovely* gives comparable insights into strategies of neo-*noir*.

Unlike earlier adaptations of Chandler's novel, *Farewell, My Lovely* is not set "today," at the time of its production in the mid-1970s; rather, it is a "period" picture, set over three decades earlier in 1941. Although the Hollywood studio system had collapsed by the late 1960s, *Farewell, My Lovely* appeared when nostalgic films set in the 1930s and 1940s – *Summer of '42* (1971), *Paper Moon* (1973), *The Sting* (1973), *Chinatown* – and films reprising genres associated with classical Hollywood – *What's Up, Doc?* (1972), *That's Entertainment* (1974), *The Three Musketeers* (1974), *Young Frankenstein* (1975) – were popular. *Farewell, My Lovely* does both: it is set in 1941 and reprises *film noir*.

Much about the film, aside from the obvious period costuming, hairstyles, sets, automobiles, and other props, recalls 1940s *film noir*. Most obviously, it stars Robert Mitchum in a trench coat and fedora as Marlowe. Mitchum was an important star in the 1940s who had appeared in numerous *films noirs*, such as *Undercurrent* (1946), *Out of the Past*, *Crossfire*, and *Macao* (1952). His co-star, Charlotte Rampling (who plays Helen Grayle/Velma), is made up, costumed, and performs in a manner that recalls Lauren Bacall in the 1946 *The Big Sleep*.

Both Mitchum and Rampling evoke presences from the history of film, and because they do, their appearance in this film works in a different way from those presences in the original films: they evoke an historical period about which 1975 audiences might have felt nostalgic. In fact, Mitchum himself could have played Philip Marlowe in *Murder, My Sweet* in 1944 since he was under contract to RKO at the time. However, his presence in a 1940s' *film noir* and, three decades later, his presence in *Farewell, My Lovely* carry entirely different significances. Furthermore, as in *Murder, My Sweet* and many *films noirs*, the detective tells the story in a retrospective voice-over narration. But, in 1975, not only did the device and the use of the 1940s vernacular recall strategies of an earlier era for audiences, but it is also Mitchum's voice, used as it was in *films noirs* like *Out of the Past*.

Unlike most *films noirs*, *Farewell My Lovely* is photographed in color, but a highly stylized color. Cinematographer John Alonzo made the film one of the first Hollywood movies to use Fujicolor because he wanted it dominated with "warm," intense colors – deep reds, browns, yellows – and a good deal of neon-type lighting. The movie's color textures resemble those of old color photographs and advertising posters of the 1940s. *Farewell, My Lovely* opens with processed color shots of Los Angeles traffic and a shot of a neon marquee showing a woman's face. The old cars, the colors, the depiction of the woman, all recall older styles, but the colors are a bit too intense, the movements a bit too slow, the stylization a bit too extreme – it recalls a dream of the past rather than a naturalistic re-creation. The camera tilts up to show Marlowe looking out of a hotel window. Mitchum visibly shows his age, nearly sixty. His voice-over says, "This past spring was the first that I'd felt tired and realized that I was getting old." He says that things are now worse for him than they were in the spring and that his only pleasure comes from following the hitting streak of the twenty-six-year-old New York Yankee's baseball star, Joe DiMaggio (Plate 19).

DiMaggio's streak is a central motif in the film: it gives Marlowe something heroic to believe in, in the face of almost universally depressing events, one of which is his own aging. Throughout the film, he is confused and endangered by the events of the case, and world events provide no

PLATE 19 *Farewell, My Lovely*: An aging Robert Mitchum as Marlowe. © 1975 The E.K. Corporation

relief. At one point, a news vendor asks, "Whaddya think of this guy Hitler? He invaded Russia." Marlowe replies, "So did Napoleon, and that's not as hard as hitting forty-two straight."

We frequently see Marlowe pick up a newspaper, ignore the world events on the front page, and turn to the sports section to learn of DiMaggio's progress. Referring to the increasing pressure upon DiMaggio during the streak, Georgie (Jimmy Archer), the ex-boxer news vendor, comments that he also knows what pressure is, that he once won nineteen straight fights. This parallels the pressure on Marlowe. Things go poorly for him throughout the film and, at the end, they look worse. His clients and a man with whom he sympathized are dead, DiMaggio's streak has been broken, and American involvement in World War II is imminent. He even gives away the money he earned.

But regardless of his circumstances, the film presents Marlowe in an unremittingly romanticized light. He maintains admirable integrity in the face of danger and loss, and the extent of his loss amplifies the courage it takes for him to go on. Although he admires DiMaggio, who is younger than he is and a "winner," he sympathizes with Tommy Ray (John O'Leary), even more of a "loser" than Marlowe. He involves Tommy Ray in the case by asking him about Moose Malloy's lost Velma. Soon, Tommy Ray is murdered. This crime profoundly upsets Marlowe. Tommy Ray was a white man married to a black woman, a fact that ruined his show business career. He and his wife appear devoted to one another, and Marlowe strikes up a friendship with their mixed-race son, also a baseball fan.

The film climaxes on the gambling boat of Laird Brunette (Anthony Zerbe), a rich racketeer who wants Marlowe to bring Malloy (Jack O'Halloran) to him. Marlowe realizes that Brunette probably intends to murder them both if they go onto the boat, but he also realizes that only by taking that risk can he solve the case. He risks his life because "otherwise that kid of Tommy Ray's will haunt me for the rest of my life for letting them kill his father." Marlowe's act of altruistic heroism inspires a comparable one from Detective Nulty (John Ireland). Nulty at first refuses to help Marlowe because he does not want his career to be destroyed by Brunette's political power. Suddenly, Nulty tells his driver to head for Brunette's boat. His thoroughly corrupt assistant, Billy Rolfe (Harry Dean Stanton), refuses to go, and Nulty screams, "Seven people are dead, Rolfe, seven, and the police are driving away." He imperils his career, is morally rejuvenated, saves Marlowe's life, and scores a major triumph on the case.

At the end, Marlowe reads of the breaking of DiMaggio's streak. He still has money he got from Brunette and says, "I had two grand in my pocket that needed a home and I knew just the place." He goes to give the money to Tommy Ray's widow and son, and the film ends. Even the DiMaggio loss does not bring him to despair, but rather stirs in him a sense of admiration for the unexpected achievements of so-called losers. "Bagsby and Smith, a couple of run-of-the-mill pitchers, stopped DiMaggio. Perhaps they had a little extra that night, like Nulty had tonight."

Farewell, My Lovely presents Marlowe as a man of prodigious integrity, an old-fashioned hero who gains nothing for himself but helps underdogs and inspires moral strength. There are no analogues to Tommy Ray's family, to Nulty's rejection of his corrupt past, to World War II, to Joe DiMaggio, or to Georgie in either of the earlier adaptations or in Chandler's novel, but they are central to the nostalgic strategies of this film. At the center of that nostalgia is the romanticized depiction of Marlowe's "old-fashioned" masculinity. Marlowe's benevolence to Tommy Ray's family is presented as evidence of his radiant moral heroism, confirmed not only by the boy's fondness for him but also by its effect on Nulty's moral rejuvenation. Furthermore, nearly everyone in the film, even Brunette, respects Marlowe.

Unlike the two earlier adaptations and the novel, Marlowe has no significant romantic involvement, and the plot is not structured around a developing romance. In the novel and in the earlier adaptations, Ann provides a romantic interest for Marlowe. This film has no analogue for her, and the supportive place she structurally supplies in the novel's plot is partially filled by the punchy news vendor, Georgie. Most women in the film are unappealing or evil. Marlowe's flashback begins as he searches for a runaway high-school girl. When he locates her in a dance hall, he must free himself from the clutches of a blowsy, middle-aged woman who has aggressively approached him. When he delivers the girl to her parents, she hits him powerfully in his groin, and he doubles up in pain. His remaining experiences with women in the film, including the drunken, disheveled Mrs Florian (Sylvia Miles), are comparable.

He is not presented as a celibate and is obviously attracted to Helen Grayle. When he prepares to leave in embarrassment after her husband (Jim Thompson) has discovered them kissing, she says, "You're old-fashioned, aren't you?" and he replies, "from the waist up." Later in the film, he invites her "to my place," and she says, "What for? You've got everything we need with you." The film then cuts to a long shot of Marlowe's car parked at the beach, and, although we only see them necking, the film implies that they have made love. Marlowe later tells Nulty, "She was incredibly beautiful. And she was something, Nulty, really something."

Velma/Helen Grayle is the film's center of desire and is destructive or deadly to all of her lovers or consorts – her husband, Malloy, Marriott (John O' Leary), Brunette – except Marlowe. The film presents most sexual activity as destructive, and it is much more explicit about sexuality and sexual deviation than earlier adaptations. It presents Marriott as homosexual, and some characters make ugly jokes about his sexual orientation. Florence Amthor (Kate Murtagh), the madam of a whore-house in which Helen Grayle once worked, is presented unattractively as a "butch" lesbian.

As in many neo-*noir* films, Marlowe finds himself surrounded by sexual excess and deviation. Hollywood's abandonment of the Production Code in the 1960s allowed many things to be shown and discussed that could only be hinted at in the 1940s. A curious pattern in many neo-*noir* films, however, is that, permitted a freedom of sexual display unthinkable in the 1940s, they display attitudes about sexuality that would have been reactionary in the 1940s. They often characterize the sexuality that they depict as degenerate and show it to be punished severely. A sign of the detective's integrity is the relative absence of sexuality from his life. In some 1940s *films noirs*, the "badness" of the black widow's sexual excess and manipulation was often counterbalanced by the "goodness" of the hero's involvement with a "good" woman. In *Murder, My Sweet*, for example, Helen Grayle's evil is contrasted with Ann's decency. The only way for Marlowe to deal with the world of "bad" sex in the post-1960 world seems to be either minimal involvement or abstinence. In this film, Marlowe does not wind up with a romantic partner of his own, as in the earlier adaptations, but rather as a kind of asexual uncle to the one traditional family unit in the film, that of Tommy Ray. The film never gives the slightest hint of sexual attraction between Tommy Ray's widow and Marlowe; his generosity will be without recompense, and avuncular. Their relationship remains "pure."

And the family is black. Like sexuality, racism was a touchy topic for films of the 1940s and seldom depicted in them. Neither of the earlier adaptations engages any of the racial themes developed in the novel. This neo-*noir* film gives that motif central importance. Marlowe warns Malloy as they approach Florian's, "Hey, this is a colored neighborhood." When they enter the bar, a bouncer tells them, "No white folks in here, just for the colored." The atmosphere, as in the novel, is racially antagonistic, and the film depicts institutionalized racism as a social fact. Nulty tells Marlowe that, although the police are indifferent to Malloy's killing of the black bar owner, they have to go through the motions of an investigation to avoid trouble from "Eleanor Roosevelt," referring to the active concern of the then-First Lady with correcting civil rights injustices.

Marlowe is aware of racial antagonism, but he himself shows no racial prejudice and, furthermore, he becomes the champion of what in a racist society is a supreme sin: a "mixed" marriage. In the 1940s, mixed-race relationships were explicitly forbidden as screen content by the Production Code Administration. This film presents mixed marriage as an act of courage: the white Tommy Ray lost his show business career because of his marriage to a black woman. He and his family become the ultimate cultural underdogs, and the film, produced at the time of heightened civil rights consciousness in the early 1970s, makes Marlowe, that defender of lost causes, their enlightened champion.

CHAPTER 5

OUT OF THE PAST

The preceding chapter discussed *Murder, My Sweet*, first on its merits as an individual film and then as one whose various components provide useful springboards for charting the overall historical development of *film noir*. This chapter looks at *Out of the Past*, made three years later, as a rich work that embodies major cross-currents of *film noir*. It also contrasts those cross-currents with their later refractions in neo-*noir*.

Since its release in 1947, *Out of the Past* (aka *Build My Gallows High* in the UK) has grown in popularity to become for many the definitive *film noir*. It can profitably be approached from many perspectives, including its place in the careers of its filmmakers and, in particular, its use of Robert Mitchum's star persona; the way in which its complex narrative structure and character ambiguity pointed toward the gradual critical acceptance of *film noir*; the way in which its retrospective narration underscores its concern with Freudian implications of repressed past experience; and its use of subtextual strategies and symbolic meanings both to circumvent censorship and to comment upon postwar gender, race, and national power dynamics. After demonstrating the value to this book of these approaches to *Out of the Past*, this chapter contrasts it with *L.A. Confidential*, a neo-*noir* made half a century later, to illustrate major differences between canonical *film noir* and neo-*noir*, focusing on their virtually opposed perspectives upon postwar American ideology and racial interactions.

Film Noir, First Edition. William Luhr.
© 2012 William Luhr. Published 2012 by Blackwell Publishing Ltd.

The Filmmakers

Robert Mitchum's complex performance is central to the success of *Out of the Past*, but the film also involved other significant contributors to *film noir*. These include not only emerging actors, like Jane Greer and Kirk Douglas, who would appear in important *film noirs* of the period, but also behind-the-camera creative people.

The movie was directed by Jacques Tourneur, photographed by Nicholas Musuraca, and written by Daniel Mainwaring. All did influential work in *film noir* as well as in other genres, particularly horror, science fiction, and earlier detective traditions, demonstrating career-long abilities to adapt to multiple generic demands. Prior to *Out of the Past*, Tourneur had directed important Val Lewton-produced horror films (*Cat People*, 1942, *I Walked with a Zombie*, 1943, and *The Leopard Man*, 1943) as well as 1930s-style detective movies in the "Nick Carter" detective series, such as *Nick Carter, Master Detective* (1939) and *The Phantom Riders* (1940). He would go on to make significant *films noirs* like *Berlin Express* (1948) and *Nightfall* (1957), as well as the horror film *Night of the Demon* (1957), while continuing to work in other genres.

Nicholas Musuraca, a cinematographer who was particularly talented in creating dark, moody scenes using chiaroscuro lighting, also worked in multiple genres. He photographed detective movies in the "Falcon" series (*The Gay Falcon*, 1941, and *The Falcon in Hollywood*, 1944) and horror movies for Val Lewton (*Cat People, Ghost Ship*, 1943, *The Curse of the Cat People*, 1944, and *Bedlam*, 1946). He shot an early *film noir* (*Stranger on the Third Floor*, 1940) and important later ones (*Clash by Night*, 1952, and *The Blue Gardenia*. 1953).

As we noted in Chapter 3, Daniel Mainwaring based the screenplay on his novel *Build My Gallows High* (both written under his pseudonym of Geoffrey Homes). He wrote other significant *films noirs* like *The Big Steal* (1949) and *The Phenix City Story* (1955) as well as the ground-breaking science fiction/horror film *Invasion of the Body Snatchers*, which shares important themes like the erosion of postwar American identity with *Out of the Past*.

Much of the power of the movie centers upon Robert Mitchum's performance, one of the most resonant in all of *film noir*. Where *Farewell, My Lovely* shows him near the end of his career and bearing the cultural weight of having become a *film noir* icon, *Out of the Past* shows him near the beginning of that career, when his image was still forming. He had appeared in numerous movies before 1947, but often in minor roles. He gained visibility in Hollywood with a Best Supporting Actor Academy

Award nomination for *The Story of G.I. Joe* (1945), but, if anything, in 1947 he was more known for his appearances in "B" Westerns. His nuanced performance in *Out of the Past* demonstrates a talent that would enable him to maintain a productive career for another half-century. He radiates a charisma that endows his character, Jeff Bailey, with dimensions beyond its role in the script. Actors playing doomed characters in many other *films noirs*, like Fred MacMurray in *Double Indemnity*, Tom Neal in *Detour*, or Edmund O'Brien in *D.O.A.*, however effective, generally give performances that function largely within parameters established by the screenplays. Other competent actors could have played those characters in similar ways. Mitchum's performance here, however, adds something extra. While it credibly conveys the dimensions of the role as written, it also adds layers of complexity and even contradiction that build a creative tension with the scripted role. Even when Jeff behaves badly, Mitchum's performance projects a deeply conflicted, melancholic personality. Although Jeff betrays his employer, his partner, and his girlfriend and meets with a dark end, Mitchum's performance gives Jeff a poetic complexity that often renders him more compelling and even sympathetic to viewers than the morally righteous characters.

Some of Jeff's complexity is indicated in the screenplay. When the gangster Whit Sterling (Kirk Douglas) first meets him, he comments on Jeff's self-containment: "You just sit and stay inside yourself. You wait for me to talk. I like that." Later, an old friend tells Jeff that he looks like he is in trouble. When Jeff asks why, the man replies, "Because you don't act like it," indicating Jeff's ability, known to friends, to conceal major tensions. Mitchum's performance adds more levels. His broad-shouldered, indolent physical presence and sleepy-eyed, detached facial expressions project raw power and impenetrable self-confidence. His periodic insolence and cynical wisecracks reinforce this and yet all exist within the context of his character's repressed despair and increasing loss of control. Jeff is an amalgam of near-contradictions that Mitchum's performance makes credible and poignant.

Narrative Complexity, Character Ambiguity, and Critical Acceptance of Film Noir

At the film's opening, Jeff enjoys an idyllic life in rural Bridgeport, California. He runs a gas station, has a loving girlfriend, Ann (Virginia Huston), and goes fishing in the mountains (Plate 20). Abruptly, Joe Stephanos (Paul Valentine), a sinister-looking man from Jeff's past, arrives

PLATE 20 *Out of the Past*: Jeff (Robert Mitchum) and Ann (Virginia Huston) fishing idyllically. © 1947 RKO Radio Pictures, INC.

in town and summons him to Lake Tahoe to see the gangster Whit Sterling. On the drive there, Jeff tells Ann about his past. His name is not Bailey, as he is called in Bridgeport, but Markham, and a few years earlier he had been a private detective in New York City. Whit had hired him to track down his runaway girlfriend, Kathie Moffat (Jane Greer), who had shot and robbed him. Jeff located her in Acapulco (Plate 21) but, instead of notifying Whit, fell in love with her himself and they fled to San Francisco together. Jeff's partner, Jack Fisher (Steve Brody), to whom Jeff had promised half of his earnings on the case, tracked them there. In a scuffle, Kathie shot Fisher to death and fled. Jeff wound up in Bridgeport, where he began a new life and met Ann.

At this point, Jeff has confessed to Ann that he betrayed both his employer and his partner for another woman. He hopes to square himself with Whit in Lake Tahoe and return to his new life. It will never be. Whit, who is once again living with Kathie, sends Jeff to San Francisco to retrieve tax records from a lawyer who Whit claims is blackmailing him. Jeff quickly realizes that Whit plans to revenge himself not only on the lawyer but also on him. The lawyer is murdered and Jeff is implicated. He attempts to extricate himself, only to find out that Kathie has murdered Whit (Plate 22).

PLATE 21 *Out of the Past*: Kathie (Jane Greer) meeting Jeff in Acapulco. © 1947 RKO Radio Pictures, INC.

PLATE 22 *Out of the Past*: Jeff's shocked reaction at coming upon Whit's body. © 1947 RKO Radio Pictures, INC.

She plans to flee with Jeff, who, in a suicidal act, notifies the police of their getaway plans. When a police roadblock stops their car, Kathie shoots him to death before being killed herself.

Jeff spends the entire film under a cloud of doom, weighed down with the certainty of malevolent forces in motion around him. One of his most resonant lines comes when he watches Kathie play roulette in Acapulco. He tells her that the way she is playing is not the way to win. When she asks him if there is a way to win, he replies, "There's a way to lose more slowly." His plight is basically one of losing more slowly, and winning has never really been an option.

One of the film's most disturbing aspects involves Ann. Clearly in love with Jeff, she believes blindly in his integrity, regardless of his reputation in Bridgeport as a man with a mysterious past and the suspicions of her own parents about him. Her love for Jeff endangers her relationship with Jimmy (Richard Webb), a local law-enforcement official who is devoted to her and pained by her love for his rival. During a particularly cruel and complex moment near the end of the film, Jimmy confronts Jeff, who is fleeing from the police, and threatens to turn him in. Jeff cruelly but perceptively tells him that, if he does turn him in, Ann will hate him forever. It does not matter that Jimmy, an uncomplicated, decent man, is more traditionally suited to Ann and more likely to provide her with a happy life. Unlike Jeff, he has no "past" involving romantic and professional betrayal. Ann fell in love with Jeff just as Jeff fell in love with Kathie, regardless of morality, logic, or consequences. In this scene, Jeff brutally makes Jimmy aware that, if he does the "right" thing and reports Jeff, Jimmy will, justly or unjustly, lose the woman he loves forever. Right or wrong has nothing to do with it.

The power of sexual desire in the film is encapsulated in Jeff's response to Kathie before they first kiss. Having told him her version of her violent departure from Whit, she asks if he believes her. He replies, "Baby, I don't care," and they kiss (Plate 23). His point is that, whether or not he knows she is lying to him, and whether or not a relationship with her will destroy them both, he cannot contain his desire. It overwhelms logic, morality, and self-preservation.

At the film's closing, Ann asks Jeff's nameless deaf/mute assistant and confidant (simply called "The Kid" and played by Dickie Moore) if Jeff and Kathie were once again running away with one another when they were killed. Jeff had assured Ann that he no longer loved Kathie, but the circumstances of their deaths seem to indicate otherwise. Although The Kid has no way of knowing Jeff's final intentions, he nods to Ann that, yes, Jeff and Kathie were running away together. As Ann leaves, he looks up at Jeff's name on the gas station's sign and nods a private gesture of affection,

PLATE 23 *Out of the Past*: Jeff and Kathie on the beach – "Baby, I don't care."
© 1947 RKO Radio Pictures, INC.

indicating his hope that, in allowing Ann to think Jeff betrayed her, she might be able to relinquish her love for him and find a future with Jimmy, as Jeff would have wanted for her.

It is a curious ending for the movie, which opens and closes with The Kid, who holds an important but ambiguous position in the film. Aside from his handicap, which often renders his motivations unreadable, the only thing we learn about him is his total devotion to Jeff. In fact, the film introduces him before it introduces Jeff and, after Jeff's death, places him at the center of the concluding scene. He is present at Jeff's service station at the opening when Joe mysteriously enters town, and he has a lit match sadistically flipped at him when, owing to his handicap, he does not respond to the stranger's verbal summons. And he is present at the film's closing when Ann inquires about Jeff's intentions. Like Ann, he has blind faith in Jeff. He helps him out repeatedly, even to the extent of killing Joe as the hitman hunts Jeff. The Kid's final gesture, based on something he has no way of knowing, has little to do with traditional story logic and exists on a strange plane known only to himself and the viewer. Jeff seems to be the only character with an empathic relationship with him, and that relationship humanizes Jeff. But with Jeff's death, The Kid is set adrift in a profoundly desolate way.

The ending is a particularly grim one, even for *film noir*. The central characters have all died violently and the survivors have little to anticipate in their lives. Ann might be able to move on to a reasonably contented life with Jimmy, although it would always be clouded for both by memories of Jeff, but The Kid's future promises nothing. The film's brief sense of uplift provided by The Kid's final gesture can hardly obscure the profound loss and hopelessness underlying it. It concludes a sordid sequence of events in which numerous people have been killed and innocent lives have been ruined – all to no good end.

The Kid's role is one of many curious and/or ambiguous elements in the film that dovetail with strategies and themes important to *film noir*.

The screenwriter, Daniel Mainwaring, then an established author, describes how when writing the source novel he was frustrated with the constraints of traditional plotting. "With *Build My Gallows High*, I wanted to get away from straight mystery novels. Those detective stories are a bore to write. You've got to figure out 'whodunit.' I'd get to the end and have to say whodunit and be so mixed up I couldn't decide myself" (see McGilligan, 2002). In writing the novel and screenplay, Mainwaring appears to have had little interest in composing a precisely structured whodunit. His script and the film frequently deviate from traditional patterns of mystery logic, as with the ambiguous presence of The Kid and the complexity of the plot.

Implicitly demonstrating respect for tropes of the newly emerging *film noir*, a number of critics praised the film while, at the same time, commenting on the almost indecipherable complexity of its plot. In this and many other *films noirs*, a tension is apparent between the clear plotting associated with earlier detective films and the growing importance of evocative subtextual structures that by their very nature defy clarity.

Two *New York Times* reviews by Bosley Crowther, a year apart, illustrate his growing tolerance for the deviations from traditional narrative clarity that *film noir* was bringing with it. In 1946 he gave a negative review to *The Big Sleep*, primarily on the basis of its confusing narrative:

> If somebody had only told us . . . just what it is that happens in the Warners' and Howard Hawks' "The Big Sleep," we might be able to give you a more explicit and favorable report on this overage melodrama. . . . But with only the foggiest notion of who does what to whom – and we watched it with close attention – we must be frankly disappointing about it. For "The Big Sleep" is one of those pictures in which so many cryptic things occur amid so much involved and devious plotting that the mind becomes utterly confused. . . . It's likely to leave you confused and dissatisfied. (Crowther, 1946b)

Just over a year later in his review of *Out of the Past*, Crowther opens by describing the bewildering plot:

> There have been double- and triple-crosses in many of these tough detective films, and in one or two Humphrey Bogart specials they have run even higher than that. But the sum of deceitful complications that occur in "Out of the Past" must be reckoned by logarithmic tables, so numerous and involved do they become, The consequence is that the action of this new film . . . is likely to leave the napping or unmathematical customer far behind. Frankly, that's where it left us. (Crowther, 1947)

However, unlike his response to *The Big Sleep,* he was unwilling to allow his bewilderment with the plot to make him condemn *Out of the Past.* Instead, he closes the review by acknowledging positive, balancing virtues and recommends the film.

> However,. . . it's very snappy and quite intriguingly played by a cast that has been well and smartly directed by Jacques Tourneur, Robert Mitchum is magnificently cheeky and self-assured as the tangled "private eye.". . . If only we had some way of knowing what's going on in the last half of this film, we might get more pleasure from it. As it is, the challenge is worth a try.

Many popular *films noirs* had appeared between 1946 and 1947, acclimating critics and the public to their tropes. By the time that *Out of the Past* opened, Crowther seemed ready to acknowledge the value of such balancing elements in compensating for the absence of clear narrative logic in it. *Time* magazine's anonymous reviewer seemed attuned much earlier than the sometimes stodgy Crowther to the changes *film noir* was bringing. The *Time* review of *The Big Sleep* acknowledged confusion over the plot while not treating it as particularly troubling. It called the film "wakeful fare for folks who don't care what is going on, or why, so long as the talk is hard and the action harder." It adds, "[T]he plot's crazy, mystifying nightmare blur is an asset, and only one of many" (*Time*, 1946).

This critical tolerance of narrative bewilderment indicates both one deviation of *film noir* from practices of earlier detective films and the growing critical acceptance of such deviations. The rules were changing.

Even though *Out of the Past* would not appear for another year, Nino Frank's influential 1946 essay that first identified *film noir* is remarkably prescient about central strategies of the film and how they differed from earlier practices, particularly with reference to convoluted plotlines and enigmatic characterization. The essay is so prescient, in fact, that it seems like a virtual blueprint for *Out of the Past*. It contrasted detective films in the emerging *film noir* with the earlier detective tradition, one that valued logical and lucid plotting. In the older films the detective was

> a thinking machine sniffing and filling his pipe. They [the older films] fall back on sets, humor, supplementary crimes – and that can't last. We are witnesses to the death of this formula. . . . The essential question is no longer to discover who committed the crime, but to see how the protagonist behaves (you don't even have to understand, in detail, the stories in which he is involved). Only the enigmatic psychology of one or the other counts, at the same time friends and enemies. . . . Thus these "black" films have nothing in common with the unusual detective films. Clear psychological stories, action, whether violent or lively, counts here less than the faces, the behavior, the words – therefore the truth of the characters, this "third dimension.". . . And that's great progress: after films like these the characters in the usual detective films seem like puppets. (Frank, 1995, pp. 9–10)

It would be hard to find a more enigmatic protagonist than Jeff, or one less resembling a "thinking machine" or a puppet.

All of this provides a useful context for the complexities, ambiguities, and contradictions centered upon Jeff's character in *Out of the Past*. And significantly, not only is he at the center of the film, but his voice also drives the first half of the narrative.

Retrospective Narration and the Power of the Past

Jeff's voice-over narration describing his earlier life serves a purpose beyond informing Ann and the viewer of his past activities; it infuses a layer of poignant suffering into the film because Ann is listening to it. Since the tale centers on his falling desperately in love with Kathie, hearing it clearly causes Ann agony. In this it resembles Neff's voice-over narration in *Double Indemnity*, made more poignant and painful because it is addressed to Neff's mentor and friend, Barton Keyes, and describes Neff's betrayal of him. Jeff's story recounts a history of uncontrolled desire, moral failures, and betrayal that Jeff hopes to escape, and escape with Ann. It will never be. The past is too strong and determining.

The movie's first half resembles an eroticized nightmare. Although the voice-over narration ends once Jeff arrives at Whit's place in Lake Tahoe, the remainder of the film retains the atmosphere of a dark dream revived and replayed. It shows the same characters – Jeff, Kathie, Whit, and

Ann – largely repeating behavioral patterns already established. Jeff is again employed by Whit in a dangerous venture. Both men again fall under Kathie's deadly thrall and all three spiral into a doom that has long been inevitable. Ann remains blindly loyal to Jeff although her loyalty causes her nothing but pain. Near the end, after Jeff discovers that Kathie has murdered Whit, the two prepare to escape. Jeff becomes more grimly resigned than ever, behaving as if he were floating in a dream world while detachedly observing his time run out. Kathie now brusquely orders him about, telling him that, because she can testify against him and even implicate him in Whit's murder, which she committed, he is forever bound to her. She tells him, "I'm running the show; don't forget," and he replies, "I doubt you'd ever let me." When she goes upstairs to get luggage, he makes a telephone call notifying the police of their where-abouts and escape plan. He knows that they will probably be killed, but the prospect of life under Kathie's domination makes that a possibly preferable fate. He has lost all hope for a future. Whatever future he might have would be yet another recycling of his failed past.

The movie's opening credits appear over spectacular natural lands-capes surrounding Bridgeport – snow-capped mountains and deep, fertile valleys. The film then shows Whit's henchman Joe, shot from behind his head and shoulders and giving his point of view, driving into Bridgeport. When he stops at Jeff's gas station, Musuraca photographed his dark overcoat and hulking body from behind, rendering him a dark, sinister presence in this sunlit rural town. The film effectively begins, then, by aligning the viewer with his point of view as he malignantly re-enters Jeff's life and besmirches the unspoiled landscape. Joe embodies the black hole of a past that Jeff so desperately wanted to escape, but that past, including Joe, Whit, and Kathie, has resurfaced and will overwhelm them all.

The title, *Out of the Past*, underscores the importance of the past and of the impossibility of repressing or escaping it. This central theme is articulated in the exchange between Ann and Jeff after he completes his tale of his earlier life. Ann optimistically exclaims, "And it's all past," to which Jeff sadly responds, "Maybe it isn't." The once-presumed and hoped-for separation of past and present no longer exists.

The ineradicability of the past was an important theme in films of the 1940s within the context of the era's growing fascination with and acceptance of Freudian ideas. One premise of psychoanalysis is that the past cannot be ignored, and that it is essential to explore one's past to gain insight into one's personality and ongoing behavior. It holds that we repress troubling memories at our own peril and that, if not confronted, those memories will eventually emerge in some form, and emerge destructively. Mirroring this pattern, Jeff's past literally returns to destroy him.

Just as the movie depicts the breakdown of distinctions between past and present, it also depicts the erosion of traditional presumptions about geographical differences. It initially seems to establish a strong symbolic opposition between the city and the country by associating urban areas like New York and San Francisco with corruption and rural areas like Bridgeport with innocence and revitalization. However, almost as soon as the "bad" city/"good" country opposition appears to be established, it breaks down. Although the gangster Joe in his black overcoat brings a menacing presence into Bridgeport, we soon learn that life was never idyllic there. Many people in the town are suspicious of Jeff's past, justifiably as it turns out, and the sad Ann/Jimmy relationship is deeply troubled. The next rural American environment depicted is Lake Tahoe, which, although beautiful, is a gangster hideout. Furthermore, when Kathie kills Jeff's partner, she does it not in San Francisco but in the forest cabin she and Jeff shared. As the film concludes, the major characters – Jeff, Kathie, Whit, even Joe – are killed in the country and Ann is left in Bridgeport, which now seems as desolate as New York or San Francisco. Just as there is no purifying escape from the past, there is also no restorative geographical escape from corruption.

Subtextual and Symbolic Meanings – Censorship, Race, Nation

Out of the Past has a rich subtextual network of meanings that are implied but not overtly stated. This includes but goes far beyond the use of indirect symbolic strategies to imply censorable activities, such as those employed when Jeff and Kathie first become lovers. After she seductively invites him to her cottage for the first time, a tropical storm breaks out as they race there through a jungle. Upon arriving, they vigorously dry one another's hair until Jeff flings the towel at the room's only lamp, knocking it over and darkening the room. The camera, which had panned away from the couple to follow the movement of the towel, does not return to the couple when the lamp topples but, instead, shows the front door that the storm has just flung open. The volume of the music on the soundtrack rises. The next shot shows the rain-drenched jungle outside. When the camera next shows the interior of the cottage, an unspecified period of time has passed. Jeff closes the door but both his and Kathie's hair is no longer tousled as it had been earlier but is now neatly combed. Combined with the growing erotic tension between the characters and the abrupt and turbulent storm that provides an external parallel for those tensions, this temporal elision is the film's strategy for bypassing PCA prohibitions against overt depictions of sexual activity. Contemporary audiences would have understood that the elision indicated what the film was not allowed to actually show them – that the two have now become lovers.

In addition to this fairly common strategy, the film establishes a complex network of indirectly developed, exotic associations surrounding Kathie. Some have no real narrative justification in the film; they exist to convey symbolic associations. Their presence also helps account for some of the narrative convolutions discussed earlier. The story that we see does not tell the whole story. Much functions on a symbolic level and tensions between the narrative and the symbolic can be confusing.

The film is the story of Jeff's downfall, which begins when he meets Kathie. His pursuit of her draws him into a whirlpool of doom, developed by means of layered associations with degradation, emasculation, self-betrayal, and corruption.

Jeff pursues Kathie to Mexico, where he falls in love with her, uncharacteristically betraying his boss as well as his business partner. Why did this happen? In New York, Jeff had a reputation for integrity and intelligence, which was the reason Whit hired him. Jeff's motivation for throwing it all away is never explained beyond his telling us on the soundtrack that he suddenly fell in love. The film, however, indicates in its symbolic use of exoticism that much more is involved.

One indication of the role of the exotic in *Out of the Past* is evident in its selection of Mexico as a setting. On a story level, there is really no need for the film to include Mexico at all; its entire justification is that it is simply a place outside of New York to which Kathie flees. The movie uses diverse locales all over the US – New York, Bridgeport, San Francisco, Lake Tahoe, and so on – so why cross the border into Mexico? The rationale exists on the symbolic level, where the film has every reason to go "south of the border" since it presents Mexico as a profoundly exotic place, more so than anything the US offers. Furthermore, it becomes the symbolic locus for other exotic associations. From the perspective of postwar US ideology, Jeff pursues one kind of exotic – a seductive and murderous woman above his class – into an exotic place, Mexico. As a result, he loses his masculinity (at the end he is literally and mortally shot in the groin), his integrity, his career, his very identity (he changes his name and occupation), as well as his American dream, shown as a working-class life running a gas station in rural Bridgeport and courting his clean-cut, blonde girlfriend, Ann.

The movie presents Mexico as an exotic locale marked by racial, linguistic, and cultural differences. For Jeff it becomes a place of temptation, feminization, indolence, and sensual overload, a place where "such things happen." And when they do, Jeff is doomed, although the film implies that, in a less exotic environment, he might not have so readily lost control over his life. In fact, at a crucial moment, he is unable to telegraph Whit that he has finally located Kathie because the telegraph office is closed for siesta. Businesses in New York or Bridgeport do not close for siesta. Had Jeff been in either of those places, he would have sent the wire, thereby completing his assignment; he could then have returned to his old life. But he is in Mexico, and the siesta gives him time to reconsider and time for his desire to grow. He never sends the wire but flees with Kathie instead, thereby sealing his doom.

In another instance of the film's selection of a setting with little narrative but great symbolic justification, Jeff begins his search for Kathie by briefly questioning her former maid in a Harlem jazz nightclub. It is the only time that both the maid and an African American cultural environment appear in the film, and the information Jeff elicits is minimal, so why the locale? Within the norms of 1947 Hollywood, the nightclub's exotic associations with people of color and with jazz made it a symbolically appropriate place for Jeff to begin his journey away from the securities of his culture. That journey leads him to Mexico (shown in the very next shot), which becomes his "heart of darkness."

Jeff's life changes irrevocably when he travels there. Later he seeks a way back. He changes his name and starts over in Bridgeport. But his past catches up with him, and he returns to Kathie. He is not alone; Whit also returns to her. She will eventually kill both men. The film not only depicts a woman who becomes more powerful than its men, but it also shows the men returning repeatedly to the woman who betrayed them, fully aware that she is likely to continue doing so.

Although Jeff tries to reclaim his life, the film indicates that there is no going back. The appeal of the exotic masks its ability to corrupt, and its seductive pleasures erode Jeff's ability to reintegrate himself into the US. When he finds out how far he has fallen, it is too late. This sentiment reflects US xenophobia of the 1940s and also appears in the popular World War I era song that opposes simple, rural American life with the exotic European experiences of returning American soldiers, asking "How 'Ya Gonna Keep 'Em Down on the Farm (After They've Seen Paree)?" Its message is that, once innocent Americans taste corrupting foreign pleasures, they will never again be satisfied with "home sweet home." Much of *film noir* exhibits such xenophobia. *The Maltese Falcon*, for example, presents all of its villains as either foreign in origin or as having traveled to exotic places, and implies a linkage between their foreign associations and their evil. In *Out of the Past*, Jeff's new life is ruined as the consequences of his Mexican trip emerge "out of the past" into his present.

As is common with many forms of prejudice, the film's racism is covert, never overt. Neither Mexico nor people of color are ever characterized as actively evil in *Out of the Past*; rather, both are associated with evil exclusively on a subtextual level. The African American patrons of the jazz nightclub have no overt connection whatsoever with the Latinos in Mexico. Their only relationship is symbolic; they are people of color. Furthermore, no black or Hispanic character does anything evil or even menacing; they are benign. This does not, however, give them equal status with the white characters. The film associates its people of color with Kathie, the *femme fatale* who betrays and kills white men. Kathie employed the African American maid, Kathie chooses to travel among Hispanics in Mexico, and those people of color and foreign places become symbolically, although never causally, associated with her evil.

As with *Murder, My Sweet*, much about *Out of the Past*'s ideology is apparent in what appear to be offhand jokes. Near the close of the movie, after Jeff has called the police who will soon kill him and Kathie, the two pause for a final drink together. Referring to the innocuous guide who attempted to sell them trinkets on the day they first met, Jeff says, "We owe it all to José Rodriguez. I wonder if he'll ever know what a bad guide he really was." The idea of blaming their subsequent history of betrayal and murder is, of course, a sardonic and preposterous joke, since there is no evidence they even saw the man more than once and, even then, they declined his offer of his services as a guide. However, on a symbolic level, it associates Rodriguez, a Mexican, with the origin of their doom, which meshes with the movie's overall association of the exotic with evil.

Neo-Noir *and* L.A. Confidential

Just as an examination of *Murder, My Sweet* alongside *The Falcon Takes Over* and *Farewell, My Lovely* illustrated shifts in the *noir* tradition, so also does a look at *Out of the Past* with reference to *L.A. Confidential*. Unlike the three Chandler-based films, these two do not share a common literary source, but like those three, they share a cinematic tradition. Although set in the same place and era, the postwar US, the two films were made fifty years apart and, when contrasted, reveal major changes in US culture, in racial representation, and in *film noir* itself.

L.A. Confidential, which appeared in 1997, the year of Robert Mitchum's death, refers to a scandal involving him from half a century earlier. One of the film's main characters, LAPD Detective Jack Vincennes (Kevin Spacey), is described as having made the widely publicized arrest of Mitchum for marijuana possession in 1948. In this manner, *L.A. Confidential* invokes a different image of Mitchum from that of the actor of *Out of the Past*, who was building a star image during the canonical *film noir* era, and a different Mitchum from that of *Farewell, My Lovely*, whose star image by 1975 had strong iconic associations with *film noir*. The image of Mitchum evoked by *L.A. Confidential* is one of offscreen scandal.

No film of the era referred to Mitchum's arrest and imprisonment, and it surprised many that, after the scandal, he was able to resume his career. The PCA prohibited drug references in films and, during the Classical Hollywood era, offscreen association with drugs could easily destroy an actor's career. At the same time, innuendo about violations of such industry prohibitions fueled a thriving market for Hollywood scandal in sleazy magazines. The title, *L.A. Confidential*, refers to *Confidential*, one of the most notorious scandal magazines of the day, and the film's main topic is the corrupt underbelly of postwar Los Angeles.

The movie is based upon James Ellroy's novel of the same name and Ellroy has described hard-boiled fiction, like his own, as "the history of bad white men doing bad things in the name of authority" (see Garner, 1997). Ellroy's description applies as well to *Out of the Past* and *L.A. Confidential*, although the two films, as well as *film noir* and neo-*noir* in general, develop very different perspectives upon what constitutes "bad white men" and "authority." In *film noir*, a bad white man is generally one who falls from the presumed cultural ideal of the responsibility and privilege of white men as depicted in Hollywood film. In neo-*noir*, the bad white men do not fall from such a cultural height; they often occupy the center of evil and, in all of this, the relationship of white males with "other" people, whether women, people of color, or people of other nations, is crucial.

Out of the Past is set in the era in which it was made; *L.A. Confidential* is set in the past. Both films center upon white American males and both depict them undergoing erosions of their presumed cultural privilege over "other" peoples and cultures, but differences in the ways the films present the "other" peoples and "other" ways of life reveal fundamental changes in American film and culture between the 1940s and the 1990s.

Out of the Past adopts a reactionary stance that laments the loss of white male power, a loss it associates with a powerful woman as well as with exoticized people of color and with Mexico. The ideological stance of *L.A. Confidential*, to the contrary, might be described as liberal. It represents the all-white and all-male Los Angeles Police Department of the early 1950s as a hypocritical center of corruption that systematically diverts blame for its own criminal activities onto immigrants and people of color. Unlike *Out of the Past* but like many neo-*noir* films such as *Chinatown, Farewell, My Lovely, Mulholland Falls,* and *Devil in a Blue Dress,* it explicitly condemns white racism and associates evil not with exoticized people and places but rather with the white power structure itself.

From a racist and sexist perspective, danger is easy to spot in much of canonical *film noir* because it is visible – it comes from another race, another gender, another country. But what if it is not so easy to spot, as is the case in *L.A. Confidential?* One reason it is not so easy to spot is that, during the half-century separating the two films, the meaning of the exotic had changed.

This points to a larger shift within Hollywood cinema and American culture from associating people of color with evil to placing them at the sympathetic center of viewer identification. Social historians have helped to explain this. The history of US political demonology, or the tendency to characterize certain types of people as "devils" and thereby scapegoat them for all things that go wrong in society, has been categorized by social historians such as Michael Rogin as having gone through three stages. The earliest stage began in colonial America and was overtly racial. It pitted whites against people of color and its targets were the red and black peoples of frontier America. Such demonization provided a rationale for enslaving blacks and displacing Native Americans. The second stage of demonization, a reaction to the waves of immigration, particularly from Eastern Europe, in the late nineteenth century, was class- and nation-based. In this stage, the demonized people might have been white, but "they" were readily identified by physical and linguistic markers. In the post-World War I "red scare" round-up and deportation of subversives by Attorney General A. Mitchell Palmer (and his subordinate J. Edgar Hoover), Palmer described his targets as "alien filth," with "sly and crafty eyes . . . lopsided faces, sloping brows, and misshapen features." He considered them the working-class "savages" of newly urbanized America (Rogin, 1987, p. 187).

The third stage of demonization, which appeared simultaneously with canonical *film noir* and referred to the perceived international menace of Soviet Communism, among other things, shifted the danger from visible body markers to the invisible mind. During the Cold War, Communists looked no different from white, US males. This presumption is fascinatingly evident in the popular 1950s television series *I Led Three Lives* (cited in Chapter 2), in which the central character, a white male, plays three radically different roles: that of a "normal" US citizen, an FBI agent, and a

Communist spy (really an FBI double agent). However, whether he was appearing as a "normal" Boston advertising executive, an FBI agent, or an agent of foreign subversion, he looked exactly the same. The message was clear: demons were no longer easy to spot because they looked just like "us." This postwar sensibility is also evident in *Invasion of the Body Snatchers*, the influential science fiction movie that was written by *Out of the Past*'s screenwriter. Its invading space aliens were not creepy-looking "little green men" but, instead, were indistinguishable from the "normal" inhabitants of small-town America. As with the era's categorization of Communists, "they" looked like "us."

In *L.A. Confidential*, the enemy does, indeed, look like "us." The movie concerns the investigation of a massacre of six people at a diner for which three African American youths are arrested; the real murderers, however, are members of the LAPD. Furthermore, a secret task force exists within the department that brutally intimidates and ejects dangerous outsiders, such as gangsters and drug dealers, ostensibly to keep Los Angeles pure, especially from the narcotics trade. It turns out, however, that the police themselves are running the drug trade, and eject or kill outsiders not for the public good but to consolidate their own hold on corruption. Although the police captain, Dudley Smith (James Cromwell), initially appears to embody the best traditions of his department, he in fact stands at the center of the corruption. He even murders members of his own department.

His LAPD consists entirely of white males, and the movie depicts incidents of ugly white racism. In one, a mob of drunken officers, acting on an unsubstantiated rumor, stampedes into the station's jail to savagely beat Chicano prisoners. In another, just referred to, police frame three African American youths for murders committed by police officers. Unlike *Out of the Past*, this film deals explicitly with racism and condemns it. The officers who resist it are its heroes.

In *L.A. Confidential*, social evil comes not from outside the white power structure but from within it. The corrupting influences associated with exotic people and places that seduced and destroyed the central characters in *Out of the Past* are, here, no dangers at all but a smokescreen for white male corruption. The system has turned in on itself. The enemy is now "us."

Why the change? One influence results from the fact that the above-described historical pattern – whereby traditional racial and/or national criteria which purported to provide visible, physical evidence for differentiating "good" from "bad" people – was losing its credibility, and many were publicly questioning its validity. Maybe "they" were not inherently bad and "we" were not inherently good. Another influence was the sea change in US culture that took place in the 1960s and 1970s resulting from the Watergate scandal, the Vietnam War, and the empowerment movements for women, various racial and ethnic groups, and gays and lesbians. The integrity of the power structure was widely questioned and it was no longer so easy to blame "others" for problems in the country.

These changes are evident in neo-*noir* films emerging in the 1970s. Where the earlier ones were about the "today" of their era, these new films were often "period" films, about the past. In ways that canonical *films noirs* never did, the new films combined nostalgia for that era with an often cynical re-examination of our national and cinematic history. In them, the nature of the exotic had changed in fundamental ways.

This shift was not confined to *films noirs*. Horror films of the 1930s (such as *Dracula*, 1931, *Frankenstein*, 1931, *Island of Lost Souls*, 1932, *The Werewolf of London*, 1935) represented evil as coming from "somewhere else," foreign places. After the mid-1950s, however (as in *Invasion of the Body Snatchers*, *Psycho*, 1960, *The Texas Chainsaw Massacre*, 1974, *Halloween*, 1978, *Friday the 13th*, 1980, *Nightmare on Elm Street,* 1984, and *Candyman*, 1992, among many others), horror films commonly depicted their evil as coming not from "somewhere else," but from "here"– the mainstream US. Neo-*noir* films made after the 1960s, such as *Chinatown, Body Heat, L. A. Confidential, Mulholland Falls*, and *The Black Dahlia*, reflect this presumption and also provide an additional perspective. Their exotic, their "somewhere else," is often the bygone world of the earlier films – the retro glamour of the clothing and hairstyles, the music, the automobiles, the colors, even the men in fedoras. These movies tend to present race in a post-1960s' "liberal" manner and characterize foreign nationals and people of color as victimized by white racism rather than as symbolic of an exotic, sinister menace. Evil in these films lies not on the fringes but at the center of the dominant power structure. It would be difficult to find a recent Hollywood film that, like *Out of the Past,* categorizes the association of white people with people of color or foreigners as an indicator of white villainy or degradation. It would be comparably difficult to find a recent film that uses belief in Communism, as in *Shack Out on 101* (1955) or *My Son John* (1952), to do the same thing. The message of many of these recent films is that mainstream white society is often corrupted by its very power and needs extensive reorganization.

A central theme of *L.A. Confidential* is that apparently benevolent social institutions, such as the LAPD, are not as righteous as they present themselves. The movie's three central and ultimately heroic detectives demonstrate this. Each finds something horribly wrong in the traditions he was raised to revere. Ed Exley (Guy Pearce), the proud son of an honored LAPD officer, wants to follow in his father's tradition, now embodied in Captain Smith. Exley is horrified to learn of Smith's corruption and ultimately kills him. Bud White (Russell Crowe) was abused and abandoned by his father, who also murdered his mother. He repeatedly goes out of his way to brutally punish abusers of women. Captain Smith, noticing his penchant for brutality, recruits him into his secret task force. Jack Vincennes is the technical advisor for *Badge of Honor*, a popular television series glorifying the LAPD that resembles the influential television series *Dragnet* (1952–9, 1967–70). But while he presents himself to the public as the "real life" model for the noble detectives on *Badge of Honor*, he also covertly accepts bribes from *Hush Hush* magazine for his participation in high-profile and possibly fraudulent celebrity arrests, such as that of Mitchum. When he attempts to reform and prevent the framing of a gay man, however, Captain Smith murders him.

Not only are the righteous images of public institutions deceptive, but so also are the physical appearances of characters. Kim Basinger plays a prostitute made up to look like Veronica Lake, the popular 1940s movie star. She is employed by a service that specializes in movie star lookalikes, and whose clientele includes powerful politicians. Some of the women have even been surgically altered to enhance their resemblance to famous actresses. In one scene, Exley accuses a woman who looks like the movie star Lana Turner of being a prostitute associating with a gangster, only to learn that the woman is, in fact, the real Lana Turner, who is, nevertheless, dating a gangster. Over and over, the message is reinforced – appearances are unreliable.

L.A. Confidential opens with nostalgia-evoking film footage of the postwar era, Johnny Mercer's upbeat rendition of "Ac-cent-tchu-ate the Positive" on the soundtrack, and enthusiastic narration by Sid Hudgins (Danny DeVito), a gossip columnist for the sleazy *Hush Hush* magazine. He describes the post-war Los Angeles that is touted by the mass media as a "paradise on earth" holding unlimited promise, but adds that the mainstream media does not show "trouble in paradise." The publicizing and exploitation of such "trouble" is the mission of *Hush Hush*. Sid describes the underbelly of Los Angeles as the criminal empire ruled by the historical gangster Mickey Cohen, and says that, now that Cohen has been sent to prison, an underworld power vacuum has opened up. That vacuum will be filled by the LAPD.

As with Jeff's voice-over narration in *Out of the Past*, Sid's narration is dropped in the middle of the film. His voice is silenced when he is beaten to death by Captain Murphy's secret task force. But he is so mired in the corruption that, until close to his death, he thinks that even his own fatal beating is simply a set-up for another scandal story. But unlike Jeff in *Out of the Past,* there is nothing confessional in Sid's narration. Instead, Sid is a publicity-hungry huckster who jubilates in the corruption he exploits, referring to his stories as "off the record, on the Q-T, and very hush-hush." He gleefully describes his subject matter as "prime sinnuendo." Like many *film noir* narrators, he is telling the story that leads to his own extinction.

The opening footage of postwar Los Angeles establishes the movie as being "about" the American past. It uses period music, a staccato, Walter Winchell-type narrational style, and authentic or mimicked film stock associated with the era, like black and white television footage, color 8 millimeter home movie footage, and promotional footage. It does not employ the "period" visual style – heavy browns and yellows, Expressionistic lighting and camera angles, and nostalgic iconic referential shots – widely associated with neo-*noir* and used in films like *Farewell, My Lovely* and *Chinatown.* The movie closes with a black and white image of a stereotypical 1950s white, suburban nuclear family avidly watching *Badge of Honor* on television (Plate 24). The shots are heavily ironic because the entire film preceding them has shown that the image of the LAPD promoted by *Badge of Honor,* as well as the image of untroubled 1950s suburban family life, is a hypocritical and carefully manufactured lie. A significant point of commonality between both of them, and one that the movie critiques, is glorified whiteness – the police in *Badge of Honor* are white, the idealized family is white. The movie makes it clear that the postwar US was very different from the idealized images it presented of itself,

PLATE 24 *L.A. Confidential:* An idyllic 1950s family watching *Badge of Honor* on television. © 1997 Monarchy Enterprises B.V. and Regency Entertainment (USA), INC.

whether in the nostalgic footage opening *L.A. Confidential*, or in the idealized families and police detectives in television shows of the era.

Just before the final scene, which appears at the end of the closing credits, we see what appears to be grainy, color home movie footage of the popular 1950s television cowboy star Hopalong Cassidy (William Boyd) riding his trademark white horse, Topper, in a Los Angeles parade and waving cheerfully at the camera. The camera pans behind him to show, in a color-matched process shot, actors playing prominent members of the Los Angeles justice system whom the film has just shown to be utterly corrupt and committing or covering up major felonies. They all parade proudly behind this popular television cowboy, a 1950s symbol of pure, righteous American masculinity.

Even though *L.A. Confidential* critiques white racism, it does so from within the perspective of white culture. It never attempts to explore an alternative point of view. Every important character in the film, good or evil, is white; they, and never people of color, are the film's normative figures of identification. Although the three central detectives are presented as ultimately heroic for their defiance of the corrupt system, all commit serious crimes against people of color or women. The movie presents these crimes, but then implicitly glosses over their importance by the end. While Bud White defends abused women, he also murders a black rape suspect in cold blood. In addition, he savagely brutalizes a black youth during an interrogation. White forces him into a terrifying variation of Russian Roulette by shoving a pistol into his mouth and pulling the trigger repeatedly. While Jack Vincennes tries to prevent the framing of a gay white male, he has a long history of corrupt activity. During a drunken riot at the police station (Plate 25), he also participates

PLATE 25 *L.A. Confidential*: Riot in the police station. © 1997 Monarchy Enterprises B.V. and Regency Entertainment (USA), INC.

in the beating of Chicano men. Although Ed Exley defies Captain Smith, he also uses his methods when he shoots Smith in the back and later participates in a conspiracy to glorify Smith's reputation and save his own career. Furthermore, he rapes a woman. But regardless of these crimes, the film invites us to sympathize with all of these characters by its end.

In this fashion, the manner in which the film presents all of its issues from the perspective of white culture makes it more similar to than different from *Out of the Past*.

CHAPTER 6

KISS ME DEADLY

The first three individual analysis chapters in this book, including this one, focus upon movies that span the classical *film noir* era and, taken together, provide an outline of that era's overall arc. The first, Chapter 4, explored *Murder, My Sweet* within the context of the emergence of the genre, and Chapter 5 discussed *Out of the Past* as a film made when the form had become established. This chapter looks at *Kiss Me Deadly*, which appeared while the *film noir* era was declining. The movie is one of the last important *films noirs* to be made when the genre was a contemporary, rather than a retrospective, one. Upon its release in 1955, it was largely dismissed as "B" movie trash or ignored by English-speaking critics while simultaneously being extravagantly championed by French *cinéastes*, particularly those at the new *Cahiers du Cinéma*. Today it is considered a masterful *film noir* milestone.

Kiss Me Deadly's storyline is straightforward. It opens as Mike Hammer (Ralph Meeker) encounters Christina (Cloris Leachman), a terrified woman who is fleeing killers along a dark California highway. The killers soon capture them both and brutally torture Christina, who dies without revealing information about the valued object they seek. They place her body alongside an unconscious Mike in his car, push it over a cliff, and watch it explode. Mike miraculously survives and pursues them, not for retribution for Christina's murder but because he presumes that

Film Noir, First Edition. William Luhr.

whatever they are so savagely seeking is "something big," and he wants a piece of it. His quest leads to more violence. His life is repeatedly menaced (by mob hitmen and car bombs), a close friend is murdered, and his trusted assistant, Velda (Maxine Cooper), is kidnapped. Mike also brutalizes people as he blunders through the Los Angeles underworld until he finds the prized object – a box containing deadly radioactive material. When finally opened, it causes a woman to burst into flames and sets off an explosion that destroys a beach house. The film ends abruptly while the explosion is still in progress, with no sense of how extensively it will continue.

Some elements of *Kiss Me Deadly* place it in continuity with classical *film noir* while others presage the genre's resurrection in neo-*noir*. This chapter examines the movie's brutal, largely amoral central character and the greed-driven, self-destructive world he inhabits; its "pulp" flavor and censorship problems; its distinctive formal strategies; its atmosphere of Atomic Age consumerism and paranoia; its use of science fiction and apocalyptic tropes; and its critical reputation

Mike Hammer and His Corrupt World

Hammer is a tough, cynical, private detective, like Sam Spade or Philip Marlowe, but he is manifestly unlike Marlowe, who, because of his strict moral code, refuses to accept divorce work and lives frugally. Hammer is also unlike many earlier hard-boiled detectives who, however flawed, prove themselves to be morally superior to those they pursue. Hammer is both morally compromised and morally contemptible. He and Velda specialize in divorce cases and drum up business by seducing people and then offering investigative services to their spouses. There is little moral distance between Mike and those whose wrong-doing he uncovers; he often precipitates the illegal or unethical activities that he investigates. He demonstrates no guilt about what he does and conspicuously enjoys the creature comforts it brings him. He is not given to soul-searching and, unlike many of his predecessors, has no voice-over narration in the film to indicate his inner tensions, if he has any. He embodies a type of brash, arrogant American masculinity that would largely die out by the 1960s.

At one point the main villain, Dr Soberin (Albert Dekker), describing the postwar era in which the film is set, proclaims that, "as the world becomes more primitive, its treasures become more fabulous." Regardless of his fashionably consumerist lifestyle, Mike is certainly primitive. He behaves in systematically brutal ways. This is not surprising in his treatment of criminals. When a switchblade-wielding thug attacks him on a street, he knocks the man down a huge stone staircase, possibly killing him, and then moves on without looking back. Later, he turns the tables on men who have kidnapped and drugged him, resulting in their deaths.

But Mike also crudely intimidates people who are not, or are just marginally, involved in the case. When he goes to Christina's rooming house to search for clues, he is met by the building superintendent and his wife. The wife demands that her husband find out what Mike wants. Without looking at her, Mike commands the husband to "Tell her to shut up" and the man instantly says, "Shut up" and admits Mike. When in Christina's apartment, Mike brazenly takes one of her books in full view of the superintendent and departs with it. The superintendent says nothing. When an elderly clerk refuses to accept a bribe to allow him access to the Hollywood Athletic Club, Mike brutally slaps him until he relents. When an opera lover does not immediately give Mike information he wants, he smashes the man's rare Caruso recording and prepares to destroy more. When a coroner will not accept a bribe, Mike crushes his hand by slamming a desk drawer on it; he sadistically smiles as he continues to hold the drawer closed while the man howls in agony (Plate 26).

Early in the movie, Mike is summoned before the "Interstate Crime Commission," whose members display undisguised repugnance at his career as a "bedroom dick." They ask him questions but then immediately

PLATE 26 *Kiss Me Deadly*: Mike (Ralph Meeker) crushes the coroner's hand. © 1955 Parklane Pictures, INC.

answer these themselves, indicating that they feel they know all they need to know about him and would not trust his answers anyway. Mike sums it up: "All right, you've got me convinced. I'm a real stinker." As he leaves the room, one of the men contemptuously says, "Open a window."

Mike differs little from the criminals; he is part of their world and they of his. When they present him with a new car as an inducement to abandon the case, he won't allow his mechanic to start it until he finds the bomb that he presumes will be attached to the ignition. He then has the man drive to his garage, where Mike again searches the car, saying, "That was the one they expected us to find." His world is so treacherous that he is not surprised to find at least one bomb in a gift/car, and presumes, correctly, that there will be at least one more.

Until the film's end, Mike has no conception of what the "something big" is that he pursues, only of the fact that others value it. Comparably, although, like Mike, she has no idea of what it is, Gabrielle (Gaby Rodgers), the movie's *femme fatale*, murders Dr Soberin, the main villain, for what Velda has termed "the Great Whatsit." She only knows that, "Whatever is in that box, it must be precious [because] so many people have died for it." It is one of the many times that the film, beginning with its title, links desire with death. Dr Soberin compares Gabrielle to Pandora, the mythological figure who opened the fabled box that unleashed evil into the world. After Gabrielle mortally shoots him in order to acquire the box for herself, Soberin, in an uncharacteristic gesture of humanity, pleads with her not to open it because of the incalculable destruction it can unleash. Ignoring his plea, she opens the box; its contents instantly set her ablaze and precipitate the film's concluding explosion.

Mike's opportunistic credo of "What's in it for me?" encapsulates the compulsive greed that pervades the film. Everyone is affected by it, generally with no idea of what it is they so desperately pursue, until they are killed or caught up in the final, climactic explosion. The movie depicts a debased world that is getting worse, with few if any decent characters and no future.

The only characters who question Mike's values are women, and he ignores them. At the beginning, Christina quickly sizes Mike up as a wholly self-centered man whose only love is himself, a man who never contributes to a relationship but only takes from one. Later, Velda, who allows Mike to exploit her for degrading sexual entrapments, acknowledges the sadomasochistic nature of their relationship, saying, "I'm always glad when you're in trouble because then you always come to me."

Velda is the only character to mount a sustained critique of the perverse values that drive most of the characters, and to lay out their inevitable consequences. When she learns that Nick (Nick Dennis), Mike's mechanic friend, has been murdered, she warns Mike that his remaining friends are all going to "get it one of these days." She asks, "What is it you're after, Mike?" When he replies, "Something very valuable," she asks, "Is it worth Nick's life, or ... or Christina's or Raymondo's or Kawolsky's or mine?" Mike says that "they" also tried to "get" Christina's roommate and Velda responds, "They? A wonderful word. And who are they? They're the nameless ones who kill people for the Great Whatsit. Does it exist? Who cares? Everyone everywhere is so involved in the fruitless search for what?"

When Mike tells her about Christina's murder, she simply asks, "What's the point of all this?" Uninterested in Christina's cryptic request to Mike to "Remember me," Velda says, "She's dead. But I'm not dead. Hey, remember me." Unconvinced by Mike's rationales for his quest, she wants him to focus on the reality of the here and now. She describes his detecting activities as "First, you find a little thread, the little thread leads you to a string, and the string leads you to a rope, and from the rope you hang by the neck." But even though Mike ignores her, she remains loyal to him. Although aware of the venality of the world she and Mike inhabit, Velda cannot escape it.

The gender politics of *Kiss Me Deadly* place it at a transitional point in *film noir*. Its men are fairly traditional for the genre. They are either hardboiled tough guys or victims. Mike is presented as heterosexual and attractive to women but so jaded and suspicious that he seldom reciprocates sexual advances, even from Velda. Before he learns how evil Gabrielle is, he allows her to stay at his apartment for her safety; when she offers him sex in gratitude, he declines it. When an attractive woman seductively approaches him at a gangster's home, he only briefly embraces her before moving on to what he considers more important things. Comparably, the gangsters present in the scene largely ignore the seductive, *Playboy*-type women hovering around them in order to gamble with one another.

The movie's women are more complex. It was a common practice in many *films noirs* to balance the "bad" of a *femme fatale* with the "good" of an innocent woman. Even though these "innocent" women are often betrayed, their presence in many films indicates that uncorrupted areas of society continue to exist outside of the domain of the evil or tormented people at the center of the movies. These "bad/good" pairings include, among many others, Phyllis Dietrichson with her stepdaughter Lola in *Double Indemnity*; Helen Grayle with Ann in *Murder, My Sweet*; Kathie with Ann in *Out of the Past*; and the demented actress Norma Desmond with the young screenwriter Betty in *Sunset Boulevard*. *D.O.A.* does not have a central *femme fatale* but rather many corrupt women who exist in stark contrast to the main character's adoring and faithful assistant, Paula. Of course there were many exceptions, like *Scarlet Street* and *White Heat*, among others, in which no innocent female character exists to provide contrast with the evil one. In *Kiss Me Deadly*, the venal, duplicitous, and murderous Gabrielle certainly qualifies as a *femme fatale*. Christina and Velda, however, who are certainly victimized, are not innocent by traditional standards or indicative of the presence in society of zones where "good" women" continue to flourish. Implicitly acknowledging this, the film uses both for spectator titillation. It emphasizes Christina's nudity under her raincoat and displays Velda in skin-tight outfits and behaving seductively toward Mike. Neither is sexually naïve by traditional norms. Velda, while loyal to Mike, is sexually sophisticated and manipulative; Christina is intelligent, embittered, and unembarrassed at Mike's awareness of her lack of clothing, but she is not sufficiently developed in the film to be able to further categorize.

Fritz Lang's *The Big Heat* (1953) may provide a model for the blendings of innocence and corruption in 1950s films. The central character's wife is established as a traditionally innocent, "All-American" woman, but she is murdered early in the film. Then, curiously, a gangster's corrupt girlfriend who is brutally scarred by the gangster seeks revenge by helping the central character out. It leads to her death but, in this case, a woman who would have traditionally been categorized as corrupt becomes redeemed by the film's end.

Many neo-*noir* films, such as *Taxi Driver*, *Body Heat*, and *The Last Seduction* (1994), focus on the *femme fatale* and either discard the option of a morally balancing *ingénue* entirely or make only passing reference to one. In many such films, the absence of "good" women implies a bleaker view of women and of society. *Kiss Me Deadly*, appearing at least two decades earlier, points ahead to the abandonment of innocent options widespread in neo-*noir*, but not fully.

"Pulp" Atmosphere and Censorship Problems

Kiss Me Deadly emphasizes "pulp" strategies that ate away at contemporary censorship norms. These begin with the choice of source material in the critically reviled but enormously popular 1952 Mickey Spillane novel with the same title. Spillane got his start by writing not for the "pulp" magazines of the prewar years but rather for comic books, a different mode of publication that in the early 1950s was itself under congressional investigation for endangering the morals of youth. In the late 1940s he moved into novel writing. His Mike Hammer novels quickly developed a following of millions of readers. The filmmakers sought to capitalize on his *Kiss Me Deadly*'s popularity and deliver a film that would meet its fans' expectations. Although the work of many earlier hard-boiled novelists, like Raymond Chandler, Dashiell Hammett, James M. Cain, and Cornell Woolrich, had initially been denounced as crude, sensationalistic, "pulp" fiction, those writers had gained some prestige by the 1950s. Spillane's fiction, although far more commercially successful than that of any of his predecessors, has never found wide literary respectability and was often denigrated as fascistic, exploitative of sadistic violence, leeringly misogynistic, and stylistically crude. Many critics dismissed the movie using similar terms. The *New York Times* did not even bother to review it.

The film's garish advertisements, combined with the lowbrow reputation of Spillane's novel, promised "cheap thrills" of sadistic violence and sleazy sexuality to its 1950s audience. As is common with exploitation cinema, the producers simultaneously promoted the film's "pulp" elements and decried moralistic criticism of it as salacious. The movie was banned for a time in England, and its distributor, United Artists, encountered difficulties advertising it in some American Midwestern and southern states. The Roman Catholic Church's influential Legion of Decency demanded numerous changes and deletions before it gave the film a "B" (Morally Objectionable in Part) instead of a commercially crippling "C" (Condemned) rating. Many of the movie's strategies are provocative and titillating, such as those in the scene depicting Christina being tortured to death with pliers. While PCA codes would not permit the display either of her naked body or of its mutilation, the scene shows her legs dangling from a table, at first spasming with pain and then motionless in death. It establishes her nakedness without actually depicting it by showing the raincoat that she had just been wearing lying crumpled on the floor beneath her. Her agonized screams continue on the soundtrack even after her legs stop spasming.

Another morally "daring" aspect of the film is Mike's sexually exploitative relationship with Velda. She is clearly in love with and sexually available to him. She masochistically allows him to use her to seduce potential clients and tolerates his involvements with other women. He has the key to her apartment, as she does to his, and he enters her apartment and even her bedroom unannounced and at will.

The movie's "cheap thrills" certainly contributed to its commercial success, which enabled its director, Robert Aldrich, to establish his own production company, for which he would direct twelve films in the next seventeen years (see Cook, 1996, p. 481). Furthermore, the very cultural disreputability of its content was employed by some French critics to praise it as signaling a new kind of cinema. They were revolting against many of the presumptions underlying the then-dominant French "Cinema of Quality," one of which valued films based upon prestigious, "high art" literary source material. Claude Chabrol's milestone 1955 *Cahiers du Cinéma* essay, "The Evolution of a Thriller," exuberantly describes *Kiss Me Deadly* as having created itself out of "the worst material to be found, the most deplorable, the most nauseous products of a genre in a state of putrefaction: a Mickey Spillane story. Robert Aldrich and A.I. Bezzerides have taken this threadbare and lackluster fabric and woven it into rich patterns of the most enigmatic arabesques" (see Chabrol, 1985, pp. 60, 163).

The film generates a pervasive atmosphere of sexual transgression. Even when no sexual activity occurs, it invokes sleazy innuendos. Soon after Mike stops for Christina, he pulls into a gas station to have its attendant remove a tree branch caught in his car's undercarriage. A close-up shows the attendant leer with the presumption that the branch became entangled because Mike and Christina had driven off the highway to engage in roadside sex.

The movie appeared at a time when PCA codes were being widely challenged, particularly by "B" movies like this one. In a few years, those codes would collapse altogether. Director Robert Aldrich and screen-writer A.I. Bezzerides depicted Mike Hammer as cruder, crueler, and more amoral than his private eye predecessors, in a film that was calculated to aggressively assault the senses and challenge PCA norms. This in itself did not deviate from practices of earlier *film noir*; indeed, many *films noirs* had pursued such an agenda from the beginning. The main difference here is that the borderlines of the permissible had been constantly changing. Many things that had been considered transgressive in the early 1940s had become acceptable by 1955, and filmmakers who wanted to produce "edgy" work for that era had to push the envelope even further.

It was an inexpensive "B" film produced by the independent studio, Parklane Pictures, Inc., at a cost of roughly $400,000 and with a shooting schedule of about a month in late 1954, much less than standard for studio productions. Where many earlier *films noirs* had investigated character interiority, this film dispensed with the novel's first-person narration and shows little interest in exploring psychological complexity. It has no voice-over narration and no flashbacks (aside from a few brief aural ones). Its atmosphere is one of speed, harsh juxtapositions, brutality, and a society spiraling toward doom.

In its challenges to traditional practices, the film fits well into Aldrich's career. In the same year (1955), he directed *The Big Knife*, another *film noir* and, two decades later in 1975, would make *Hustle*, an important neo-*noir*. But Aldrich was not only, or even predominantly, a *film noir* director. Like many directors of important *films noirs*, such as Billy Wilder, Fritz Lang, John Huston, Howard Hawks, and Orson Welles, Aldrich made successful movies in numerous genres. He is perhaps best known for working in established Hollywood genres, such as the Western (*Vera Cruz, 1954, Apache*, 1954, and *Ulzana's Raid*, 1972), the war film (*Attack*, 1956, and *The Dirty Dozen*, 1967), and the male action film (*Fight of the Phoenix*, 1965, *Emperor of the North*, 1973, and *The Longest Yard*, 1974). He repeatedly challenged censorship codes, a practice associated with but by no means exclusive to *film noir*. A decade after *Kiss Me Deadly*, the enormous popularity of his *The Dirty Dozen*, despite its critically condemned graphic violence, marked a signal moment in the fatal erosion of Hollywood censorship codes. In the following year, 1968, he made *The Killing of Sister George*, which dealt explicitly with lesbianism and became one of the first movies to be released with an "X" rating in the United States. The inevitable collapse of the PCA in the late 1960s would become important to the revival of *film noir* in the 1970s.

Formal Strategies

Like many *films noirs*, *Kiss Me Deadly* employs disorienting, even disturbing, formal strategies. Cinematographer Ernst Lazlo used off-center framing, considerable location shooting, often of seedy areas in Los Angeles, and night-for-night cinematography which drenches some shots in intense darkness. Many interiors appear as shadowy mazes of staircases and banisters, shot from overhead or at odd camera angles, suggesting an oppressive, malevolent environment. The editing is often bold and abrupt. The film depicts graphic, often sadistic violence and a world of pervasive, exploitative sexuality, both of which are linked in the title, *Kiss Me Deadly*.

Many of the movie's formal strategies are evident in its opening sequence, including its disorienting visuals, its harsh editing, its intrusive use of sound, its abrupt introduction of dramatic situations about which the viewer has virtually no understanding, and its "pulp" implications of transgressive sexual and violent content, at times depicted and at times implied. The movie begins at night *in medias res* and ends in the same way, at night and in the middle of a possibly nuclear explosion. At its beginning, we have no clue as to who Christina is or why she is so desperately running; at its end, we have no idea when or if the explosion will end or whether any characters will survive.

Highly unusual for 1955, *Kiss Me Deadly* begins abruptly with no establishing shot, no narrative context, and no credit sequence. A high angle shot shows Christina's legs running frantically along a dark highway. She desperately solicits help from passing cars but is ignored. Finally, she almost suicidally stands in the middle of the road and throws her arms into the air, causing Mike to lurch off the road and stop. As she enters his car, he expresses no sympathy for her plight but petulantly tells her that she almost wrecked his car. We then get an odd shot as Mike drives on, with the camera placed in the car behind and between him and Christina, showing the dark road ahead with its winding white center lines through the car's windshield. Then the shot gets even stranger as the film's credits begin. They are bizarrely scrolled down from the top of the frame to the bottom and in backwards order, forcing us to read them from the bottom up, so we first see "DEADLY" and then "KISS ME," and so on.

At this point we know nothing about either Mike or Christina. When they begin to converse, we get provocative and mysterious clues. She repeatedly looks back at the road behind them; he notices that she is naked under her coat and at first assumes that she is fleeing a rapist. At a police roadblock set up to capture her, she cuddles next to him, inducing him to tell the police that she is his wife, even though he learns that she has escaped from a mental institution, or what Mike soon crudely terms a "laughing house." Later, she tells him that her clothes were seized to keep her confined in the asylum. She also gives a caustic appraisal of Mike, perceptively noting his vanity, his indifference to others, his love of consumer goods, and his obsession with his appearance. The sequence ends after the killers in a large car suddenly cut them off, torture Christina to death, and then push both Mike and Christina over a cliff, where his car explodes, presaging the film's final explosion.

The pacing of the sequence is dominated by abrupt intrusions, first by Christina into the film itself, next by Christina into Mike's path, and then by her killers. It emphasizes speed – of the editing, of the cars, and of the ambush. The explosion of Mike's car establishes formal and thematic patterns that are logical extensions of the film's dynamic of reckless speed and the frenzied pursuit of "the Great Whatsit." In this corrupt society, everything will blow up in everyone's face. At the end of the opening sequence, Dr Soberin thinks he is killing Mike and Christina in the exploding car. Later, he will have two bombs placed in a car, hoping to blow Mike up. Mike's friend Nick repeatedly exclaims "Va-Va-Voom," by which he means speed or sex, but the term also connotes an explosion. Dr Soberin, who had tried twice to blow Mike up, is himself consumed in the exploding beach house.

The opening sequence's disorienting images include the strange, upside-down credits; the initial characterizing of both Christina and the killers by shots of their legs; the slightly off-screen scene of Christina's fatal torture with her legs spasming in agony; and the big close-up of the leering gas station attendant who presumes that Mike and Christina have just engaged in roadside sex.

More unusual is the soundtrack, which periodically violates Hollywood continuity norms. At the beginning we hear Christina's heavy panting much more loudly and more intrusively than in comparable scenes in traditional films. This contrasts harshly with the mellow, traditionally balanced sound of Nat King Cole singing "I'd Rather Have the Blues than What I've Got" on Mike's car radio. On numerous occasions, generally when characters are terrified or in danger, we hear what sounds like poorly synched and overloud sound, a strategy which amplifies the almost unworldly strangeness of the scenes. At times there is a strange disconnect between the sound and image tracks when we hear continued sounds of agony on the soundtrack even after the action on the image track indicates that those sounds should have ended. We continue to hear Christina's agonized screams even after her legs have stopped spasming. Comparably, when Mike crushes the hand of the corrupt coroner by smashing a desk drawer upon it, the man's agonized screams dominate the soundtrack, even after we see that he has stopped screaming. When the box containing "the Great Whatsit" is opened, we not only see blinding white light but we also hear growling sounds, as if from demons in hell.

Atomic Age Consumerism and Paranoia

Kiss Me Deadly emphasizes jazzy, atomic age, consumer culture, evident in the set design; in Mike's expensive sports cars, wardrobe, modernist apartment with up-to-date gadgets like his telephone answering machine; and the film's overall obsession with speed. The mechanic Nick's repeated exclamations of "Va-Va-Voom" indicate jubilation in modern forms of excitement like readily available sex and speed.

The film also stresses the flip side of the era's self-satisfied consumer culture – 1950s paranoia. *Kiss Me Deadly* depicts a world in which paranoia is not only justified but also necessary. Mike is systematically suspicious, with abundant cause. When we first see him enter his apartment, he carefully and anxiously explores it, as if expecting intruders to be present. As he does so, his telephone rings and we hear a disembodied woman's voice answering it. This unexplained voice comes as more of a disorienting surprise to the viewer than to Mike. However, we soon see that the voice comes from a tape recording on his answering machine. His telephone answering machine was a device virtually unheard of in 1955 that must have struck contemporary viewers as bordering on the futuristic, like nuclear power.

During this scene, two thugs are watching Mike's apartment from a car outside. He will be shadowed throughout the film and later he will be kidnapped. When he parks his car on an isolated street, a thug with a switchblade knife follows and attacks him. In this and numerous cases, he is able to turn the tables on his attackers. He thwarts kidnappers who plan to murder him and escapes death from the two car bombs planted in his car because he expected them to be there. He accepts such danger as omnipresent in the jungle-like world he inhabits. His ability to anticipate and deal with most of it underscores the smug arrogance he habitually displays.

He appears confident in his ability to handle threats from local power structures like the Interstate Crime Commission and the Los Angeles mob, but he gradually discovers layers of power and danger that surround him of which he knows nothing and with which he is unequipped to deal. When, late in the film, he locates the sought-after box, he is surprised to find that it is hot. He opens it slightly but immediately slams it shut, finding his wrist severely burned. His sometime friend, police Detective Lieutenant Pat Murphy (Wesley Addley), tells him he is way out of his depth on this case and ominously utters a few cryptic words, including "Manhattan Project, Los Alamos, Trinity," which refer to highly classified atomic energy programs of the era. Hearing these culturally charged words, Mike is stunned and mutters, "I didn't know. . . ." He suddenly realizes that Dr Soberin represents a menace far beyond his ken. Velda has been kidnapped and he does not know by whom.

Mike understands local power structures but knows little of national ones like the FBI or atomic energy agencies, and less of international criminal groups that traffic in stolen nuclear materials. The dark side of postwar internationalism was the expansion of barely understood dangers from around the world and from new technologies, and in this film their menace encroaches upon Mike's world.

But then everyone is out of their depth. At the beach house, Gabrielle murders Dr Soberin for the box without knowing what it is or how she can profit from it. Dr Soberin, who exudes smug condescension throughout the movie, is shocked when his greedy mistress Gabrielle suddenly shoots him. Gabrielle also shoots Mike when he bursts into the room searching for the kidnapped Velda. Finally, she opens the box. Its contents instantly set her ablaze and cause the entire house to explode. At the film's end nobody, including the audience, knows the extent of the devastation the box is unleashing. The movie's atomic age paranoia is more than justified.

The unknown extent of the catastrophe applies to whichever of film's two endings one sees. For more than half a century after the film's release, the only prints in circulation ended with shots of the exploding beach house with no indication that Mike and Velda had escaped it. During that time, however, rumors had circulated about a different ending, reinforced by production stills showing Mike and Velda in the surf outside of the house. A print containing that ending surfaced in 1997 and its conclusion is now considered to be the original one that, for unknown reasons, was shortened after the film's original release. It shows Mike and Velda escape the beach house using an exterior staircase, stumble across the beach, and stand in the surf watching the explosion. Robert Aldrich has said that the only print he ever saw ended with Mike and Velda watching the explosion from the surf, and added that, even though Mike had escaped, he had to have been contaminated with radiation.

The editing in the recently released ending seems more professionally integrated than that in the other version but, thematically, it makes little difference which ending one sees. In either case, whether Mike is inside the house or outside watching it explode, he is probably doomed – from having just been shot at close range by Gabrielle, from the radiation, and from the explosion in progress. Both endings are open-ended and neither bodes well for Mike.

Nuclear Fission, Science Fiction, Apocalypse, and Resurrection

Fueling the movie's theme of paranoia and marking some of its deviations from earlier *films noirs* are its tropes of thermonuclear devastation, dystopian science fiction, apocalypse, and resurrection.

The Mike Hammer of Spillane's novel dealt with mafia thugs and drug money, fairly conventional issues for crime stories of the era. The tropes of nuclear fission, science fiction, and apocalypse are entirely new to this movie and open up a vastly broader spectrum of dangers. Early on, Mike encounters a man with burn scars on his face. Later when he briefly opens the box, he gets a radiation burn on his wrist. He is then struck virtually dumb when his friend Pat Murphy refers to nuclear power. These things place radioactive material at the center of the case and touched upon widely publicized social fears of the era.

Nuclear devastation was a very recent phenomenon in the 1950s. It had abruptly entered the popular consciousness in August 1945 after the bombings of Hiroshima and Nagasaki and, for many, seemed like an unimaginable science fiction menace suddenly and shockingly become real.

The most extravagant danger was the specter of an uncontainable nuclear chain reaction. Before the first atom bomb test in 1945, Edward Teller, a prominent physicist who worked on the project, purportedly expressed concerns that the bomb could initiate such a chain reaction, one that might never be able to be stopped until it consumed the earth itself. Throughout this era, this nightmare scenario remained a widespread fear, particularly considering the very limited but anxiety-inducing nature of popular knowledge of the rapidly escalating potential of atomic energy. The plutonium bomb dropped on Nagasaki was more destructive than the uranium bomb dropped only three days earlier on Hiroshima. By the late 1940s, the Soviet Union had developed atomic bombs and the arms race had begun. In the early 1950s, the more powerful hydrogen bomb had been developed. By the time of *Kiss Me Deadly*, the prospect of a never-ending explosion was no longer science fiction; it had assumed the mantle of a "real-world" version of a biblical Apocalypse.

The era's "Red Scare" fueled anxieties about Soviet spy networks stealing US nuclear secrets and enabling a "first strike" nuclear attack that would instantly and decisively cripple the country. Many people built fallout shelters on their property for protection not only from bombs but also from contamination by the subsequent radioactive fallout. Furthermore, many feared possible human or animal mutations resulting from exposure to nuclear testing and radiation. Popular science fiction and horror movies like *Them* (1954), *Godzilla* (1954), and *The Incredible Shrinking Man* (1957) capitalized on such anxieties. The best-selling novel *On the Beach* and its popular 1959 film adaptation depicted a moribund world after a nuclear war whose few remaining inhabitants stoically await inevitable extinction from drifting clouds of radiation.

All of this was very much in the air when *Kiss Me Deadly* appeared, and 1955 audiences would have had little doubt about the extravagantly dangerous contents of the box when Mike first opens it. But although science fiction and movies about nuclear anxiety were popular genres in the 1950s, they seldom intersected with *film noir*. Comparably, while some *films noirs* had employed apocalyptic imagery, most notably the ending of *White Heat* in which James Cagney's psychotic gangster blows himself up in a huge industrial explosion, none had implied the literal obliteration of the planet that, for the first time in history, nuclear power had made possible. Many *films noirs* developed themes of characters weaving their own doom and consequently ending their own lives; this one raises the specter of the end of the world itself. Furthermore, its conclusion depicting a possible nuclear chain reaction and potentially the end of the world itself has a symbolic aptness for a film appearing at the end of *film noir*.

The mysterious Dr Soberin links all of the layers of power of which Mike is initially unaware. He is a cryptic character. For most of the movie we do not see his face, only his trouser legs and shoes, but we hear his imperious, condescending voice. He is a brutal killer, overseeing the murder of Christina and attempted murder of Mike at the beginning, among others. He alone knows what the box contains and to whom it can be sold, although the purchasers are never identified. He provides the link among the film's tropes of crime, science, "high" culture, and mythology. He is presumably a physician because we see his name on a prescription label; he is also established as literate and conversant in modern art. He speaks pretentiously and introduces the extraordinary layers of "high cultural" reference that pervade the film, from the Bible to classical Greek mythology. When he refers to these things, those to whom he speaks, whether Mike, or Gabrielle, or one of his thugs, have no idea what he is talking about.

Soberin's pronouncements are the lynchpin that propels events of the film beyond those of traditional detective films into a crazy-quilt of cultural contexts. He alone seems to understand the danger of the material in the box from the outset – a danger almost unimaginable and far beyond others in Mike's world. On the one hand, the film is about brutal people and events framed in traditional generic molds but, on the other hand, Soberin casts them into the realm of past culture that is ever-recycling its contexts onto contemporary activities. Soberin's character pushes the film's extravagant imagery one step further by linking the scientific and the mythic. The final explosion might materially be categorized as a massive physical destruction, but it can also be described in biblical terms as an apocalypse. While Soberin causes literal physical destruction, he often places things in which he is involved in a wholly different context by describing them in biblical or mythic terms. And amid these grand notions of death and extinction, a central theme is also that of resurrection. At the beginning, one of Soberin's thugs, after brutally torturing Christina to death with a pair of pliers (Plate 27), asks Soberin if he wants him to revive her.

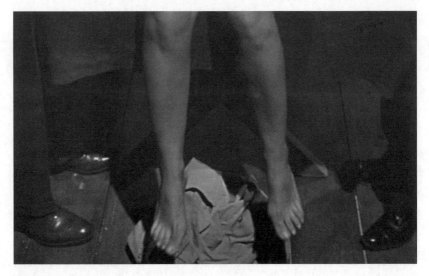

PLATE 27 *Kiss Me Deadly*: Christina (Cloris Leachman) tortured as Mike lies unconscious on the bed. © 1955 Parklane Pictures, INC.

Soberin pretentiously responds by referring to divine powers, "If you revive her, do you know what that would be? Resurrection, that's what it would be. And do you know what resurrection means? It means raise the dead. And just who do you think you are that you think you can raise the dead?" After Mike miraculously survives the explosion of his car, Nick tells him, "I'm sure glad you're back, Mike, like Lazarus rose out of the ground." Later, when a gangster watches Mike emerge from a drugged state, he says, "Back among the living, eh?"

Soberin refers to Lot's wife, fire and brimstone, Cerberus and Medusa. His high-flown talk points to numerous, preexistent contexts for the film's events that come from diverse historical cultures. Such horrific crimes have happened before and will happen again. On one level, this moves the significance of the events from the local to the universal; on another, it can simply be seen as resulting from the cynicism of the filmmakers about the material. Screenwriter A.I. Bezzerides explained away many of the cultural references as simply things that were in the air that he used as a result of his contempt for Spillane's novel: "I wrote it fast, because I had contempt for it. It was automatic writing. Things were in the air and I put them in" (see Naremore, 2008, p. 152). But they do form a pattern in their very excess.

Soberin is pompous and bombastic in his pronouncements, which is one way in which the filmmakers distanced themselves from him and what he says. However, another aspect of his character contradicts traditional notions that culture is "good for you," that knowledge of cultural traditions is civilizing and morally uplifting. Soberin is urbane and well educated; he is also a monster.

The only character likely to have understood Soberin's references is Christina, but, although he oversees her murder, we never see them converse. When she asks Mike if he reads poetry, he gives her an arrogant "Are you kidding me?" look in response. She tells him that she is named after the Victorian poet Christina Rossetti, and cites the Rossetti sonnet "Remember." Regardless of his apparent contempt for poetry, he remembers and it provides him with a major clue to the case. Later, Mike takes a book of Rossetti's sonnets from her apartment. Near the end of the movie, a remarkable shot shows a Los Angeles coroner, Gabrielle, and Mike from the point of view of the morgue slab where Christina's body lays, the literal point of view of the dead (Plate 28). Looking at her body, Mike speculates on the poem "Remember," and recites part of it, including, "For if the darkness and corruption leave/A vestige of the thoughts that once I had." From this, Mike concludes that the clue that Christina wanted to give him, the "vestige" of her thoughts, had to have been something that she concealed on her body. He determines that the clue, the key to the case, is a literal key that she had concealed within her body by swallowing it. He soon learns that, during the autopsy, the coroner

PLATE 28 *Kiss Me Deadly*: Coroner, Gabrielle (Gaby Rodgers), and Mike, photographed from the point of view of the morgue slab on which Christina's body lies. © 1955 Parklane Pictures, INC.

had found that key. Mike forces the coroner to give him the key and it leads him to "the Great Whatsit."

The use of the Rossetti sonnet to uncover a major clue in the case underscores the film's repeated references to past culture. The evocation of old poems, old Caruso recordings, and biblical and mythological figures in a sense brings those things to life again, resurrects them into new contexts. Christina Rossetti was long dead and Christina dies at the beginning of the film but then "comes back" to solve the case. These evocations are part of the film's pattern of presenting renewed contexts for old cultural meanings, from Trinity to Victorian poetry to Christina – the first person we see in the film and the first to die.

Mike's discovery of the key is one of the last times in the movie when he has control over anything. Keys generally imply entry into locked places that lead to resolutions of mysteries, but, from this point on, events spiral into contexts that Mike barely understands.

The key leads him to a locker in the Hollywood Athletic Club. When he begins to open the box inside, searing light and growling sounds emerge. Bewildered, he slams it shut. His wrist is seared. He then returns to his apartment to find Detective Lieutenant Pat Murphy and other policemen waiting for him. Murphy tells him that Gabrielle, with whom Mike had been pursuing clues about Christina's murderers under the impression that she was Lily Carver, Christina's bereaved roommate, was a fraud. Gabrielle was Soberin's mistress and the real Lily Carver's body had been found in the harbor a week earlier. Mike soon telephones the Hollywood Athletic Club but no one answers. The clerk has been murdered and the box is gone. Since Gabrielle had earlier been in Mike's car when he had found the box in the Athletic Club but had disappeared by the time that he came out of the club, it is likely that she had informed Soberin of the box's location and that Soberin's murderous thugs had retrieved the box. Soon after, when Detective Lieutenant Murphy sees Mike's burned wrist, he tells Mike that he has gotten involved in something that is way over his head and ominously tells him to carefully listen to "harmless" words like "Manhattan Project, Los Alamos, Trinity," indicating nuclear power. Numbed, Mike mutters, "I didn't know. . . ."

The next time we see the box it is at the beach house. Dr Soberin is preparing to depart with it without taking Gabrielle with him. Even though she has no idea what the box contains, she wants her share, first asking for half and then demanding it all. Soberin tells her that she deserves a share but that it is undividable. He invokes mythological references like Pandora's Box and the head of the Medusa. He cautions Gabrielle to heed his warning "as if I were Cerberus with all his heads barking at the gates of Hell." He warns that, if she opens the box, she will turn not to stone but rather to brimstone and ashes, which, in effect, she soon does. Gabrielle has no idea what he is talking about. She simply shoots him and, dying, he begs her never to open it.

Searching for the kidnapped Velda, Mike bursts in. Gabrielle asks him to kiss her, then shoots him. She greedily opens the box and stares directly into it. Sheer, blinding light emerges as she opens it wider and wider: she soon bursts into flame. Mike staggers from the room, rescues Velda from an adjacent room, and flees with her, only to stand in the surf outside and watch the beach house explode in what may be a thermonuclear explosion, accompanied by growling, demonic sounds (Plates 29, 30).

The key Mike found led him to something of which he had no comprehension and which will very possibly kill him, and maybe destroy the earth. He and Gabrielle are caught in a world of meanings that preexist them – culture, science, religion, and myth. They proceed as they do in pursuit of what they don't understand – but think they understand the value others place on it. They are fatally wrong.

Amid all of this modern technology, Soberin's statement that, as the world becomes more primitive, its treasures become more fabulous has resonance. Audiences of the 1950s had recently experienced the unparalleled devastation caused by World War II and feared the prospect of

PLATE 29 *Kiss Me Deadly*: Gabrielle opens the box containing "the Great Whatsit" – blinding, deadly light. © 1955 Parklane Pictures, INC.

PLATE 30 *Kiss Me Deadly*: Explosion at the beach house. © 1955 Parklane Pictures, INC.

greater devastation in a nuclear war. A major strain of science fiction in the postwar years was dystopian science fiction, which rejects the traditional utopian notion of historical "Progress," of an opposition between the primitive and the modern in which the modern signifies a moral advance over the primitive. Dystopian science fiction often categorizes those things that are the most modern, the most technically advanced, like the atomic bomb, as the most primitive.

One of the clues that give Mike a sense of what "the Great Whatsit" involves is the simple, but religiously loaded, word "Trinity." Trinity was a term given to one of the atomic bomb projects by J. Robert Oppenheimer, the head physicist of the program. He took the term from the title of a seventeenth-century poem by John Donne on the mysteries of religion. In this film the term links the dangers of modern atomic energy with those of biblical Apocalypse.

The film is also concerned with the new. It can be seen as an end and as a beginning, as pointing toward an exhausted past or an imminent, frightening future.

Critical Reputation

Kiss Me Deadly has often been cited as an endpoint of the canonical *film noir* cycle. In their 1979 "Postface" to their seminal 1955 book on *film noir*,

Borde and Chaumeton call the movie "in every respect, a point of no return" and describe it as "the desperate flip side of the film that had opened the noir series fourteen years earlier, *The Maltese Falcon*" (Borde and Chaumeton, 2002, p. 155). They add, "But between 1941 and 1955, between the eve of the war and the advent of consumer society, the tone has changed. A savage lyricism hurls us into a world in manifest decomposition, governed by dissolute living and brutality; to these intrigues of wild men and weaklings, Aldrich offers the most radical of solutions: nuclear apocalypse" (p. 155).

They note similarities with *The Maltese Falcon* and other *noir* detective movies – a search for a treasure, a cynical private eye, and a *femme fatale*. In its chronicling of a quest for a fabulous treasure that turns out not to be what its seekers expected it to be, the movie resembles *The Maltese Falcon*. The fabled and fetishized Maltese Falcon that everyone seeks, and some die for, turns out to be a fake. At the film's closing, a detective asks Sam Spade what it is and he replies, "The stuff that dreams are made of." Earlier, when a villain had asked him if he knows what the Maltese Falcon is worth, Spade replies that he has no idea, only that "I know the value in human life you people put on it." Like those seeking "the Great Whatsit," many of those involved in its pursuit have little idea of what it is, only that others value it.

In their listing of similarities among *Kiss Me Deadly* and other *films noirs*, Borde and Chaumeton might have added a tone of despair, a disorienting visual and aural style, and a chaotic, malevolent world in decline. The movie's very title, *Kiss Me Deadly*, links death and sexuality in a way that resembles other *films noirs*, either literally in their titles (like *Murder, My Sweet*, *Kiss of Death*, 1947, *Killer's Kiss*, 1955, or *A Kiss before Dying*, 1956) or thematically.

As noted above, the film was largely ignored or dismissed by English-language critics at the time of its release. However, at the same time it was championed by many of the influential critics at *Cahiers du Cinéma*, which had recently been founded in 1951 with an agenda of overturning dominant tenets of the contemporary French critical establishment. Among other things, they rejected the notion of "quality" cinema by categorizing it as polished, respectable, and stale, and in its place championed the harsh, unpolished, and disrespectable aspects so evident in American genre film. *Kiss Me Deadly* provided them with an ideal example. Furthermore, many of the critics writing at the time for *Cahiers du Cinéma*, like Jean-Luc Godard, François Truffaut, and Claude Chabrol, among others, would soon become filmmakers themselves, participating in the new movement known as the French *Nouvelle Vague*. Their films incorporated their critical tenets and referred widely to

Hollywood genre cinema. *Kiss Me Deadly*'s strong generic markers, its harsh juxtapositions, and its dynamic of speed and the new anticipated and influenced *Nouvelle Vague* films like *Breathless*, *Shoot the Piano Player*, and *Alphaville*.

Kiss Me Deadly looks both back to canonical *film noir*, whose era was winding down, and ahead toward neo-*noir*, or resurrected *noir*, which would not emerge for more than a decade. Death and resurrection are central themes. Like the neo-*noir* films *The Long Goodbye* and *Seven*, which will be discussed later, it generates a strong sense of embodying the baroque endpoint of an exhausted genre, of pushing that genre's tropes to, and beyond, their limits. This involves much more than the movie's apocalyptic conclusion.

Although science fiction motifs had largely been absent from *film noir*, they would become important to neo-*noir* in films like *Blade Runner*, *The Matrix*, and *Minority Report*. As discussed earlier, prior to World War II, much science fiction included notions of a technologically advanced future with utopian potential. In the postwar era, however, advanced technology was not always seen in a positive light, and novels like *Nineteen Eighty-Four* popularized the prospect of a dystopian future to the postwar consciousness. The conclusion of *Kiss Me Deadly* fits this pattern, one which would appear frequently in dystopian neo-*noir*. Where much of *film noir* dealt with the local, with the individual on a social level, neo-*noir* tends towards the generic and mythic.

Aside from parallels with science fiction, *Kiss Me Deadly*'s conclusion presages an apocalyptic/mythic theme which would appear widely in neo-*noir* films surrounding the millennium such as *The Terminator*, *The Butcher Boy*, 1997, and *End of Days*. This is evident in the religious and biblical imagery pervading the movie. Other cultural contexts come from the worlds of art, ballet, and opera, but literature is the most pertinent.

From the initial mention of the Rossetti sonnet, the theme of literature and the remembered past is developed repeatedly. The film contains many references to individual lives or worlds that no longer exist, from ancient Greek culture to the biblical Sodom and Gomorrah to Lazarus to Enrico Caruso to Christina Rossetti. Christina presumes that she is likely to die but asks to live on in Mike's memory. Much of *Kiss Me Deadly* evokes a strange past tense; it deals with things passing away, including *film noir* itself. And its apocalyptic ending implies a time when civilization itself might become nothing more than a memory.

Kiss Me Deadly embodies much about *film noir*; indeed some claim it culminates it. It encompassed doomed characters working out their own

PLATE 31 *Kiss Me Deadly*: Oppressive visual environment – the stairway near Gabrielle's rooms. © 1955 Parklane Pictures, INC.

destruction, an unstable world, nightmares coming true, the link of doom with sexuality as well as an often mysterious-looking, heavily shadowed environment (Plate 31), not to mention the illusory prospects of fabulous wealth and creature comforts like cars, ritzy apartments, and the world of the arts. From the beginning, *film noir* was about a world in decline, one where everything goes wrong. It is, however, a convenient overstatement to claim that *Kiss Me Deadly* marked the end of *film noir*. Other candidates would serve as well to mark the end of the era, such as *Touch of Evil, Experiment in Terror,* and *Underworld USA*. But *Kiss Me Deadly* does provide a useful instance of a complex film that looks both backward toward *film noir* and ahead toward neo-*noir*.

CHAPTER 7

THE LONG GOODBYE

The Long Goodbye (1973) is one of the earliest neo-*noir* films. Following the precipitous commercial decline of *film noir* around 1960, crime and mystery films distanced themselves from its tropes for over a decade. The new films were in color instead of black and white and tended to regard those tropes, which had been widely appropriated on television in the 1950s, as being as outmoded as those of silent films had appeared to many audiences in the early 1930s. Not until the 1970s did filmmakers began to reengage *film noir* in a serious and non-patronizing manner. Films such as *Klute* (1971) and *Dirty Harry* provide early examples and *The Long Goodbye* and *Chinatown* were of the first to do so wholeheartedly. Neo-*noir* begins here.

Although *The Long Goodbye* questions the value of *film noir*, it engages it with great seriousness and, as the conclusion of this chapter will show, has much more in common with the genre than is generally understood. It is a substantial film but enjoyed neither critical nor commercial success on its release; it took years to develop the high reputation it now holds. By comtrast, *Chinatown*, appearing the following year, almost instantly achieved great acclaim and set the neo-*noir* standard for years to come.

Film Noir, First Edition. William Luhr.
© 2012 William Luhr. Published 2012 by Blackwell Publishing Ltd.

The Film

The Long Goodbye begins with what seems like an endless series of meandering tracking shots through the messy apartment of Philip Marlowe (Elliott Gould). Nothing seems to be going on: it is 3 am and he is asleep, fully clothed, on his bed. Then his cat awakens him to be fed. Marlowe stumbles out of bed, lights a cigarette, and places cat food in a bowl, but the cat rejects it, knocking the bowl off the countertop. Realizing that it wants its favorite "Curry Brand" cat food, Marlowe drives to an all-night supermarket. When he finds that the market doesn't have the brand, he buys another. Returning home, he enacts an elaborate subterfuge to fool his cat. He furtively stuffs the different brand of cat food into a discarded "Curry Brand" can, then ostentatiously removes it from the can in front of the cat, and places it into the cat's bowl. The cat refuses to eat it and soon disappears forever.

This goofy sequence seems out of place in a mystery and/or a detective film, particularly since it has no relationship to subsequent plot events. Soon after Marlowe returns from the market, however, a traditional mystery plot does begin. Marlowe's friend Terry Lennox (Jim Bouton) shows up with his face and hands badly scratched from what he says was a fight with his wife. He asks Marlowe to immediately drive him to Mexico. Marlowe complies, only to later learn that Terry had killed his wife and lied to him.

In the supermarket, Marlowe had spoken briefly with an employee about his fruitless search for "Curry Brand" cat food. When the man asked why Marlowe had gone to such trouble, Marlowe asked him if he had a cat. The man replied, "What I need a cat for? I got a girl" (Plate 32).

PLATE 32 *The Long Goodbye*: Marlowe (Elliott Gould) in the supermarket looking for cat food. © 1973 United Artists Corporation

Marlowe mutters to himself, "He's got a girl, and I got a cat." Sadly, it's all he has, and he doesn't have it for long.

At the film's conclusion, Marlowe travels to Mexico to confront Terry about having deceived him. Terry shrugs off his cynical manipulation of Marlowe's friendship by saying, "Nobody cares." He adds that the only reason that Marlowe cared was that "You're a born loser." Marlowe replies, "Yeah, I even lost my cat" and abruptly shoots Terry dead.

The opening sequence involving Marlowe's cat had been intercut with shots of Terry driving purposefully toward Marlowe's apartment. By traditional narrative standards, the long cat sequence is irrelevant since it has no causal relationship with subsequent events in the film. Many directors would have cut it out, or never have shot it in the first place. The scenes of Terry driving to Marlowe's apartment, however, set the plot in motion, motivating all subsequent narrative action. He has just killed his wife, he is fleeing with $355,000 stolen from the gangster Marty Augustine (Mark Rydell); and he seeks Marlowe's help in getting him out of the country. He has also been having an affair with Eileen Wade (Nina van Pallandt), who, impressed with Marlowe's loyalty to Terry and/or struck by his manipulability, will soon hire him.

Upon his return from driving Terry to Tijuana, Marlowe is met by homicide detectives investigating the death of Terry's wife. When he refuses to tell them where he drove Terry, they arrest him for aiding in his escape. After spending three days in jail, Marlowe is abruptly released and told that the Lennox case has been closed because Terry had confessed to killing his wife and subsequently committed suicide. Bewildered, Marlowe refuses to believe any of it.

He is soon hired by Eileen Wade to locate her missing husband, the drunken novelist Roger Wade (Sterling Hayden). He is also threatened by the vicious gangster Marty Augustine, who holds Marlowe responsible for the money that Terry stole from him. Marlowe locates Roger Wade and returns him to his wife but, in doing so, discovers suspicious connections among the Wades, the Lennoxes, and Augustine. Eventually, he learns that Terry did, in fact, kill his wife and steal Augustine's money. After fleeing to Mexico with the money, Terry faked his own death, assumed a new identity, and was waiting for Eileen to join him. Realizing that he has been betrayed by everyone, Marlowe goes to Mexico and kills Terry.

The unavailable cat food storyline goes nowhere; the Terry–Marlowe–Eileen–Marty–Roger plot resembles one in a traditional mystery in that it presents a causal trajectory of events filled with sex, violence, greed, betrayal, and surprises. But within the film's thematics, the two storylines are similar in that their empty characters and empty actions begin and end with Marlowe alone, feeling betrayed, and without the resources to understand or to cope with his situation.

Marlowe is pathetically out of touch with the world around him; he is an anachronism who is anchored to the values of a past, irrelevant era. The film's depiction of Marlowe parallels its approach to *film noir*. Appearing early in the neo-*noir* period, *The Long Goodbye* took a different posture toward *film noir* than that of most neo-*noir* films. Where they generally adopt a nostalgic approach to the genre, *The Long Goodbye* does precisely the opposite. It not only questions the merits of reviving *film noir*, but it also challenges the merits of the genre itself, even during its classical period.

In its practice, the film raises questions about *film noir* and the neo-*noir* era such as: Why revive *film noir*? What meaning, if any, does it hold for the "today" of 1973? Why has such uncritical nostalgia arisen for *film noir*, for Raymond Chandler's idiom, and for the postwar Hollywood in which they had appeared?

Vilmos Zsigmond's cinematography for *The Long Goodbye* used a "post-flashing" technique that bled most of the primary colors out of the images, diminishing their intensity and giving much of the film a washed out, too-much-California-sunshine look. Many of its images look as if their vitality has been drained from them. This differs from the warm color tones that a number of neo-*noir* films cultivated, tones that gave the images the look of faded old photographs and contributed to their evocation of nostalgia. The movie's rejection of the widespread nostalgia in neo-*noir* fueled much of the angry critical response to it. Some critics considered it almost a desecration of the chivalric Marlowe myth and of the ways in which *film noir* was regarded and being reinvented at the time.

This chapter, the book's first detailed analysis of a neo-*noir* film, focuses upon the following issues: the reasons for the initial hostile critical reception of *The Long Goodbye*; the film's non-traditional depiction of Marlowe; the creative challenges faced by its screenwriter, Leigh Brackett, and in particular her understanding of the difficulties involved in adapting the cultural milieus of a 1953 novel and a postwar film style to that of a 1970s movie; the film's distinctive formal strategies, particularly its constantly roving camera and its unusual soundtrack; and its profound kinship, on multiple levels, with canonical *film noir*, particularly with those films that did not feature detectives.

Hostile Initial Reception

As with *Kiss Me Deadly*, the critical reputation of *The Long Goodbye* has grown substantially in the decades since its release. It is now widely regarded as a rigorous, insightful film with a revisionist vision of *film noir*. Upon its release, however, many considered it to be an inept and/or a sacrilegious failure.

From its conception, the movie courted associations with Chandler's work and with *film noir*, upon which his work was so influential. It was an adaptation of a major Chandler novel whose central character is his hard-boiled detective, Philip Marlowe; it was set in Los Angeles; and its screenplay was written by Leigh Brackett, who, a quarter-century earlier, had been one of the screenwriters on the *film noir* classic *The Big Sleep*. It comes with a strong *film noir* pedigree.

In 1973, neo-*noir* was in its formative stages. Filmmakers working in it did so with the awareness that they were engaging with, and in some way resurrecting, a dead tradition, one that had not only lost commercial viability around 1960 but that also involved filmmaking practices which, owing to the sea changes in Hollywood filmmaking, could no longer even be replicated as they had existed prior to 1960. Furthermore, this occurred in a context in which many things bound up with *film noir* had also died, such as the studio system, black and white cinematography, the PCA, and the masculinity and femininity of a bygone era.

The period between the precipitous commercial decline of *film noir* around 1960 and the rise of neo-*noir* in the early 1970s is a curious one of uncertainty and overlap. Although some have described 1958's *Touch of Evil* as marking the end of *film noir*, its declining period continued into the early 1960s and produced many rich *films noirs*, notably *Psycho, Underworld USA, Cape Fear* (1962), *Experiment in Terror, Shock Corridor* (1963), and *The Naked Kiss* (1964).

It was not until the mid-1970s that Hollywood films self-consciously engaged the *film noir* tradition and develop neo-*noir*'s recognizable generic patterns, such as a moody, expressionistic use of color and music; complex narrational structures which sometimes involved a retrospective point of view and sometimes aligned the film's point of view with a demented or evil character (as with *The Killer Inside Me*, 2009); graphic sexuality and violence; and periods of ominous, lugubrious pacing. Some of these films remade canonical *films noirs*, like *Farewell, My Lovely* and the 1981 *The Postman Always Rings Twice*. Others, while not remakes, revealed multiple affinities with the genre, like *Body Heat, At Close Range* (1986), *Blue Velvet, Sea of Love* (1989), *China Moon* (1994), *Devil in a Blue Dress, Lost Highway* (2000), *The Salton Sea* (2002), *Kiss Kiss Bang Bang*, and *Out of Time*.

Such films are different in texture from numerous color films made in the late 1950s and 1960s with narrative or thematic structures that might have qualified them as *films noirs* had they been made in black and white and/or during the early postwar era. However, they are seldom discussed as such. Color crime films like *Harper* (1966), *Point Blank*, *Bullitt* (1968), and even Hitchcock's *Vertigo* (1958), as well as color domestic melodramas like *Peyton Place* (1957) and *A Summer Place* (1959), seemed to avoid associations with the then-unfashionable *film noir*. As late as 1973, the made-for-television remake of *Double Indemnity* went virtually unnoticed. Some films of this era, like *Gunn* and *Marlowe*, contrasted central characters with *film noir* associations, like Peter Gunn and Philip Marlowe, with "Swinging Sixties" characters, but they focused more on recuperating an older, middle-aged masculinity in a debased culture than on *film noir* concerns. During this period, films that self-consciously embraced the *film noir* tradition, or referred to it, appeared primarily in foreign cinemas, most notably the French *Nouvelle Vague* with Godard's *Breathless* or *Alphaville* and Truffaut's *Shoot the Piano Player* and *The Bride Wore Black*.

But in the 1970s, after *film noir* as well as many of the genres associated with classical Hollywood seemed to have died out, a new generation of American filmmakers emerged who were eager to revive it. They were the first generation of filmmakers who had not worked their way up within the industry but rather had graduated from film schools, and included Francis Ford Coppola, George Lucas, Steven Spielberg, Martin Scorsese, John Milius, and others. They held great affection for the then-outdated genres of classical Hollywood and nostalgically evoked them in their projects. Those genres included the jungle adventure film (*Raiders of the Lost Ark*, 1981), the outer-space science fiction film (*Star Wars*, 1977), the gangster film (*The Godfather*, 1972), and *film noir*.

Robert Altman, who was somewhat older than that generation, pursued a diametrically opposed vision, one to which the critics of *The Long Goodbye* vehemently objected. Altman's film aggressively rejected the nostalgic approach to the perceived legacy of *film noir*, characterizing such an approach as not only misguided but also damaging. The film presents Marlowe's nostalgia for the Hollywood past as a sign of his vacuity as a character. *The Long Goodbye* is not only indifferent to nostalgia for *film noir*; it holds it in palpable contempt.

Jay Cocks's dismissive review of the movie, and of Altman's approach to Marlowe, in *Time* magazine is representative of many at the time: "Altman's lazy, haphazard putdown is without affection or understanding, a nose-thumb not only at the idea of Philip Marlowe but at the genre that this tough-guy-soft-heart character epitomized. It is a curious spectacle to see Altman mocking a level of achievement to which, at his best, he could only aspire" (see Cocks, 1973). Cocks and others considered the film to be an insult to *film noir* rather than a serious critique of it. Their outrage provides a revealing inroad into contemporary perceptions of *film noir* as well as into Altman's agenda. Such negative reviews led the studio to withdraw the film for six months and then re-release it with a new advertising campaign, including a cartoon-like poster designed by Jack Davis of *Mad* magazine, to emphasize its satirical nature. Although the film did well in New York, it did poor business in most of the rest of the US and only slowly developed the widespread prestige it now holds.

When Cocks described *film noir* as "the genre that this tough–guy–soft-heart character epitomized," he reveals his perception of *film noir* as a sentimental genre. Many of the filmmakers who nostalgically revived it shared that view. But that view belies an understanding of the profoundly anti–nostalgic, anti–sentimental cynicism and despair that pervaded the actual films themselves, as well as *The Long Goodbye*.

A first point to be made is that Altman's movie shares much in common with *film noir*: its themes and incidents, such as murder, betrayal, adultery, and theft, are widespread in *film noir*; its character types – a lonely, betrayed private detective; a traitorous friend; a mysterious beautiful woman; cynical police detectives; and a brutal gangster – are comparably wide-spread, as is the movie's environment of endemic futility and corruption.

Intriguingly, *The Long Goodbye* resembles many neo-*noir* films in its use of representational strategies that differ substantially from those of *film noir*. It was photographed in color and not black and white, and it contains nudity, profanity, and graphic violence that the PCA would never have permitted. Its narrative is not organized around retrospective, point of view narration so common to *film noir* but, instead, is linear and chronological. It is set not in the immediate postwar era in which the novel was set but rather at the time of its production in the 1970s. Most neo-*noir* films employ similarly "updated" strategies but very few have triggered the kind of hostility directed toward *The Long Goodbye*. A major reason is the extent to which many neo-*noir* films are constructed upon nostalgia; very few of them critique the widespread nostalgia for *film noir*, for classical Hollywood cinema, and for the postwar era as confrontationally as does *The Long Goodbye*.

All of the post-1960 movies based upon Chandler novels engage the fact that the era in which those novels were set has passed and, with the exception of *The Long Goodbye*, they illustrate various nostalgic strategies developed by neo-*noir* filmmakers to acknowledge that fact. The earliest, Paul Bogart's *Marlowe* (1969), was set in the late 1960s, at the time it was made, and not during the 1949 setting of its source novel, *The Little Sister*. It was the first Marlowe movie photographed in color and the first in which Marlowe does not wear a fedora. But however up-to-date

Marlowe (James Garner) appears, the movie characterizes him as an anachronism. He might live in the "Swinging Sixties" but he represents older and more conservative values, an attribute that this film presents as ennobling. The values he represents are, in effect, those reflective of the Marlowe films made two decades earlier in the 1940s.

The times have changed but this Marlowe has not. The movie even acknowledges changes in the mass media and in popular taste. Where a major character in the novel had been a movie star, the comparable character here is a television actress. In one scene Marlowe talks with the actress's business representative in the control booth of a television studio as a show is being shot. Before them, we see live performers through a large window. We also see five television monitors, four of which show the action being filmed onstage in color; the fifth, in black and white, shows a scene with Greta Garbo from *Grand Hotel* (1932). Marlowe watches the film and comments, "She was great, wasn't she?" and adds, with directional emphasis, "on the film." The perturbed representative considers the old movie irrelevant and replies that "the show we're doing is out there."

By contrast, *Farewell, My Lovely*, made two years after *The Long Goodbye* and discussed earlier in Chapter 4, is not set contemporaneously in 1975 but in 1941, at roughly the time in which the novel is set. But where 1944's *Murder, My Sweet*, based upon the same novel (also discussed earlier), is set in that same era, that movie was "contemporary," or set at the time of its production, whereas *Farewell, My Lovely*, using roughly the same storyline and characters, was a "period" film, about what, by 1975, had become a bygone era. Robert Mitchum's Marlowe, like that of James Garner, is a highly romanticized throwback to an earlier time. Although *Marlowe* and *Farewell, My Lovely* are set in very different eras, they, like many neo-*noir* films, share nostalgia for *film noir*. *The Long Goodbye*, to the contrary, rejects such nostalgia. Like *Marlowe*, it is set at the time of its production and presents its detective as a character attuned to a bygone era. However, unlike *Marlowe*, this attribute is not used to ennoble him but rather to establish his profound inadequacies.

Marlowe

The Long Goodbye is very much the movie that Robert Altman and Leigh Brackett wanted to make. They considered many of the things that annoyed its critics, like the casting of Elliott Gould, the anti-nostalgic tone, and Marlowe's murder of the Terry Lennox character, to be central to their vision of the film, and the development of Marlowe is essential to that vision

Long before *The Long Goodbye* went into production, producers Jerry Bick and Elliott Kastner had secured adaptation rights to Chandler's novel and sought the right blend of creative talent for the film. Among the directors they approached were Howard Hawks and Peter Bogdanovich. Hawks was an obvious choice since he had directed the legendary 1946 Chandler adaptation, *The Big Sleep*, starring Humphrey Bogart. Bogdanovich was also a likely choice since he was building a career based upon his deep affection for classical Hollywood films, directors, and genres. His *The Last Picture Show* (1971) and *Paper Moon* (1973) included homages to works of John Ford, and, in fact, in 1971 he made a celebratory documentary, *Directed by John Ford*, about Ford's career. His *What's Up, Doc?* (1972) was an affectionate homage to Howard Hawks's 1938 screwball comedy, *Bringing Up Baby*. Clearly, the producers' rationale behind approaching both directors was to make a neo-*noir* with a nostalgic tone. Although those directors declined the project, Bogdanovich suggested Robert Altman, who, after the success of $M^*A^*S^*H$ (1970), was at a career peak as a talented, "hip" director attuned to 1970s sensibilities. Altman's notion of the Marlowe character was radically different from what would have been likely from either Hawks or Bogdanovich, but he agreed to direct the film if he could cast Elliott Gould in the role.

Although just prior to this film Gould had experienced career difficulties after a few flops and reports of contention on sets of his films, the 1970s as a whole marked the peak of his popularity. He starred in a number of successful anti-establishment films that reflected the cultural mood of what would soon be termed the Watergate Era, including *Bob and Carole and Ted and Alice* (1969), *Getting Straight* (1970), and $M^*A^*S^*H$. His star image centered upon a rebellious, new kind of masculinity that implicitly rejected older models, one that spoke to the anti-establishment, anti-Vietnam War, sexually liberated, youth culture so visible and so influential in the era. At earlier stages of the project, producers had proposed Robert Mitchum and Lee Marvin for Marlowe, actors whose star images embodied the older masculinity. Gould's image differed substantially from theirs as well as from those who had played the character in the Marlowe films immediately preceding and following this one. In 1969, James Garner had played the title role in *Marlowe*; in 1975, Mitchum would play Marlowe in *Farewell, My Lovely* (as well as in the 1978 *The Big Sleep*). Both actors fit the mold of leading men in classical Hollywood hard-boiled films. Garner, Marvin, and Mitchum were two-fisted, strong, silent types who could as credibly play modern-day tough guys wearing suits and ties or gunfighters in Westerns. It would be hard to see the semi-hippie, urban, 1960s era Gould looking comfortable in a suit and tie or coolly facing down outlaws in a Western. He was less bourbon from the bottle and more marijuana haze.

Altman renders Gould doubly out of place in *The Long Goodbye* by costuming him in a suit jacket and tie. Not only did such attire, then associated with an older generation, not fit Gould's image, but he is also virtually the only character to dress in that manner. Most other characters wear chic 1970s Southern Californian casual attire. Gould's wardrobe reflects the shoddy, outmoded past that imprisons his Marlowe. His jacket and tie do not make him look glamorous or retro-chic, just shabby and out of touch, closer to a derelict than a noble echo of a better age.

But even though Gould's image ran counter to those of traditional hard-boiled detectives, his Marlowe does credibly share some attributes with earlier private eyes. He is honest and loyal to his friends, competent at his job in locating both Roger Wade and Terry, he lives by his own moral code, he is not intimidated by either police or gangsters, and he is able to uncover the "real" truth behind the "official" story.

Despite these points of similarity, however, fundamental aspects of his character distance him from the traditional mold. The most significant of these is the simple fact that, throughout the film, in whatever he does, he is out of place. This is not because of his strict professional code or because of his shabby lifestyle; it is simply because he doesn't fit in anywhere. He is weird. He wears a mismatched suit jacket, slacks, and tie that he sleeps in and never changes. He smokes cigarettes incessantly in a non-smoking culture. Where smoking was fashionable and even glamorous in postwar movies, it was no longer so in Los Angeles of the 1970s. He constantly talks to himself and, even when conversing with others, he makes references that few understand. His amalgamation of characteristics does not, as with Chandler's Marlowe, render him Byronically aloof from a debased world; they are just a cluster of disconnected, dysfunctional, self-delusional character traits that hover uselessly about him. Screenwriter Leigh Bracket found her key to writing the role of Marlowe, and to the film, in Altman's description of the character: "I see Marlowe the way Chandler saw him, a loser. But a *real* loser, not the fake winner that Chandler made out of him. A loser all the way" (see Brackett, 1988, p. 140). He is out of his time, and time is important to neo-*noir*.

Chandler's Marlowe was a romanticized figure, likened to a medieval knight-errant in a debased world. His novels and the movies based upon them generally present the character as following his own moral compass in a world with a deeply flawed justice system. Tough and intelligent, he seeks little for himself, often risks death, and receives scant or no compensation for his work. A lonely man living under straitened financial circumstances, he is characterized as heroic because of the sacrifices he makes to maintain his integrity. Chandler structures the novels so that, while many characters in them consider Marlowe a loser because of his isolation and relative poverty, the reader is positioned to realize that it is society and not Marlowe that is corrupted, hence Altman's description of him as a fake loser.

Furthermore, a dominating influence on the popular perception of Marlowe has become Humphrey Bogart's charismatic, heroic portrayal of the character in *The Big Sleep*, which is often conflated in the popular mind with Bogart's portrayal of Sam Spade five years earlier in *The Maltese Falcon*. At times, when people invoke the popular image of Marlowe, they are really referring to Bogart playing both Spade and Marlowe.

But Bogart had been dead nearly two decades when Altman made *The Long Goodbye*. As we noted in Chapter 1, on the set while shooting the movie, Altman referred to the character as "Rip Van Marlowe" – a man who has been asleep for twenty years and is now out of step and out of touch. Appropriately, the very first time we see him he is sound asleep on his bed. Altman considered the novel less a tightly constructed mystery plot and more a loosely connected collection of thumbnail essays. Altman was interested not so much in the novel's plot as in Chandler's depiction of his era, and in fact he claimed never to have finished the novel. Instead of suggesting that the cast and crew read Chandler's *The Long Goodbye* as background for the film, Altman circulated a collection of Chandler's letters and essays. He felt that Marlowe embodied a cluster of outmoded attitudes about life, including his notion of masculinity and his sense of his culture, revealed in his dress, comportment, and abrasive social interactions. Although Chandler's worldview struck resonant chords for audiences in the 1940s and 1950s, Altman felt that, by the 1970s, those perceptions had become outmoded and ossified, and his Marlowe embodied them. Like the jacket and tie he wears, what was current in the 1940s had become archaic by 1973. Altman's Marlowe feels that he lives according to superior values of the past but the movie gives no indication that those values were any better even then. Like the gateman who constantly does star imitations from old movies, Marlowe is playing largely, and irrelevantly, to himself.

Both Robert Aldrich and Robert Altman are known as creative genre directors, but where Aldrich generally worked within the norms of the genres he attempted, while sometimes pushing the borders of those norms, Altman repeatedly critiqued the genres he engaged, particularly in the 1970s. This difference in approach also applies to the work of both in *film noir*. Although Aldrich's *Kiss Me Deadly* was largely ignored by critics in the US upon its release, those who did comment upon it tended to view it as existing in continuity with other movies in the genre. Many reviewers of *The Long Goodbye*, however, greeted it with scorn upon its release, partially because it was not "another" private eye film but something altogether different and subversive. Unlike Aldrich's practice, Altman had no desire to make a *film noir* that pushed the limits of the genre; instead, he made a film that subverted the rejected the genre.

This applies as well to the two directors' work in other genres. Enthusiasts of war movies tend to enjoy Aldrich's *Attack* and *The Dirty Dozen* in ways that some Western fans do not enjoy Altman's *McCabe and Mrs Miller* (1971) or *Buffalo Bill and the Indians, or Sitting Bull's History Lesson* (1976). Aldrich's war films presented tough, dedicated combat soldiers, reinforcing the heroics of many war films. Altman's Westerns subvert expectations of many Western fans. They do not celebrate heroic individualism but, instead, mourn its failure. There is no heroic gunfighter in *McCabe and Mrs Miller* but rather a petty opportunist crushed by encroaching capitalist interests. Altman's Buffalo Bill is not a noble man of the West but a charlatan.

Indicative of Marlowe's isolation in *The Long Goodbye* is his lack of a romantic life. This sets him doubly apart because it contrasts sharply with the norms both of the setting and of the genre. First, the movie has a hip "Los Angeles in the 1970s" atmosphere, drenched in sexuality. Setting Marlowe's lack of romantic companionship in bold relief, all other main characters have multiple sexual partners. Terry just killed his wife and was having an affair with Eileen Wade; her husband, Roger Wade, had an affair with Terry's wife; the gangster Marty Augustine travels with his mistress and talks about wife and children. An apartment adjacent to Marlowe's is occupied by a group of spaced-out young women who are often drugged and topless or naked. Every male who comes to Marlowe's apartment stops in disbelief to ogle them. Except Marlowe. He repeatedly goes back and forth to their communal elevator, politely says hello to the women, who are generally in full view in the area in front of their apartment, does small favors for them, and shows no sexual interest whatsoever in them.

Secondly, Marlowe's monastic celibacy goes against the grain of all previous Marlowe films as well as other Hollywood hard-boiled detective movies, in which the detective is commonly presented as sexually charismatic. Marlowe appears virtually asexual. Attempts by other characters to demean his heterosexual potency – at one point Augustine threatens to have him castrated; at another a police detective insultingly asks him if he is "a fag" – are beside the point; he seems to exist outside of any sexual realm. Traditional detective films often posited strong sexual tension, if not an affair, between the detective and the *femme fatale*. Here, Eileen Wade, the central female character, who is involved both with her husband and with Terry, is depicted as a stunningly attractive woman. At one point she seems about to seduce Marlowe but no romance develops, or is likely. There is no sexual chemistry or tension between the characters.

Altman's Marlowe is alone in a hypersexualized society, placing him in bold contrast to other screen Marlowes, before and since, who are generally presented as enormously attractive to women and have at least one romantic partner.

Leigh Brackett, Chandler, Generic Change, and Marlowe

Leigh Brackett, *The Long Goodbye*'s screenwriter, had been one of the screenwriters for the hugely successful and influential 1946 *The Big Sleep*, based upon the Chandler novel of the same name and starring Humphrey Bogart and Lauren Bacall. For Brackett, a major challenge in tackling *The Long Goodbye*'s script was that American culture had changed so much since 1946 that it was impossible to approach the project as she had done in the 1940s. She wrote:

> Twenty-five years had gone by since *The Big Sleep*. In that quarter-century, legions of private eyes had been beaten up in innumerable alleys by armies of interchangeable hoods. Everything that was fresh and exciting about Philip Marlowe in the forties had become cliché, outworn by imitation and overuse. The tough loner with the sardonic tongue and the cast-iron gut had become a caricature. Also, in twenty-five years, the idiom had changed. (Brackett, 1988, p. 139)

She felt that her new script needed to reflect the fact that times had changed and to underscore the dangers of ignoring that reality.

Brackett's perceptions provide a key to the movie's approach. She knew that, when she wrote the screenplay for *The Big Sleep*, the idiom of the World War II era was still a fresh one, and the hard-boiled private detective was a culturally resonant character. By the 1970s, the idiom had become clichéd through overuse, in radio, film, and on television, and the character of Marlowe had become a caricature. Brackett and Altman agreed that an attempt to re-create the milieu of that era would be folly. Furthermore, Los Angeles as a cultural environment had changed. The LA of the 1940s was long dead. Brackett knew that the character of Marlowe had always been a fantasy but one that had resonated with cultural chords in the 1940s; the 1970s had clichés also, but they were ones that touched very different cultural chords.

She acknowledged that Elliott Gould was a different screen presence from Bogart, but she added that, were Bogart still performing, he would not have played the role in the same way he had done it in the 1940s. He would have adapted to changing times. The same went for Chandler, who, in the two decades during which he wrote his seven Marlowe novels, constantly sought to refresh and update the formula. He repeatedly altered his depictions of both Marlowe and Los Angeles. Consequently, *The Long Goodbye* is a very different kind of novel from *The Big Sleep*. In his final novel, *Playback*, Chandler largely abandons Los Angeles as a setting in favor of a fictionalized San Diego. And in the fragment of a Marlowe novel that he left at his death, Chandler further pushed the boundaries of the genre by having Marlowe get married.

While Chandler's Marlowe had become a prototype for the hard-boiled private detective in both fiction and film, and while Chandler's writing style had not only been widely imitated but also, perhaps more than any other, come to represent the verbal style and strategies of *film noir*, they were all subject to changing times. The very extent of Chandler's popularity and influence, even during his lifetime, had created problems for him. The fact that his writing style had become so quickly and so widely imitated became a creative impediment to his work since at times he felt like he was imitating his imitators. What had once been new became quickly old.

Aside from the problems raised by changing times, Brackett realized that, as a novel, *The Long Goodbye* was constructed very differently from *The Big Sleep*. *The Long Goodbye* was much longer, more narratively complex, much slower in movement, and much more depressive than its predecessor. In constructing her screenplay, she eliminated the novel's World War II context and a substantial number of plot threads to largely focus on the Roger Wade story. She also changed the novel's quiet, sad climax and invented the abrupt, violent ending of Marlowe killing Terry. All centered on her vision of Marlowe. Agreeing with Altman, she saw him as a loser. Referring to Marlowe's lack of a romantic life, she said that "the girl" did not leave him; she just did not know he was there. This is the way in which the half-naked women next door behave toward him; they only acknowledge him when he is literally in front of them, and then they quickly forget him. Brackett's Marlowe is not a hero and is not taken seriously by other characters; he is simply a patsy.

Hence, Brackett, Altman, and Chandler were all conscious of the fact that, in order to remain vital, a genre had to continually reinvent itself and adapt to changing times. Once a generic formula becomes established and successful, it risks becoming imitated, overused, and stale. A writer or filmmaker working in a generic tradition cannot rest on old laurels but, instead, must constantly seek fresh imaginative directions. At times, however, such new directions can antagonize the mood of the times, as with *The Long Goodbye*.

Brackett was a talented screenwriter who had successfully worked in many genres, from *film noir* (*The Big Sleep*) to the Western (*Rio Bravo*, 1959, *El Dorado*, 1966, *Rio Lobo*, 1970) to science fiction (*Star Wars: The Empire Strikes Back*, 1980) to comedy (*Man's Favorite Sport*, 1964). She had a firm sense of ways in which genres and cultural circumstances change over time and of the need to adapt new films to those changes. *El Dorado* is an elegiac, half-comic Western about aging and is very different in tone from the earlier *Rio Bravo*, which was about rugged individualism. The differences related to the aging of the film's star, John Wayne, as well as to that of the genre.

Illustrating one example of changed circumstances, Brackett noted that in 1973 they no longer had to deal with the PCA. In *The Big Sleep* and much of *film noir*, nudity, profanity, sexual activity, graphic violence, and drug use were prohibited. Certainly, as described earlier, there were ways of hinting at these things, but overt representation was impossible. *The Long Goodbye*, however, appeared under different representational structures since the PCA, which actively forbade the depiction of transgressive content, was abolished in the 1960s and replaced by the Classification and Rating Administration (CARA), which did not prohibit any depictions but rather gave age-appropriate classifications to films. Intriguingly, the increased leeway that CARA allowed makes little difference in *The Long Goodbye*. The women next door to Marlowe are shown topless, there is frequent profanity and reference to drug use, but these things do not give the film a particularly transgressive tone. Marlowe is indifferent to them and, with the exception of the two scenes of sudden and graphic violence, the film does not represent any of this previously unrepresentable material as shocking. The mood resembles that in some post-apocalyptic films – nothing matters or is meaningful. Terry says "Nobody cares" and Marlowe repeatedly says, "It's OK with me." The film gives no sense that the things permitted by greater representational freedom are either degenerate or empowering; they are just there in a desensitized society.

This mood is informed by the two-decade gap between *Kiss Me Deadly*, as well as *film noir*, and *The Long Goodbye*. *Kiss Me Deadly* is very much part of the *film noir* era in that much of its aesthetic is modernist. The world might be degenerate and falling apart, but that sad state still has the power to upset people; such things still matter. Even the corrupted and cynical Mike Hammer is horrified by the implications of Soberin's evil, and the explosion concluding the film is presented as apocalyptic. In *The Long Goodbye*, with the neo-*noir* era in place, only isolated incidents are presented to court either audience sympathy or outrage. It is almost as if the world itself has become drained of meaning. One strategy for grasping at meaning is nostalgia for the past, but *The Long Goodbye* rejects that as an option.

The Long Goodbye eschews much about the classical Hollywood style; it also presents classical Hollywood itself as outdated and irrelevant, as well as a central clue to Marlowe's character. It does not make romanticized citations of old movies and, even though it is set in Los Angeles, no one aside from Marlowe and a goofball gateman even acknowledges Hollywood.

The gateman is singular in that, as a way of livening up his tedious job of admitting cars to the exclusive, gated "Malibu Colony," he constantly does mediocre imitations of old Hollywood stars – Barbara Stanwyck, Cary Grant, James Stewart, Walter Brennan. Aside from Marlowe, no one pays him any attention. At one point Marlowe fools him up by telling him that a gangster who is following Marlowe is a Walter Brennan fan. When the gangster drives up, the gateman greets him while imitating Walter Brennan's mannerisms. The gangster has no idea of what the gateman is doing, considers him crazy, and drives off.

Comparably, Marlowe constantly refers to his own private mythology of once vital but now archaic movies that few recognize; these references isolate him from nearly everyone. He calls a dog blocking his car "Asta," referring to the dog in the "Thin Man" movies of the 1930s and 1940s. In a police interrogation room, he smears fingerprint ink on his face and sings "Swanee," referring to Al Jolson's blackface performances in early sound movies. When Marlowe is hospitalized after being hit by a car, his roommate's entire body is bandaged. Marlowe tells the man that he's seen all of his movies, referring to the "Invisible Man" movies in which the title character was frequently bandaged. The man gives him a miniature harmonica, which Marlowe pulls out at the very end to accompany "Hooray for Hollywood."

The musical score for *The Long Goodbye* is, with a single exception, a multitude of arrangements of the same song, "The Long Goodbye" by John Williams and Johnny Mercer, going from soulful ballads to a song heard on the radio to a dirge played by a Mexican marching band, even to the sound of the doorbell ringer at the Wade house. The one exception to this comes at the very beginning and at the very end. It is an old, scratchy recording of "Hooray for Hollywood" by Richard A. Whiting and Johnny Mercer, a song used in the 1937 Busby Berkeley movie, *Hollywood Hotel*. We hear a few bars of it at the opening and then the full song at the very end as Marlowe walks down a rural Mexican road. He even does impromptu dance steps to it and at one point briefly twirls a woman. He does not speak Spanish, has never been on that road before, and no one has any idea what he is doing, just as in the rest of his life. The outdated quality of the recording is marked by the performance style of the vocalists, the orchestration, and its poor, scratchy, audio quality. These things categorize it, like the Hollywood that it celebrates, as an artifact from a past era.

Marlowe leaves, alone, as the movie ends to the tune of "Hooray for Hollywood."

Formal Strategies

The movie's pacing differs from classical Hollywood pacing. It begins very slowly, not by presenting the viewer with a puzzling crime or a mysterious, menacing situation but, rather, with what seems to be an aimless scene involving Marlowe and his cat. Many other scenes also initially seem meandering. As opposed to classical Hollywood style, where cinematography, editing, and blocking generally conspire to provide a clear focal point to each shot, Vilmos Zsigmond's Panavision camera in *The Long Goodbye* seems constantly to be roving through the sets and among the characters in what at times seems an arbitrary manner. Some shots have multiple focal points and the viewer must work to determine what the scene is about. Sometimes this leads to abrupt and shocking surprises. Altman reinvented the character of Marlowe in this film; he also in a sense reinvented the destabilization and visual disorientation of *film noir* by employing new strategies to produce comparable effects within the audience.

Altman and cinematographer Zsigmond developed a unique visual style for the movie. They did not want harsh shadows and intense colors; rather they sought a flat, semi-washed-out look for 1970s Los Angeles. As noted above, they used a "post-flashing" technique – exposing the film, after shooting but before developing, to pure light – which has the effect of reducing color intensities to pastels and muting contrasts. This differs substantially from the visual strategies used by cinematographer John Alonzo two years later for *Farewell, My Lovely*. In that film and for one of the first times in a Hollywood movie, Alonzo used Fujicolor film stock, which he considered uniquely equipped for emphasizing warm colors and endowing the images with a comfortable, nostalgic "feel." By contrast, many images in *The Long Goodbye* have a cold, plastic "feel," suggesting neither warmth, depth, nor anything below the movie's hard surfaces.

The scene in which Roger and Eileen Wade argue in their beach house is brightly lit, visually dominated by the large glass panels admitting sunlight from the beach outside. Marlowe stands outside, able to see through the glass that they are arguing but unable to hear their voices. In some shots we see all three characters, who, although they are in separate spaces – inside and outside – appear visually together, whether shown directly or by means of their reflections on the glass. The shot serves to unite them visually but also to reduce them to their surface appearances.

Many of the film's sets contain a considerable amount of glass, like the beach house, Marty Augustine's penthouse apartment, and the police station. Such "surface" and/or reflected images often reveal more about the characters and their relationships than does what those characters actually say or do. This relates to the constantly roving camera, which frequently seems to conceal nothing and gives the impression of a free-ranging look at a society's many facets, big and small. At times, the camera itself seems to provide the action in a scene where the habitually aimless Marlowe does not. Because of the constantly meandering camera, we often are not sure what we are looking at in shots, or what to look at in them.

At times, we are presented with competing focal points. When the police interrogate Marlowe about Terry's disappearance, we see him in an interrogation room through a one-way mirror from an adjacent obser-vation room. Marlowe knows it is a one-way mirror and has placed a black handprint on the glass. The shot has five different focal points. In the interior room, we see the seated and alternately enraged and wisecracking Marlowe, responding both to the policeman in that room and to those he knows are watching on the other side of the one-way mirror. We also see the abrasive interrogation officer and his attempts to provoke Marlowe. On the intervening window, we see the ridiculous, black handprint Marlowe has placed there. And in the observation room, two racially antagonistic detectives – one black and one white – watch and argue between themselves. The viewer hardly knows what to watch, and, of course, throughout all of this, the camera continues to move (Plate 33).

The roving camera also allows for remarkable surprises and shocks. The boldest comes when Marty Augustine comes to Marlowe's apartment looking for the money that Terry stole from him. Marty's mistress, Jo Ann (Jo Ann Brody), follows him into the apartment. Marty asks for a Coke and talks of his love for his mistress while the camera moves around her face in a series of caressing shots. Suddenly the camera stops and Marty brutally

PLATE 33 *The Long Goodbye*: Police interrogation scene with five focal points. © 1973 United Artists Corporation

smashes the bottle into her face, horribly disfiguring it. Even Marty's goons are aghast. Marty tells Marlowe, "Now that's someone I love, and you I don't even like," and demands that Marlowe find his money. It is an extraordinary moment of shocking and graphic violence.

It also reverberates throughout the movie. It has shown us that Altman is capable of presenting graphic explosions of violence and the possibility of a recurrence pervades the mood of the rest of the film. During an argument with his wife, Roger Wade, a hulking, swaggering, mountain of a man, suddenly takes her chin in his hand and slowly steps back. He seems to be preparing to hit her with a virtually decapitating roundhouse punch. He doesn't do it, but the earlier mutilating violence we saw has let us know that Altman is capable of making it happen, and this gives the scene greater tension (Plate 34).

PLATE 34 *The Long Goodbye*: Roger Wade (Sterling Hayden) in a potentially violent scene with his abused wife (Nina van Pallandt). © 1973 United Artists Corporation

Later, Marlowe is brought to Marty's penthouse, where he sees Jo Ann, whose face is now grotesquely wired with reconstructive devices and bandages. Marty again rants on about her beauty and Marlowe becomes tense, since it is altogether possible that Marty might once again explode and abruptly smash the reconstructive devices into her face, further mutilating the woman. Marty does not do it, but the earlier scene of her disfigurement hovers menacingly over this one.

The movie has other moments of surprise involving the roving camera. One remarkable scene occurs after Marlowe and Eileen Wade have just eaten dinner at her beach house in the evening. Earlier, her drunken husband had again disgraced himself and then fallen asleep in a stupor. Marlowe had advised her to leave and stay in a hotel or with a friend but she says that she did that once only to find on her return that her husband had wrecked the place. She had asked Marlowe to stay with her for a time and prepared a candlelit dinner for them both.

After the dinner, they stand quietly in front of large panel windows. She asks Marlowe to call her "Eileen" and the scene has the potential to become a romantic one. The camera moves in closer to them, apparently to intensify the potentially romantic atmosphere. Abruptly, Marlowe breaks the mood by asking her about her husband's involvement with Marty Augustine. The mood instantly becomes tense. Now the scene seems to be about a romantic mood suddenly shattered by a confrontational question. But the camera keeps moving in – now going between the characters and showing the dark beach outside. A white blur has begun to emerge from the bottom of the frame that we soon learn is Roger Wade in a white shirt. He is purposefully walking into the ocean to commit suicide (Plate 35).

It is a remarkable scene that repeatedly changes its meaning, all in one slowly moving shot whose significance repeatedly changes. It is structured around the "invisible" glass panels which separate the "inside" from the initially irrelevant "outside" until the "outside" suddenly becomes a dynamic presence. At first the shot seems to be "about" a romantic situation, then "about" the abrupt breaking of that mood to refocus onto the facts of the case, and finally "about" the discovery and shock of Roger Wade's suicide. It is constantly changing. The shot encapsulates the movie's pervasive atmosphere of instability and unexpected discoveries, as well as its formal, thematic, and narrative strategies. While Roger Wade's suicide comes as a surprise in the scene, it is also quite logical considering Wade's incoherent alcoholism and his humiliation earlier in the day (see below). Although Eileen appears open and truthful in the shot, she is still consistently lying to Marlowe. Marlowe appears to be doggedly

PLATE 35 *The Long Goodbye*: Marlowe and Eileen Wade inside her home. Through the window, we see Roger Wade on the beach outside as he slowly emerges from the bottom/center of the frame to commit suicide. © 1973 United Artists Corporation

pursuing the case but is ineffective in foreseeing or preventing Wade's suicide. Each surprise brings a new and unpleasant revelation about the world of the movie.

Although the movie presents Marlowe as hollow and deluded, no one else comes off any better; it does not give us an alternative or more admirable way of life. Virtually everyone in the film is manipulative, self-deluded, or evil. It depicts a world without a moral center, something which the Marlowe of other movies often provided. *The Long Goodbye* shows us a world going nowhere, like its vision of the revival of *film noir*.

Marlowe is clearly ineffectual and out of date, but the other men in the film also radiate desperation, particularly the two who appear the most powerful and commanding, Roger Wade and Marty Augustine. Roger Wade is a physically powerful man as well as a wealthy, successful novelist with a beautiful wife, but we learn that he has been impotent, that he fears his writing skills are gone, and that he is a hopeless alcoholic. He presents himself as hyper-masculine, constantly bellowing and assuming dominating postures. However, when he is challenged, he collapses. In one scene, Dr Verringer (Henry Gibson) confronts him about an unpaid bill at a party at Wade's house. The diminutive Verringer appears dwarfed by the big, blustering Wade, who cruelly capitalizes on their size difference: Wade mockingly calls him "Minnie Mouse" and refuses to pay the bill. Abruptly, Verringer harshly slaps Wade; everyone is shocked and stops to watch what will happen next. Wade seems to gather his strength to easily destroy the man but suddenly and meekly agrees to pay. He gives the impression of a balloon suddenly and humiliatingly deflated. Later that night he commits suicide.

Hollywood is not the only cultural myth that Altman critiques in the film. Roger Wade appears to model himself on Ernest Hemingway, a writer who epitomized one model of twentieth-century masculinity. Wade is huge, bearded, loud, and constantly swaggering. But like Altman's view of Hollywood, he is hollow. His talent has dried up, his wife is cheating on him, none of his friends come to his defense, and his suicide is a desperate, lonely end, like that of Hemingway just over a decade earlier. Wade is attempting to enact a dead, desperate myth, like Marlowe. Wade's inadequacies are transparent, like those of Marty Augustine, who surrounds himself with hired thugs and incessantly brags about his power and possessions. The thugs seem like a mobile audience hired to massage his profoundly insecure ego. When he mutilates his girlfriend, it is a cowardly act done by surprise and among people unable to challenge him. Altman's novelist, detective, and gangster all critique the myth of rugged masculinity that they so desperately attempt to embody.

The Long Goodbye illustrates one of the strategies available to neo-*noir*. It takes an old tradition that was being revived in nostalgic ways at the time and references it in an anti-nostalgic film that critiques that tradition as well as the very value of reviving it. It does so, as *Little Big Man* (1970) did with the Western, by questioning the generic premises of that tradition, both at the time of its revival and even for the earlier era when the genre was contemporary.

The Long Goodbye *and* Non-Detective *Films Noirs*

Intriguingly, *The Long Goodbye* is in many ways more attuned to canonical *film noir* than are the nostalgic evocations of many neo-*noirs*. Although some critics initially considered the movie an outrage to their memories of *film noir*, it is worthwhile to compare their responses with many critical reactions to *films noirs* of the canonical era, especially to films that did not have detectives as central characters. Negative responses to such films often foregrounded the culturally abrasive components of *film noir*, and comments of critics about the immorality or offensive elements of the films, when contrasted with conventional Hollywood product, echo some of the outrage decades later against *The Long Goodbye*.

Detective films, even in *film noir*, often allowed space for heroism or culture-affirming personalities, regardless of the film's grim events, characters, and social commentary. Private detectives like Sam Spade in

The Maltese Falcon or Marlowe in *Murder, My Sweet, The Big Sleep,* and *Lady in the Lake,* even Mike Hammer in *Kiss Me Deadly,* as well as many "official" detectives, whether police detectives as in *The Naked City,* FBI agents in *Walk East on Beacon* (1952), Treasury agents in *T-Men,* or Immigration agents in *Border Incident* (1949), could often be seen as heroic agents for justice, however flawed, whose actions reinforced traditional values and courted audience sympathy. Such characters provided a comfort zone in a dirty world and were often revived nostalgically in neo-*noir.*

But many *films noirs* without central detective characters lack such a balancing, potentially regenerative presence, and this lack renders overt their severe critique of the American Dream and its social institutions. Such institutions included the insurance industry (*Double Indemnity, The Postman Always Rings Twice*), Big Business (*The Big Clock,* 1948, *T-Men, The Asphalt Jungle*), the penal system (*Brute Force,* 1947), small-town business (*Act of Violence*), and Hollywood (*Sunset Boulevard*). Such a critique is also evident in many films featuring detectives, such as *Out of the Past, The Big Heat,* and *Touch of Evil* but, with many of them, analysis can become sidetracked by discussions of the detective's personality.

Film noir has been called a cinema of failure and disillusionment, and many of the films were initially reviewed with distaste for their violence, sexuality, and downbeat narrative arcs. Some critics characterized the films as guides to crime, or as glorifications of immoral, repellent, or anti-social characters. French commentators in the 1940s characterized such dark perspectives as signaling a new American maturity, but many American critics characterized them as perverse and distasteful, even immoral.

The Long Goodbye can be viewed from both perspectives. Deeply cynical, it depicts a superficial contemporary society with nowhere to go but down. This certainly fits many *films noirs,* in which central characters are often morbidly aware of the futility of their actions. At the beginning of *Double Indemnity,* the already-doomed Walter Neff says he committed murder for money and for a woman and that he didn't get the woman and he didn't get the money. The film follows his point of view throughout. *The Postman Always Rings Twice* is similar in that it is narrated by Frank Chambers and depicts his crimes of passion and greed; at the end we learn that he has been narrating the film as he is about to be executed for those crimes. Paul Sheridan, the police detective in *Pushover* (1954), knows that his involvement with Lona McLane, the *femme fatale,* will end catastrophically for him but pursues it anyway. *The Long Goodbye* begins with Marlowe going to considerable trouble to please his cat but being abandoned by it. He then spends most of the film trying to rehabilitate his friend Terry's reputation but finally kills Terry. Throughout, he is entirely alone for reasons he never understands. However, like Neff, Chambers, and Sheridan, he deserves his fate. *The Long Goodbye* mounts a trenchant critique of contemporary society – its wealth, sexuality, masculinity, etc. – and as with *Detour*, everything in that society is alienating, circular, and hopeless. *Film noir* has always been a loose amalgam of generic tropes, but one of its central themes is that you can't go home again, that many beliefs and places that once promised hope and regeneration are illusory. Films like *High Sierra, Out of the Past*, and *The Asphalt Jungle* show the presumption of a restorative rural America to be a dead myth; in *The Long Goodbye*, Hollywood provides such a myth. For much of his career, Altman critiqued the national myth machine of Hollywood (*The Player*, 1992) as well as its genres, such as Westerns and *film noir*, as providing seductive yet hollow and erosive myths by which people live. In *film noir*, characters often attain the American Dream only to find it to be built on sand, as in *Double Indemnity, Act of Violence, The Big Clock, Citizen Kane, The Stranger* (1946), *T-Men*, and *The Big Heat*. Most *film noir* is contemporaneously-set and anti-nostalgic, like *The Long Goodbye*, and centers upon failed masculinity, black widows, and false dreams. Nostalgia for their memories of *film noir* blinded many critics of *The Long Goodbye* to the actuality and cultural abrasion of *film noir* at its inception.

Film noir lacked the presumptive affirmation of traditional moral and social values widespread in other genres during the classical Hollywood era: Westerns often ended with the triumph of the forces of civilization over those of savagery and corruption; crime films often ended with their "public enemies" captured or killed; the comedies of Charlie Chaplin, the "common man" films of Frank Capra, the brash young-man-on-the-rise films of Douglas Fairbanks or Harold Lloyd, or the coming-of-age Andy Hardy films, affirmed over and over again the values of optimism, hard work, and adherence to the Protestant Ethic. World War II combat films showed American determination and moral righteousness in overcoming evil foes. Many of John Ford's films of the era contextualized their stories within a complex and resonant historical tradition.

Citizen Kane is a significant film within this context. Made at the height of the classical Hollywood era, it has been cited by many as among the most important and influential of all American films. It is arguably a *film noir*, although it is not generally discussed as such, perhaps because it so resolutely resists generic classification and has little interest in traditional crime. But however *sui generis* a film it is, it shares with much of *film noir* its critique and rejection of contemporary American cultural myths. It assaults the notions of a unified subject, of the present purposefully building on valuable traditions of the past and paving the way for a progressive future, of righteous masculinity, and of the ongoing potency of traditional values. It gives no cause for social optimism or reverence for the American Dream. Aside from its thematics, it also shares many formal strategies with important *films noirs* that would follow it, such as its fragmented and retrospective voice-over narration, its multi-layered soundtrack, and its Impressionistic lighting and staging.

The implications of many of the titles of *films noirs* of the canonical era, like *Desperate* (1947), *Cornered*, *Kiss of Death*, *Pitfall*, *The Killers*, *Psycho*, and *No Way Out*, should be taken literally as indications of contemporary desperation, failure and loss, hysterical delusion, and even insanity.

The Long Goodbye presents an abrasive and unsympathetic depiction of contemporary society without hope or a real future. Its future is all behind it, as in much of *film noir*. It does have a detective who solves the crime, although he also commits murder; but whatever he does matters little anyway. Instead of an insult to the memory of *film noir*, as some critics contended, it reveals a profound understanding of the genre and exists in direct continuity with some of *film noir*'s finest work.

CHAPTER 8

CHINATOWN

As much as any film, *Chinatown* qualifies as the launching point for neo-*noir*. Although *The Long Goodbye* is a film of considerable merit, it was neither a critical nor a commercial success upon its release and quickly faded from the popular consciousness, only to grow in reputation over the years. *Chinatown*, to the contrary, was immediately successful on its release in 1974 and set the standard for neo-*noir* for the next decade. It demonstrated that an engagement of *film noir* need not be a recycling of yesterday's tired clichés but offered fertile potential for both creative filmmaking and trenchant social commentary.

Like many 1970s "New Hollywood" movies, *Chinatown* was a "big" film that revived a genre that had fallen into decline. Its budget (roughly six million dollars, very substantial at the time) was much more expensive than those of many of its predecessors, its cast featured "A-list" stars, and its plot was developed within a context of weighty historical and cultural issues. These things signaled audiences that *Chinatown* was much more than "another" private detective movie that promised predictably light genre entertainment. Similar strategies were used during the era by studios like Twentieth Century Fox with the outer space action/adventure movie *Star Wars*, but were particularly visible in the films produced by Paramount Pictures when Robert Evans was Head of Production. They include the enormously successful Western *True Grit* (1969), which both

Film Noir, First Edition. William Luhr.
© 2012 William Luhr. Published 2012 by Blackwell Publishing Ltd.

parodied and reified the aging John Wayne's star image; the supernatural thriller *Rosemary's Baby* (1968, like *Chinatown*, directed by Roman Polanski); the Mata Hari-type World War I aviation musical *Darling Lili* (1969); and the blockbuster revival of the then-marginalized gangster genre in *The Godfather*. This strategy countered industry presumptions that, since many of these genres had been widely employed by network television and radio in the 1950s, they had been "cheapened" by overexposure and were, therefore, unsuitable for feature film consideration. Why would people go to the movies to see what had been available in their homes on television and radio for years? The "New Hollywood" agenda of generic rebranding and revival resembled the successful 1950s marketing of television Westerns as "Adult Westerns," with the "Adult" asserting that these "new" Westerns (such as *Gunsmoke*, 1955–75, and *Have Gun, Will Travel*, 1957–63) were not the same old children's entertainments, which is how the popular Hopalong Cassidy and Roy Rogers television Westerns were perceived, but rather represented an innovative and mature approach to the genre.

The success of this formula was evident at the Academy Awards ceremony for 1974, when *Chinatown* received eleven nominations. The fact that it only won in one category, Best Original Screenplay, has been attributed in part to competition from another film produced that year by the same studio using a similar formula, *The Godfather, Part 2*, which received eleven nominations and won six awards, including Best Picture. However, among numerous other awards, *Chinatown* received the Golden Globe Best Motion Picture award, as well as Best Director, Best Actor in a Motion Picture – Drama (for Jack Nicholson), and Best Screenplay. It enjoyed great critical and commercial success and, in 1991, was honored by being entered into the National Film Registry.

The movie also received post-release publicity as the last one that Polanski directed in the US. He fled the country in 1978 after having pled guilty to unlawful sex with a minor but before being sentenced, and the crime took place at the home of *Chinatown*'s star, Jack Nicholson. The highly publicized legal proceedings surrounding the scandal frequently referred to the film.

This chapter discusses *Chinatown* with relation to the following issues: its engagement of *film noir*; its central tropes of deceptive appearances, prejudicial blindness, and popular perceptions of Los Angeles's Chinatown; its employment of Los Angeles social history as a context for plot development and character interactions; its utility as one instance underscoring the contributions to *film noir* of immigrant directors like Polanski; and its illustration of major patterns of genre transformation.

Chinatown *as* Neo-Noir

Released a year after *The Long Goodbye, Chinatown* engages *film noir* in a radically different manner, one more representative of the majority of neo-*noirs* that would follow it. Rather than critique and reject the conventions of the genre, *Chinatown* accepts and mostly works within them. Unlike *The Long Goodbye* also, it is a "period" movie, set in 1937 during the historical era associated with *film noir* and nearly four decades earlier than the time of its production, and it makes the world it depicts nostalgically attractive. Where *The Long Goodbye* gave its world a cold, brittle appearance by often using too-bright, washed-out looking cinematography and emphasizing hard glass or plastic surfaces, *Chinatown* has a sumptuous look, often focusing on warm, deep brown wood paneling and luxuriant fabrics of expensively tailored clothes. Cinematographer John Alonzo (who would also photograph *Farewell, My Lovely* the following year in a similar manner) developed a visual palate that emphasizes rich brown, amber, and gold colors reminiscent of faded old photographs and prewar color magazine advertisements. The movie's look is designed to make its era attractive to viewers.

Although its storyline neither mentions nor depicts 1930s filmmaking, *Chinatown* evokes the world of old Hollywood in numerous ways. It opens by giving us the impression that we are not watching a 1970s movie but rather a 1930s one. Its first image is the iconic Paramount Pictures logo showing a majestic mountain peak with a halo of stars. However, as with the logos of other studios with long histories like Warner Brothers, Universal, and Metro-Goldwyn-Mayer, Paramount had repeatedly updated its logo's appearance over the years, while retaining the same basic design concept. *Chinatown* does not begin with the brightly colored, mountain peak logo used by the studio in the 1970s but, rather, with the outdated one that the studio had used in the 1930s. The logo and the credit sequence that follows it use black and white cinematography tinted with a sepia wash, recalling old sepia tone movies of the 1930s, and they employ art-deco calligraphy and iconography. During these credits, both sides of the frame are masked to make the image resemble the 1:33-1 aspect ratio of 1930s movies, as opposed to the more modern 2:35-1 widescreen ratio used in the remainder of the movie. The soundtrack for the credits is dominated by a mournful trumpet solo of the sort that is often employed to evoke the *film noir* era. Although it deals with crime and depravity, the movie seldom looks grungy. Most characters are well groomed, well dressed, drive fashionable, well-polished automobiles, and are photographed in flattering light. In this movie, the world of the past, the world of *film noir*, looks glamorous, however much evil occurs in it.

Roman Polanski's casting strategies in *Chinatown* consistently carried echoes of *film noir*. The role of the semi-sleazy private detective, Jake "J.J." Gittes, was largely written for Jack Nicholson, who was so comfortable playing it that he was willing to appear in a significant portion of the movie with a large, silly-looking bandage splattered across his nose (Plate 36), something many stars would refuse to do on the grounds that it might tarnish their leading-man image. Nicholson's Gittes resembles Mike Hammer of *Kiss Me Deadly* in that he has a seedy reputation, is skilled at sweet-talking clients out of their money, and specializes in divorce cases. However, he is not as much a lone, two-fisted tough guy as he is the head of a team of detectives, a small businessman in a dirty business. Some critics at the time spoke of Nicholson's then-developing, insolent star persona as having the potential to make him a screen successor to Humphrey Bogart. John Huston, who plays the villain Noah Cross, had directed Bogart in *The Maltese Falcon* and other films and the two were widely known as great friends and kindred spirits. Huston had also directed other *films noirs* like *The Asphalt Jungle* and had acted in more recent movies, often taking villainous roles. Polanski's casting of him in this movie brought with it Huston's associations with old Hollywood and *film noir*. As Cross's daughter, Evelyn Cross Mulwray, Faye Dunaway, in period wardrobe and makeup with thin, plucked eyebrows, looks like an exotic *femme fatale* from 1930s movies. Dreamlike images of her face framed by picturesque smoke floating from a cigarette being smoked by Nicholson dominated the posters for the film.

The Long Goodbye had systematically avoided such romanticized evocations of the world of *film noir*, beginning with its brightly lit, 1970s setting, its seemingly aimless opening sequence, and its unconventional casting of

PLATE 36 *Chinatown*: Gittes (Jack Nicholson) and Evelyn (Faye Dunaway). ©1974 Long Road Productions

Elliot Gould in the lead role. No one in the film resembles actors or character types from the 1940s. The only actor in *The Long Goodbye* whose presence might have been used to evoke *film noir* was Sterling Hayden, who had appeared in *films noirs* like *The Asphalt Jungle*, *Crime Wave* (1954), and *The Killing* (1956). However, Hayden's star image had never been primarily associated with *film noir* and, furthermore, with his aged and craggy face, white beard, and Lord-of-the-Manor wardrobe in this film, he looks little like his 1950s self. Revealingly, he was Altman's second choice for the role after Dan Blocker, the original choice, died before shooting began (Altman dedicated the movie to him). Blocker's star persona was largely limited to his semi-comic, "gentle giant" role in the Western television series *Bonanza* (1959–73) and, with Gould, Blocker would have struck 1970s audiences as an unconventional casting choice but one which fit Altman's strategy of avoiding nostalgia for *film noir*. The other featured actors – Nina van Pallandt, Mark Rydell, and Jim Bouton – were either appearing in movies for the first time or had no established screen persona, certainly not one that could evoke old Hollywood movies. Furthermore, the frame of reference for *The Long Goodbye* is rigorously confined within the 1970s era in which it is set. When references to Hollywood history emerge, they are either trivial, like the gateman's impersonations of old movie stars, or pathetic, like Marlowe's attachment to the dead past, but never nostalgic.

In stark contrast, *Chinatown*'s frame of reference is much broader and extends to Los Angeles history and the tropes of *film noir*. Aside from its opening credits, its warm color palate, and its casting, *Chinatown* evokes past movies and the times in which they were set in numerous ways, including its period automobiles, wardrobe, outdated slang, and black and white display pictures of then–President Franklin Delano Roosevelt. Not only does the film carefully detail its 1930s setting, but its plot also employs narrative tropes common to *film noir*. Unlike many neo-*noirs* (including *L.A. Confidential*, *Marlowe*, *Taxi Driver*, *The Godfather*, *Reservoir Dogs*, and *Pulp Fiction*, 1994), however, *Chinatown* never references specific old Hollywood movies or moviemaking. Nevertheless, it is set during the heyday of the classical Hollywood Cinema; its central character is a hard-boiled private detective in prewar Los Angeles under the spell of an apparent *femme fatale*; its complex plot involves multiple layers of deception and betrayal; and major themes concern personal failure, urban corruption, and sexual transgression. Like some canonical *films noirs*, including *The Maltese Falcon* and *The Big Sleep*, it does not use a retrospective, voice-over narration but presents its narrative events primarily as the detective experiences them. We learn about the case as Jake Gittes does.

However resonantly the movie evokes *film noir*, it is manifestly a neo-*noir*. It dramatically underscores its ongoing tension between the two forms at the outset with its abrupt transition from the sepia-toned, black and white credit sequence to the widescreen, Technicolor body of the film. In other words, it begins looking like an old film but quickly shows us that it is also a new film. Furthermore, its plot turns on the consequences of incest and pedophilia and includes graphic violence, sexuality, and profanity, things whose very presence PCA censorship would have forbidden in canonical *film noir*.

Some of the negative critical reaction to *The Long Goodbye* resulted from sentimentalized and often inaccurate recollections of *film noir*. On a parallel plane, some of *Chinatown*'s strategies to evoke the past also reveal ways in which *film noir* has become distorted in our collective memory by repetitive evocation over the years, with each new recollection drawing upon earlier ones and sometimes altering the original thing remembered. We have all had the experience of being shocked when a long-cherished memory of ours turns out to be inaccurate, which sometimes happens when we compare our recollections with photographs taken at the time of the event or with the recollections of others who had shared that experience with us. Somehow, over the years, we have unconsciously altered our memory of the event. The same thing happens with the way we remember movies and genres. James Cagney never said, "You dirty rat," and Cary Grant never said, "Judy, Judy, Judy," in any of their films, even though impersonators used those expressions to characterize them for decades and many people misremembered having heard the actors repeatedly uttering those signature expressions. After the introduction of color television in the 1960s, stations broadcasting *The Wizard of Oz* (1939) received outraged telephone calls from viewers who misremembered the film as having been entirely in Technicolor. Those viewers had forgotten that the opening and concluding segments of the film were in sepia-toned black and white, and that Technicolor only appeared when Dorothy opened the door to the Land of Oz. When they saw the black and white sepia images, they had presumed that something was wrong with their television sets or with the broadcast. Only later did they realize that the movie had always mixed color with black and white but that, perhaps partially because Technicolor was an exciting recent innovation in feature-length movies in 1939, they had misremembered the entire movie as having been in color.

An instance in which *Chinatown* employs distorted memory involves the music used in the credit sequence. It consists largely of a moody jazz trumpet solo against a light string background that, for audiences of the

1970s, evoked movies of the 1930s and 1940s. However, as noted by David Butler in his book *Jazz Noir* (2002), such orchestration had more to do with a false memory of past film music than with the actual films. Although many neo-*noir* movies have used single-instrument jazz solos to evoke the *film noir* era, it is difficult to find a canonical *film noir* that opens in that way. Most used full orchestral scores, as was standard studio practice. However, as *film noir* was dying out, many of its tropes became filtered into *noir*-ish television series with popular jazz scores like *Peter Gunn* and *Johnny Staccato*. Jazz and single-instrument solos then became retrospectively associated with *film noir* and its era. Regardless of the historical actuality, many people now recall *films noirs* in that way and are often surprised to learn how little jazz was actually used in canonical *film noir*. But, building on this misperception, jazz has been widely used in neo-*noir* to evoke *film noir* for the past forty years. This underscores the fact that much of neo-*noir* is set in a landscape defined less by historical specificity and more by recollections and reconstructions of a reimagined past. This shift from the world of "today" represented in much of canonical *film noir* to the imaginatively reconstructed "yesterday" of neo-*noir* may be one of the reasons why neo-*noir* has provided such fertile ground for science fiction hybrids, like *Alphaville* or *Blade Runner*.

Chinatown also exploits audience presumptions about *film noir* as part of an effective narrative strategy to mislead and then surprise the viewer. For most of the movie the Evelyn Mulwray character appears to be a classic *femme fatale*. She is an attractive, fashionable, and seductive woman married to an older, diminutive-looking man who had been her father's business partner and who dies mysteriously early in the movie. Evelyn is arrogant, wealthy, and repeatedly lies to Gittes. The viewer is led to suspect that she is evil by the generic associations of her appearance and behavior as well as by Gittes's reaction to her. The more he learns about her, the more convinced he becomes that she is concealing something sinister. When he sleeps with her, his suspicions grow.

All generic signs point to her as a manipulative *femme fatale*, like those in *The Maltese Falcon, Double Indemnity, Scarlet Street, The Killers*, or *Out of the Past*. The big surprise in the film comes when Gittes forces her to reveal the secret she has been concealing. She finally admits that she has been lying all along – not for profit or power, however, but rather to conceal her victimization. She had repeatedly been raped by her father, Noah Cross, who intends to have the same relationship with their young daughter. Throughout the film, Evelyn has attempted to hide her daughter from her rapacious father. Her husband had not been betraying her by having an affair but, to the contrary, had been compassionately helping her to protect her sister/daughter. After Gittes saw Evelyn and her sister/daughter together, he presumed that the jaded and sexually manipulative Evelyn was protecting her husband's mistress and confronts Evelyn, demanding to know about the relationship between them. He is so convinced that she is concealing her own nefarious involvement in the ugly net of betrayal, murder, and corruption that he has been uncovering that he slaps her, hoping to jolt her into revealing the truth. As he repeatedly slaps her, she says the woman is her sister, then her daughter, and finally her sister *and* her daughter, shocking Gittes with the realization of Noah Cross's incestuous behavior as well as the long-endured agonies of Evelyn's own life (Plate 37). This scene is particularly shocking for first-time viewers whose familiarity with the tropes of *film noir* would dispose them to expect Evelyn to be a villain instead of a victim.

Chinatown ends as Evelyn is killed by police and her father takes the daughter, a horrible note of evil recycling itself, as Gittes stands helplessly by (Plate 38). Now fully aware of Cross's horrid crimes, Gittes can expect no help from the police because, as Evelyn has said, referring to her father, "He owns the police." The movie depicts Noah Cross as a villain of Shakespearean proportions. He not only devastates his own family by raping his own daughter and planning to do the same with his incestuous granddaughter, but he is also a figure of monstrous municipal corruption who is orchestrating a murderous scheme to manipulate the water supply of Los Angeles in order to profit from fraudulently acquired real estate. He appears to succeed in all.

At the film's conclusion, Gittes is impotent to stop Cross from continuing his monstrous behavior. Such an ending would have been impossible in canonical *film noir* due to PCA requirements that evil never

PLATE 37 *Chinatown*: Evelyn – "My sister *and* my daughter." ©1974 Long Road Productions

PLATE 38 *Chinatown*: Noah Cross (John Huston) seizes Evelyn's daughter. ©1974 Long Road Productions

succeed but be punished in some way. Many films used barely believable *deus ex machinas* at their conclusions as a way to get around this requirement. In *The Woman in the Window*, for example, a married man becomes involved with a seductress and hopelessly ensnared in an ugly murder and blackmail plot. But at the end, he abruptly wakes up – it has all been a dream and he is free to happily resume his life. At the conclusion of *Cornered*, scarcely credible plot developments conspire to imply that the main character will avoid his inevitable fate of lifetime imprisonment. In the neo-*noir* era, such constraints on the triumph of evil characters had disappeared; films no longer needed to give lip service to the notion of justice as eternally triumphant. Many neo-*noir* films, unfettered by the PCA restrictions, drop the pretense and conclude with criminals succeeding with their crimes, as with *Chinatown, The Getaway* (1972), *Taxi Driver, Body Heat, The Silence of the Lambs* (1991), *The Last Seduction, The Usual Suspects*, and others.

Deceptive Appearances, Prejudicial Blindness, and Los Angeles's Chinatown

From its opening shots, *Chinatown* develops the theme of deceptive appearances. Following the credits, we see a glossy black and white photograph showing a couple having sex in a wooded area. That photograph is suddenly flipped away to reveal another shot of the same couple, and then another. While this is going on, the camera dollies back to show a full-color, side-angle image of Curly (Burt Young), who is viewing the photographs and exclaiming "Whew" and "Wow." Gittes is quietly sitting in the back of the frame. Curly's comments initially seem like those of a man voyeuristically leering at "dirty" photographs. We soon learn, however, that such an apparently reasonable interpretation of Curly's reactions is profoundly inaccurate: he is not making sounds of voyeuristic pleasure but rather groaning in pain. The photographs show his wife with another man. Hence, what had initially appeared to be a scene of a man enjoying pornographic pictures turns out to be something entirely different; he is deeply pained by them.

Curly had hired Gittes to investigate his wife's infidelity, and when Gittes escorts Curly out of his office, an associate introduces him to a woman calling herself Mrs Evelyn Mulwray, who hires him to investigate her husband's involvement with another woman. Gittes investigates and soon produces what appear to be compromising photographs of Hollis Mulwray (Darrell Zwerling) boating with a teenaged girl. The photographs wind up being published in a tabloid newspaper and cause a scandal. Gittes later learns, however, that the woman who hired him was not Mrs Mulwray at all but an impersonator (Diane Ladd) hired to deceive him and, furthermore, that the photographs of Mr Mulwray and the young girl were entirely misleading. The girl was Mulwray's wife's sister as well as her incestuous daughter and Mulwray was not having an affair with her but, rather, was behaving in an avuncular manner toward her with the full knowledge and gratitude of his wife.

This pattern of misleading appearances pervades the film. Curly was not enjoying the photographs of sexual activity at all but agonizing over them, the first "Mrs Mulwray" was a phony hired to damage Hollis Mulwray's reputation, and the appearance of infidelity on his part was nothing of the sort. Gittes's initial sense that he had triumphed in his pursuit of the case soon becomes his embarrassment at having made a catastrophic blunder. Furthermore, when we meet the actual Mrs Mulwray, she appears to fit the pattern of a manipulative *femme fatale* with a "past." However, one of the film's narrative surprises is that she turns out to be a profoundly wronged victim.

The pattern of misleading appearances is reinforced by the tendency of characters to assess, and often misread, what they see through the prisms of their own prejudices. This is underscored, and linked with the film's metaphoric use of Chinatown, in the scene in which Gittes finally confronts Noah Cross with his suspicions. Cross tells him,"You may think you know what you're dealing with, but believe me, you don't." When Gittes smiles in response, Cross asks, "Why is that funny?" Gittes replies, "It's what the district attorney used to tell me in Chinatown." Chinatown becomes the film's central metaphor for its mysteries, its layers upon layers of deception and misleading appearances, and the traumas that characters incur as they uncover the realities underlying those mysteries.

Chinatown's title may at first seem odd since the movie features no Asian characters and only one of its scenes, its horrifying conclusion, is set in Los Angeles's Chinatown. Geographically, the area is a Chinese enclave within Los Angeles. Some Chinese characters appear outside of Chinatown in servile positions, but, when they do, they are largely ignored as socially "invisible." All of the servants in the Mulwray mansion seem to be Chinese, and one of them, the butler Kahn (James Hong), clearly helps Evelyn to conceal her sister/daughter from her/their monstrous father. Anglo characters in the film repeatedly make racist jokes about Chinatown, revealing their blindness as to what is really going on.

References to Chinatown often deflect attention from important issues or underscore character misunderstandings of those issues. Early on, Gittes flies into a rage at a barbershop when another patron, referring to the scandalous Mulwray newspaper pictures, calls his job sleazy. The barber prevents a brawl by telling Gittes a racist and sexist joke, the import of which is that a man (presumably white) not only discovers that his wife had been unfaithful but also that her lover had been Chinese, considered a disgrace in a racist culture. Immediately after this, Gittes jubilantly recounts the joke in his office to his associates, unaware that Evelyn has entered the room and stands behind him. His associates try unsuccessfully to stop him. When he learns of her presence, Gittes is embarrassed. In the barbershop, the racist joke deflected his rage over the insult to his job; in his office, his joy in repeating it prevents him from noticing Mrs Mulwray. Both instances show Gittes ignorant of much more than he is aware. He does not yet know that he had been tricked into taking the photographs of Mulwray or that they maligned the innocent man. He also has no idea that Mrs Mulwray has been the victim of horrible sexual abuse. He at first presumes his embarrassment results from telling a "dirty" joke in the presence of a woman (he had asked a female secretary to leave the room before he told the joke) with no awareness that the implications of what is going on will continue to go deeper and deeper. For Mrs Mulwray, the experience of listening to Gittes reveling in a sexual joke while knowing that he had publicly maligned her husband for sexual malfeasance was deeply painful in ways that Gittes cannot begin to understand.

After first having been shocked to learn that she has overheard his off-color, racist joke, he is further shocked to learn that she, and not the impersonator who hired him to investigate Mr Mulwray, is the real Mrs Evelyn Mulwray, and that she will be suing him as a result of the scandal caused by his photographs. But later, when he goes to the Mulwray home, he is again shocked when she agrees to drop the lawsuit. And soon after, her husband is found dead.

All of this hits Gittes unexpectedly, so much so that, when Evelyn abruptly offers to drop the lawsuit against him, he tells her not to do it. He says that it is bad for his reputation as a savvy detective to be so publicly caught with his pants down and that he believes that larger forces are at work. He needs to learn what those forces are, who has deceived him, and why. As the film progresses, his probing leads, literally and symbolically, to Chinatown.

While Gittes shares the racism of the white characters, he is also troubled by the mysteries that Chinatown holds. He had formerly been a policeman assigned there. When he encounters his former partner, now a police lieutenant, he mockingly asks the man if he is "still putting Chinamen in jail for spitting in the laundry," referring to the racist presumption that all Chinese are launderers. The film's policemen consider an assignment to Chinatown to be the lowest rung of their career ladder, and something to get out of. This perception resembles the racist complaints of the corrupt detective Billy Rolfe in *Farewell, My Lovely* that he has been assigned to "another shine killing," indicating his belief that the murder of an African American in 1941 Los Angeles is beneath police concern and that a detective assigned to the case can expect neither publicity nor career advancement, even if he finds the culprit. When Gittes is asked what he did in Chinatown, he replies, "As little as possible," indicating that, to the all-white police force, Chinatown simply didn't matter. At the film's end as Gittes stands in shock over Evelyn's death and Cross's success, an assistant urges him to quickly leave the scene by saying, "Forget it, Jake, it's Chinatown" (Plate 39). It has all turned back on him.

PLATE 39 *Chinatown*: "Forget it, Jake. It's Chinatown." ©1974 Long Road Productions

Gittes's racism leads him to misinterpret and ignore a major clue that, had he pursued it earlier, might have saved Evelyn's life. During his first visit to the Mulwray house, he observes an Asian gardener remove some moss from a pond in the garden and say it is "bad for glass." Gittes mockingly repeats it, saying, "Yeah, sure, bad for the glass," thinking that the man is incapable of saying "grass." Only later does he realize that the man was referring not to the moss but to the fact that the pond contained salt water, not fresh water, which is certainly bad for grass, and the man also finds a pair of spectacles in the pond. They turn out to be a central clue to Cross's murder of Hollis Mulwray. Gittes learns that, although Mulwray's body had been found near a freshwater drain and he had been presumed to have been drowned there, his lungs contained salt water. In actuality, he had been drowned in the salt-water pond by Cross and his accomplices, who had then moved his body to the drainage area. Had Gittes taken the gardener's comment seriously instead of dismissing it as a racially based mispronunciation, he might have connected the dots and solved Mulwray's murder earlier. Here and elsewhere, Gittes is repeatedly deflected from the central aspects of the case.

Chinatown initially appears to be about Gittes's investigation of Hollis Mulwray's presumed marital infidelity. Mulwray was a water commissioner, and while Gittes follows him seeking evidence of adultery, he is puzzled at the extent to which Mulwray spends his free time at dried-up drainage sites. Gittes's assistant even jokes that Mulwray has "water on the brain." Gittes is also puzzled by seemingly senseless pourings-off of large amounts of water onto desert land, particularly since Los Angeles is in the middle of a drought. But his main focus is on what turns out to be a diversionary adultery investigation. When Mulwray is found drowned, a coroner comments on the irony of the water commissioner drowning in the middle of a drought. Gittes soon learns that huge tracts of desert land are being bought up by dead or senile old people, unknown to them, as part of Cross's land scam. Gittes realizes that all of this has nothing to do with adultery and everything to do with water, land, and fraud on a huge scale. Whether concerning "glass," Hollis Mulwray's adultery, or Evelyn's character, Gittes is repeatedly led astray.

Noah Cross and his associates had put all of this in motion. They engineered the sex scandal to discredit Hollis Mulwray's public opposition to an eight and a half million dollar dam project that was important to Cross's real estate fraud scheme. Gittes pursues the sex scandal until Mrs Mulwray's true identity is revealed and her husband is found dead. When he realizes he has been duped, he begins to piece together the things he had ignored in his investigation, particularly Mulwray's own investigation of the inexplicable, enormous water runoffs into the desert during a drought.

Chinatown also has personal resonance for Gittes far more profound than his smug, knee-jerk racism. When Gittes and Evelyn sleep together, she asks him what is so strange about Chinatown and, linking his sense of the mysteries of Chinatown with his inability to understand her motives, he replies, "You can't always tell what's going on – like you." This echoes the warning Noah Cross had earlier given him by saying, "You may think you know what you're dealing with, but believe me, you don't" (Plate 40). Gittes tells Evelyn that he once failed to save the life of a woman he cared for there and that his attempt to save her got her killed. This eerily presages his unintentional involvement in Evelyn's later sudden death. The movie establishes Chinatown as a profoundly "other" place for its white characters, one they can never decipher. Hence, the major mysteries of the movie – Cross's grand plot and Evelyn's victimization – all become linked in Gittes's mind with the mysteries of Chinatown.

As the movie ends, Gittes is aghast at the abrupt catastrophe of Evelyn's death. His last statement in the film comes as he stands, horrified, and mumbles what he had earlier told Evelyn when she asked what the police do in Chinatown: "As little as possible."

Chinatown does not end, as many traditional movies would have, when the different story threads of the story are wrapped up and Gittes is pulled away. The camera lingers and rises for a relatively long time before the end credits roll. After Gittes leaves, dozens of anonymous Chinese faces crowd in, curious about what has just happened in their neighborhood. The white police quickly shoo them away, telling them to get off the street and onto the sidewalk. The message is clear; they don't count.

PLATE 40 *Chinatown*: Noah Cross and Gittes. ©1974 Long Road Productions

It is intriguing that this scene appears in a film made by a Polish immigrant director, one sensitive to ways in which the globally dominant US culture has marginalized and ignored people from other cultures. Such marginalized people assume growing importance in neo-*noir*. As discussed earlier with reference to *Out of the Past* and *L.A. Confidential, films noirs* commonly privileged white American culture and associated people from other nations and races with evil; neo-*noir* films, however, frequently do the opposite. In *Chinatown* the white patriarch, Noah Cross, stands at the center of corruption.

This theme is explicit at the end of *Devil in a Blue Dress*, a neo-*noir* whose central character and point of view are not white, as is dominant in *film noir*, but African American. The movie, set in Los Angeles in the late 1940s, deals with African American identity in a racist society. The plot involves an affair between a powerful white politician and a mixed-race woman who "passes" for white. At the end, as the African American central character, Easy Rawlins, watches the politician end his relationship with the woman, he is jolted with the realization of how deeply racism pollutes both sides of the equation, not only the oppressed class but also the dominating one. Although the politician is one of the most powerful men in Los Angeles, he does not have the courage to acknowledge his relationship with the woman he loves. He considers the racial divide too powerful to challenge.

Chinatown underscores the presence of marginalized cultures within the dominant white culture that hardly acknowledges them, primarily Chinatown, but also Mexico, where Evelyn plans to flee to avoid Noah Cross before her sudden death. The shot of gathering and then dispersed Chinese observers in the last shot stresses the presence of people whose perspective had seldom been acknowledged in a genre that had traditionally been dominantly Anglo-centric, but was changing.

Los Angeles History and Identity

Part of the strategy to endow *Chinatown* with cultural weight and to present it as more than a simple genre entertainment is evident in its references to identifiable Los Angeles history. This is not only a film that revives *film noir* tropes; it is one that comments on a dark chapter of American history.

Los Angeles has always had a strong presence in *film noir*. The Hollywood industry resides there and many of the films are entirely or partially set there, including *Double Indemnity, Murder, My Sweet, Mildred Pierce, The*

Postman Always Rings Twice, *The Big Sleep*, *Detour*, and *Kiss Me Deadly*. In neo-*noir* films like *L.A. Confidential*, the presence of the film industry in Los Angeles is often used to intensify associations with *film noir*. Although *Chinatown* employs *film noir* tropes and character types, it has nothing to do with Hollywood and characterizes Los Angeles as a city whose history involves much more than the movies. Screenwriter Robert Towne originally conceived of it as the first film in a trilogy about large-scale corruption in Los Angeles history that involved exploitation of the land. *Chinatown* concerns Los Angeles's historic "water wars." The second film (*The Two Jakes*, 1990, directed by and starring Jack Nicholson) concerned natural gas development in the 1940s. The third script, called *Cloverleaf*, focused on the development of the Los Angeles freeway system in the late 1940s. It was never made into a film but some of its ideas appear in the comic, *noirish*, mixed-live action/animation *Who Framed Roger Rabbit?* Themes like the corruption of Los Angeles by Noah Cross were potent topics during the Watergate era in which *Chinatown* appeared. While many *films noirs* dealt with political malfeasance and even domination of towns or small cities, they seldom indicted identifiable national figures or the foundational history of a major city. Dark as those films were, they did not depict the nation itself as corrupt. During the Watergate era, however, the national mood invited the exploration of wrong-doing in the highest of places.

Noah Cross's activities have rough analogues in Los Angeles's "water wars" of the early twentieth century, and the career of William Mulholland, the engineer who built many of the aqueducts bringing water from the High Sierras to Los Angeles through the San Fernando Valley. As General Manager of Los Angeles's Bureau of Water Works and Supply, he was instrumental in orchestrating the purchase of cheap land and water rights for Los Angeles by speculators. These events have been referred to as the Owens Valley "Rape" and the San Fernando Valley land grab. In 1928, The St Francis Dam failed the day after Mulholland inspected it, leading to over 450 deaths and burying the town of Santa Paula.

Early in *Chinatown*, Gittes attends a public meeting that alludes to the St Francis Dam failure. Hollis Mulwray is booed after declaring that he will not support Cross's new dam project. He says that, when an earlier dam project failed, over 500 lives were lost, and that the new dam idea is just as faulty. He refuses to make the same mistake twice.

Many have argued that Los Angeles could not have become a city without its water wars. Since it is situated in a desert, only a reliable supply of a huge volume of externally supplied water could have allowed it to expand to the extent that it has. The water wars concerned the diversion of Colorado River water from its natural route to Los Angeles, in the process depriving much of the southwest of that water. Hence, the film posits the city itself as built upon the corruption of Noah Cross. Furthermore, Cross's murderous public villainy is paralleled by his private, incestuous villainy (Plate 40).

Knowledge of these things comes in successive, numbing shocks to Gittes, and the film's complex interweaving of personal, social, and historical issues endows it with a more culturally dense context than that of many traditional private detective films. Its invocation of Los Angeles history gives it a near-epic scope.

Immigrant Directors

Many foreign filmmakers and critics, assessing American film from a great geographical and cultural distance, have called *film noir* the preeminent American film form. In 1946, Nino Frank described it as having already replaced the Western in dynamism. It has also become linked with the appeal of American culture, and it is no surprise that many directors like Polanski who emigrated to Hollywood wanted to make *films noirs*.

Foreign-born directors like Billy Wilder, Fritz Lang, Alfred Hitchcock, Robert Siodmak, and Otto Preminger have always made important contributions to *film noir*. The fact that they came to the United States from another national and cultural heritage has perhaps given them a distance and an imaginative perspective upon the often alienating structures of *film noir* and American culture that might not be accessible to native-born Americans. They contributed substantially to the origins of *film noir*, drawing on their own national traditions like German Expressionism and French poetic realism, and even at the beginning the genre showed a crazy-quilt of influence. The German Fritz Lang made *Scarlet Street*, which itself was a remake of the 1931 French film *La Chienne* by Jean Renoir. The first adaptation of *The Postman Always Rings Twice* was made in Italy. The cycle of influence can be bewildering at times. And *film noir*, which was influenced by French, German, and other traditions, in turn influenced the French *Nouvelle Vague*, the New German Cinema, and the Hong Kong action cinema.

A strong appeal of *film noir* has always been a fascination with the "other," often born of watching the films from a literal distance. It began with French critics watching American films and, for neo-*noir* directors, American or not, with watching films of the past.

Many of the "New Hollywood" movies of the 1970s were made by American-born directors who developed their passion for classical Hollywood genres from a distance. These were the films not of their generation but from those of their parents and grandparents. Their great affection for classical Hollywood is evident in their passion for revivals and remakes of genres and films from that era.

Polanski did not share that past in the same way. Like the young American directors of the 1970s, he had graduated from film school and shared a love for Hollywood movies. However, he had been born in France and raised in Poland, graduating from film school and making his first movies there. He came to Hollywood movies as an immigrant director trained in a foreign tradition and not the product of American film schools. Much of his sense of America's past was formed by old Hollywood movies. *Chinatown*'s very title references a place that is within America but culturally separate from it, and such places often exist on the margins of the dominant culture. Immigrant directors often have a special sensitivity to such marginalization, and Polanski has known what it feels like to be an outsider throughout his life. Not only did his French/Polish background complicate his sense of his origins, but his Jewish ethnicity in Nazi-occupied Poland made him a fugitive. During World War II, his parents were interned in concentration camps from which only his father survived. Polanski spent much of the war years being hidden by Polish Catholic families and, during the postwar era, survived as a displaced naïf under often brutal circumstances. Even after he found success in the Polish film industry and, later, Hollywood, his life was shattered in 1969 by the murder of his wife by the Manson "family" and, nearly a decade later, by a sex scandal that has kept him out of the United States since the late 1970s, even while maintaining a successful film career in Europe. Another such director who came to *film noir* (with *Mulholland Falls*) after having established himself in another culture by making a distinguished film about that culture (*Once Were Warriors*, 1994) was Lee Tamahori from New Zealand. The perspective of such artists on the American cinematic past is an important one.

Genre Transformation

This multi-national, multi-generational cycle of influence provides an ideal context for "*Chinatown* and Generic Transformation in Recent American Films," John Cawelti's milestone essay on genre transformation that elucidates important cultural contexts for *Chinatown*. Cawelti (1985) discusses the movie's roots in the hard-boiled detective tradition as well as its place in the 1970s revival of classical Hollywood genres. He traces the hard-boiled detective tradition to its origin as an alternative to the British detective tradition in fiction and, outlining its dominant narrative and character patterns, shows how it evolved over time. His work is particularly important for understanding the many shifts in *film noir*, particularly its transition to neo-*noir*. He was one of the first to depict the specific workings of the process, describing the changes in the tradition as having resulted from the collisions of different cultural myths with one another, generally of established myths with emerging ones. He outlines four major patterns in which 1960s and 1970s movies revived the Hollywood past: (1) films that burlesqued old conventions, such as the comic Western *Blazing Saddles* (1974) and the comic horror film *Young Frankenstein* (1974); (2) films that cultivated nostalgia for past conventions, such as *True Grit* and *Farewell, My Lovely*; (3) films that invoked established generic structures to demythologize those genres by characterizing their conventions as inadequate and even culturally erosive, such as the gangster film *Bonnie and Clyde*, the Western *Little Big Man*, and *The Long Goodbye*; and (4) films, often by older directors, that initially appeared to critique the generic conventions but ultimately reaffirmed the myths upon which they were constructed (*The Man Who Shot Liberty Valance* and *The Wild Bunch*).

Cawelti does not categorize these patterns as rigid or exclusive, and acknowledges that some movies fit into more than one category. Curiously, he places both *The Long Goodbye* and *Chinatown* primarily under the category of films that demythologize old genres. His main rationale is that both movies deromanticize the code/myth of the private eye. However, Cawelti gives perhaps too romanticized a description of the private eye myth. *Chinatown* is more complex. Gittes is certainly less altruistic and more financially well off than either Sam Spade or Philip Marlowe, but the film charts his growing moral investment in the case. He is no less sleazy than Mike Hammer, many other private detectives of the 1950s, or many characters in non-detective hard-boiled fiction and film, such as Frank in *The Postman Always Rings Twice*, Walter in *Double Indemnity*, and Johnny in *Gilda*. The movie closes on a note of Gittes's wholesale failure. He failed to protect Evelyn and her daughter and he failed to stop Cross's corrupt plans. This, however, is nothing new in private eye tales or *film noir*. Regardless of Gittes's failure, the film confers a growing integrity on him. As with Jeff in *Out of the Past*, his moral failures do not erase his building integrity in the audience's eyes. Unlike Marlowe at the end of Altman's *The Long Goodbye*, Gittes's horror and the warm nostalgic look of *Chinatown* lend a melancholy romanticism to his plight.

One value of Cawelti's work lies in its acknowledgment and delineation of generic fluidity. It provides a strong corrective to critics who condemn films like *The Long Goodbye* as insults to their genre on the presumption that genres are unchanging entities. Such rigidity has never been the case, even with genres often considered the most fixed, like the Western, the biblical epic, or the Shakespearean adaptation, and *film noir* has been more visibly elastic than most genres.

Cawelti makes a compelling case for *Chinatown* as a new film that invigorates and transforms an old genre, and his essay illustrates how that process works.

CHAPTER 9

SEVEN

Seven (aka *Se7en*) is an ideal film with which to conclude this book. It contains basic elements of *film noir* that were first identified by postwar critics while, simultaneously, reflecting fundamental shifts in the genre over the past seventy-five years. Appearing in 1995, it was widely recognized as both a neo-*noir* and a film perceptively attuned to cultural anxieties of the 1990s. One acknowledgment of its continuity with *film noir* appears in the jacket blurb of the first English-language edition of Arnaldur Indridason's *Jar City* (2005), written by Michael Malone, winner of the Mystery Writers of America's prestigious "Edgar" award. Malone writes, "Indridason's detective is, like his predecessors from Philip Marlowe to Somerset in *Seven*, a deeply appealing hero." Since *Jar City* is part of the popular twenty-first-century wave of Nordic detective fiction and film, Malone, by drawing a direct line from Philip Marlowe through *Seven* to Indridason, is placing *Seven* at the center of the evolution of *film noir* over the past seventy-five years. Furthermore, like early writers on *film noir*, he blends reference to hard-boiled fiction and *film noir*, since Marlowe is a literary as well as a film figure and Indridason's novel was the basis for a well-received 2006 Icelandic film as well as a 2012 English-language one set in Louisiana. Only Somerset is a figure confined exclusively to film (excepting a seven-issue 2006 comic book miniseries on *Seven* from Zenescope Entertainment with each issue focusing on one of John Doe's

Film Noir, First Edition. William Luhr.
© 2012 William Luhr. Published 2012 by Blackwell Publishing Ltd.

victims before their deaths). In addition, *Seven*'s director, David Fincher, has throughout his career made films finely attuned to troubling, destabilizing aspects of the contemporary world. His movies tend to be contemporaneously set and strongly influenced by *film noir*, like *The Girl with the Dragon Tattoo* (2011), *The Social Network* (2010), *Zodiac* (2007), *Panic Room* (2002), *Fight Club* (1999), and *The Game* (1997). His first feature, *Alien 3* (1992), reflects the strain of neo-*noir* that blends with dystopian science fiction.

Seven is not an exercise in nostalgia for *film noir*, like *Body Heat*, which, while dealing with grim topics like destructive desire and murderous betrayal, invites viewers to find comfort in its evocations of past film styles. Like the best of *film noir*, *Seven* contains little that is comforting for viewers and much that is troubling.

The movie follows the police pursuit of a serial killer. Although the two detectives assigned to the case ultimately apprehend the murderer, their investigation becomes profoundly unsettling and ends catastrophically for them. They are at opposite stages in their careers. William Somerset (Morgan Freeman), with seven days remaining before his retirement, had anticipated escaping forever from the urban cesspool in which he had spent his professional life. David Mills (Brad Pitt), to the contrary, naïvely anticipates such a life. He has just arrived in the city from a small town, eager to begin this new phase of his career (Plate 41). The movie initially appears to resemble those in which a mature professional passes on his knowledge and experience to a younger novice, hence preserving the integrity of the profession while acknowledging the inevitable changing of players. But that does not happen here. When the detectives solve the case, things go horribly wrong, obliterating hopes for a productive transition into the future, or any future at all.

PLATE 41 *Seven*: Somerset (Morgan Freeman) and Mills (Brad Pitt) meeting for first time. © 1995 New Line Productions, Inc.

The serial killer (Kevin Spacey), who calls himself "John Doe," follows an elaborate, moralistic plan that Somerset describes as "his sermons to us." Each murder invokes one of the Seven Deadly Sins described in medieval Christianity. John Doe believes that the ongoing presence of these sins in society demands bold retribution, so he "punishes" a glutton by forcing him to eat himself to death, he "punishes" a prostitute by having her sexually mutilated, he "punishes" a wealthy lawyer by cutting a pound of flesh from his body and bleeding him dry, and so on. To underscore the purpose of his "sermons" as well as his belief that they apply to many more people than the individual victims, he scrawls the names of the sins, such as GLUTTONY, LUST, and GREED, in blood at the crime scenes (Plate 42). But when, covered in blood, he abruptly surrenders to the police before all seven killings are discovered, the detectives realize that the case is not yet over and fear that he has now enfolded them into his plan. John Doe had earlier told Mills that he envied him for the normality of his life, one with a wife he loved and a profession that gave him satisfaction. Just prior to surrendering himself, John Doe had raped and murdered Mill's wife, Tracy (Gwyneth Paltrow), also killing her unborn child, of whose existence Mills had been unaware. These acts climax John Doe's scheme of provoking Mills into exploding in rage and murdering him, hence sacrificing himself as a martyr to the completion of his plan with the final two killings, his "sermons" on ENVY (his own) and RAGE (Mills's).

This chapter will first show how *Seven* is aligned with the earliest categorizations of *film noir* and then demonstrate ways in which it also reflects the ongoing pattern of change and evolution in the genre from its beginning through the neo-*noir* era. Finally, it will show how the film is manifestly a neo-*noir* of the 1990s, not one mired in nostalgia for the past

PLATE 42 *Seven*: Mills at one of John Doe's murder scenes. © 1995 New Line Productions, Inc.

but rather reflecting contemporary anxieties about serial killers, graphic crime scene forensics, omnipresent surveillance, and social and religious fears about the then-imminent Millennium.

Continuity with Film Noir

During *Seven*'s closing credits, David Bowie's song "The Heart's Filthy Lesson" plays on the soundtrack. One of its lyrics is "If there was only some kind of future." In this film, as with so much of *film noir*, there will be no future to anticipate; it is all in the past. The youthful, dedicated Mills initially seemed to represent hope for society's future. By the end, however, John Doe has obliterated Mills's future – his anticipated new career, his happy marriage, and his unborn child – as well as his own existence. Although Somerset is horrified by this, it fits the worldview that he has held from the beginning, even before he meets Mills. A curious presence in the film, Somerset participates in its events while, at the same time, standing at a philosophical distance from them. He is an isolated character, living alone in an almost monk-like existence and resigned to an unjust world. At the film's conclusion, he quotes Ernest Hemingway to the effect that the world is a fine place and worth fighting for, commenting that he agrees with the second part. In effect, he is saying that he will continue to struggle for justice even though he has little respect for his world and feels there is little efficacy in fighting to improve it. His depressive worldview is consonant with that of *film noir* from its outset.

One indication of his distance from other characters is his habit of asking questions that reveal a broader perspective than common upon issues at hand, questions that others consider irrelevant or even annoying. At the beginning, he arrives at a crime scene in which a man had been shot to death by his wife. After examining family photographs on the refrigerator, he asks another detective, "The kid see it?" The detective, annoyed at what he considers an irrelevant question, says that his colleagues are going to be glad to see Somerset retire, blurting out, "It's always these questions with you. 'Did the kid see it?' Who gives a fuck? He's dead. His wife killed him. Anything else has nothing to do with us." Soon after this, Somerset meets Mills for the first time and asks what the younger detective considers an irrelevant question, "Why here?" to which Mills replies, "I don't follow." Somerset asks him why he would actively seek an assignment to this city. Mills says, "Maybe I'm not understanding the question." They are on different wavelengths. When he conducts after-hours research at a public library, Somerset tells the evening workers that he can't understand how they can play cards every night while ignoring the wealth of learning that surrounds them. They do not get angry at him but just chuckle, and continue with their game. Again and again, Somerset sees things differently. Although *Seven* is not directly presented from his point of view, it is largely aligned with it as he pursues the case. His reflective involvement and the implications of his seldom-answered questions make the scope of the film far broader than that of a traditional police procedural. One of the earliest descriptions of *film noir* by Nino Frank (see below) described its central characteristics as the "enigma to be solved" and the fact that the genre broke with crime film tradition by placing greater emphasis on the enigma than on the solution. In this film, Somerset is as much an enigma as the case he investigates.

Early critics

Let us return to the important early writings on *film noir* which we discussed in Chapter 3: the French examples of Nino Frank's 1946 essay, "A New Type of Detective Story" (Frank, 1995) and Raymond Borde and Etienne Chaumeton's first book-length study from 1955, *A Panorama of American Film Noir, 1941–1953* (Borde and Chaumeton, 2002); and the English-language examples of Raymond Durgnat's 1970 essay, "Paint It Black: The Family Tree of the Film Noir" (Durgnat, 1998), and Paul Schrader's 1972 essay, "Notes on *Film Noir*" (Schrader, 1998). Each characterized the genre in ways that are singularly prescient about *Seven*.

Nino Frank's seminal essay of enthusiastic discovery described *film noir* as having its origins in the detective genre but as having reformulated the treatment of the criminal behavior that is essential to that genre in fundamental ways. Earlier films had emphasized the detective's logical solution of the crime with the resultant restoration of justice to society, thereby giving those films uplifting, "happy" endings. *Film noir* concentrated instead on the crime itself and the sometimes deranged psychology of the criminal. The films often ended badly but, even when some ended happily, such resolutions frequently seemed tacked on to avoid censorship and largely irrelevant to the overall depiction of a failed world. A decade after Frank's essay appeared, Borde and Chaumeton's book described *film noir* as crime presented from within and from the point of view of the criminal. They felt that the genre had emerged from a shift in film conventions that occurred during World War II, one that resulted in the abandonment of the traditionally presumed moral center in films. The effect of this reorientation on the viewer was a loss of psychological bearings, a malaise. With such observations, Borde and Chaumeton underscored a major focus of future *film noir* commentary: the genre's destabilizing effect on the viewer. In effect, the films not only depicted tormented or disoriented characters but also sought to emotionally draw viewers into the affect of such disorientation. Instances include the ominous credit sequence in *Double Indemnity* in which the silhouette of a man on crutches directly approaches the viewer (see Plate 1, p. 2), Marlowe's hallucinations in *Murder, My Sweet* (see Plate 17, p. 80), the palpable despair evident in Jeff's voice-over narration in *Out of the Past*, The Swede's eerily tranquil and inexplicable awaiting of the men who are coming to murder him in *The Killers* (see Plate 9, p. 30), Frank's frenzied pursuit of his own murderer while he is dying in *D.O.A.* (see Plate 5, p. 8), and the quasi-experimental *Lady in the Lake*, arguably the first Hollywood feature presented almost entirely from the literal point of view of the main character (i.e. with the camera showing what his eyes see). Such strategies conspired to develop in the viewer the discomfiting sense that they have entered an environment in which everything is off-base, disturbing, not coming out as it should – just wrong.

Early commentators described the narration of such films as no longer clear and logical as in traditional mystery films but often convoluted and confusing, reflecting disordered or malignant states of mind. The films no longer centered upon the solver of the crime and his/her reassuring alliance with the traditional forces of morality but rather on the culprit and his/her deviations from such forces. One example is the scene in *Double Indemnity* in which the murderers find themselves unable to start their getaway car. The scene positions the viewer to hope that they will succeed in starting the car and, hence, succeed with murder. In such cases, the viewer finds her/himself sympathizing with the devil, a new subject position for Hollywood cinema.

Retrospective narration

In another of the shifts in Hollywood conventions that occurred during World War II, many of the films are narrated retrospectively, so the viewer (or at least the narrator) knows their outcomes from the beginning. The events that the viewer watches unfold are part of a story that has already failed. This strategy deviated radically from those of traditional detective stories, in which discovering the outcome is considered the main appeal of the entire story. Their readers or viewers would be furious were someone to reveal "whodunit" since that knowledge would ruin the pleasurable challenge of puzzling this out while reading. Much of *film noir*, to the contrary, shows greater interest in the puzzle itself than in progress toward its solution. As we noted in Chapter 1, from a viewer's perspective, the retrospective narrations of many *films noirs* resemble those of crime reportage in tabloid newspapers which render suspense irrelevant because the story's headline has already revealed the outcome (as in "Bank Robber Shot to Death by Police!"). But the readers continue to read on, not to discover how it turns out – they already know – but to savor the details of the crime.

Tensions between the older narrative model and the new one are evident in the influential *Citizen Kane*, which is organized around the quest for the meaning of "Rosebud," the title character's dying word. At the end, the viewer, but no one in the film, sees "Rosebud" written on the man's childhood sled just as it is being burned as trash. On a superficial level, this gives the viewer an "Aha!" moment, a sense that the sled is the key to understanding the film since it represents the cynical Citizen Kane's lamented lost innocence. But Welles often acknowledged that the sled was little more than a trick to give structure and the illusion of closure to the many questions raised in the film, most of which remain unanswered. The film was much more concerned with the posing of those questions than in definitively answering them with its transparently flimsy resolution.

The dwelling of many *films noirs* upon the specifics of crimes and the mentalities of the criminals led some contemporary reviewers to denounce them as immoral, as wallowing in the seamier sides of life, even as guides to crime. Raymond Durgnat, one of the earliest English-language commentators on the genre, vigorously rejected such characterizations of *film noir* as "Hollywood decadence" by contextualizing it among Greek tragedy, Jacobean drama, and Romantic Agony, earlier dark forms with doomed characters and unhappy endings that were produced by alienated cultures (Durgnat, 1998).

Such forms were often indifferent to happy endings, moral uplift, or spectator suspense. Few people who have seen *Oedipus Rex* or *Hamlet* over the centuries have gone to the theater to discover how the stories turn out; they knew the outcome from the outset. They attend the plays to reexperience their delineations of worst-case scenarios playing out. Furthermore, Durgnat, a British Marxist, found in *film noir*'s focus on the world of crime a fertile platform for investigations of the dynamics of social dysfunction.

The secondary attention that many *films noirs* give to "whodunit" or "How will it turn out?" narrative suspense relates to Paul Schrader's assertion of the importance of the "choreography" of *film noir*. For him, a major value of the films lies not in gleaning their moral lessons but in watching the way they unfold. He considers *film noir* more enduring than 1930s crime films that boldly proclaimed their "Crime Does Not Pay" moral themes. He felt that *film noir*'s delineation of the complex workings of a society in which evil things occur – their "choreography"– is more profound (Schrader, 1998). In discussing the primacy of choreography over theme in *film noir*, Schrader and others linked the style of the films with their effect on the viewer, privileging the films' emotional affect over their logically stated themes.

In the 1980s, the Coen brothers named their neo-*noir Blood Simple* after a term from Dashiell Hammett's hard-boiled novel *Red Harvest* (1929). The term refers to the disordered mental states that involvement with murder produces in people. They no longer act logically or even in their own best interests; they become "blood simple," consumed by the passion, guilt, confusion, and terror of discovery that the crime produces. Part of the appeal of *film noir* has been its drawing of viewers, often by means of a first-person point of view, into an experiential sense of this, what Borde and Chaumeton (2002) termed "a malaise." As audiences often privilege musical numbers over narrative structure in musicals and sex scenes over plot in pornography, the "choreography" of *films noirs* has often proven more compelling than either their storylines or their moral lessons.

Seven plants viewers in the midst of an unfolding series of shocking murders. From the beginning, Somerset understands that the crimes are not isolated but part of a pattern. He ominously predicts, "This is beginning," and asks his captain to remove both him and Mills from the investigation. Correctly intuiting that the case will draw them into its "blood simple" mania, he does not want it to be his last case or Mills's first one. Intriguingly, Somerset's captain tries to dissuade him from retiring, telling him that he shouldn't leave because "You were made for this." As much as Somerset is repulsed by his deep understanding of what is going on, his captain realizes that that very understanding makes him the best person to investigate it.

The contemporary fantastic

At a later point, Somerset objects to a description of John Doe as a lunatic. He feels that, however monstrous, he is a product of the normal, and not abnormal, world. John Doe's very name is a widely accepted term meaning Everyman, one of us. The world of *Seven* is depressing – a grungy, unnamed American city in which it nearly always rains, although nothing ever appears either cleansed or refreshed. The only scenes that are set outside of this city occur at the conclusion, in a wasteland with little but scrub brush and large power poles alongside a desolate highway. But although the film's events are horrifying, they occur in a world that would appear familiar to contemporary viewers. This is not a horror film set in Transylvania or on a distant planet with supernatural occurrences; it is one set in today's "normal" world with events that, however appalling, resemble those commonly shown on popular weekly television series whose popularity is underscored by their multiple spin-off series, like *Law and Order, CSI, NCIS,* and *Criminal Minds.* John Doe, however monstrous, is part of this normality; he fits right in.

Nino Frank (1995) perceptively described the setting of *film noir* as the "contemporary fantastic." It is a setting in which horrific events of the sort traditionally associated with horror and fantasy are implanted in the everyday world of the normal. Borde and Chaumeton (2002) elaborated upon this with their observation that, while *film noir's* individual shots often have a semi-documentary appearance, their cumulative effect is that of a nightmare. For their initial audiences, most *films noirs* were about "today." The characters, styles, automobiles, landscapes, that they saw on the screen corresponded to the world they saw when they left the theater. But the films imbued those commonplace things with a growing sense of surreal menace. Similarly, *Seven* is set contemporaneously in an environment similar to what a 1995 viewer would have seen outside of the theater. But it is ultimately a horrifying environment, one dominated by the mind of John Doe.

The police procedural and Seven

Seven has the trappings of a police procedural. Borde and Chaumeton (2002) excluded the procedural from *film noir* on the grounds of its optimism and formal strategies (the procedurals focused on the police, not the criminals, they incorporated neorealist techniques, used oratorical "Voice of God" rather than depressive, first-person narrations, and often ended happily with the criminals brought to justice). But Borde and Chaumeton were writing in the early 1950s, during *film noir's* canonical era, and procedurals of the 1940s and 1950s worked differently from *Seven.* They presumed the rectitude of social agencies like the police and FBI as well as the positive social effects of their activities; *Seven,* while not concerned with police corruption, concludes with the sense that police efforts have little effect on limiting crime and that any hopes of improving society are folly.

For much of its duration, *Seven* appears to be a procedural. Clue by clue, the detectives seem to be closing in on the killer. However, we gradually realize that the film's driving force is not the police investigation at all but rather the enfolding of that investigation into John Doe's plan. Although it is unclear to the viewer at the time, the opening credits show John Doe assembling the notebooks that motivate his plan. By the end of the film, that plan has been successfully accomplished. John Doe will be dead and Mills will be ruined. Somerset will live on but, from the perspective of the film, the characters' lives or deaths will make little difference since all the action plays out in a ruined world. While reading John Doe's notebooks, Somerset comments that he is pouring his mind out on the pages. John Doe possibly views his writings as a form of scripture, hoping in his megalomaniacal way that potential future followers will consult them for inspiration. Hence the film's structure comes from his plan and not the police investigation. While *Seven* initially seems to be a procedural, we realize by its conclusion that its apparent procedural structure was misleading. Instead, the film is a detailed depiction of the crime itself, planned long before the film begins. The detectives were pawns in John Doe's scheme. Thus the movie has a circular and not a linear structure; the end returns to what we have seen, though not understood as such, at the beginning – John Doe's plan.

Change and Evolution in Film Noir

In addition to describing what they considered the basic elements of *film noir*, many early critics allowed for continued change in the genre. Borde and Chaumeton (2002) as well as Schrader (1998), for example, stressed that *film noir* was a product of its historical moment – the postwar era – with meanings specific to people of that era, while allowing that those meanings might change for viewers of subsequent eras. *Film noir* is substantially concerned with depicting a world gone wrong and with undermining traditional viewer expectations about a just society. Its strategies for accomplishing this often sought to disturb the viewer. However, many commentators on *film noir* understood that those things that disorient viewers have expiration dates and that what is currently new and shocking can quickly become dated and anticipated. After the initial jolts, viewers become familiar with and even bored by them. A genre that hopes to destabilize its audience over time must adapt its strategies and tactics and constantly reorient itself to evolving social and cultural realities.

The many shifts in *film noir*, from its early stages to the influence of neo-realism, documentaries, and the police procedural, to neo-*noir* and dystopian science fiction, evidence the genre's continual adaptation to changing times. And as the times to which *film noir* has adapted have changed, so also has the psychological makeup of its viewers. The anxieties produced by the Great Depression, World War II, and the Cold War were potent in the 1940s and 1950s but often strike twenty-first-century viewers as quaint or even irrelevant. Most of them were born after *film noir* had died as a commercial form. They have no memory of black and white as a normative film stock and many even cringe and rush to change the station when it appears on television. The appearance and social behaviors of the 1940s and 1950s are as foreign to their experience as are those in Westerns. But regardless, *film noir* has resonantly endured among filmmakers, critics, and viewers.

Kiss Me Deadly *and* Seven

One way of illustrating *Seven*'s continuity amid the pattern of change and evolution in *film noir* is to compare it with a film from the canonical era that was analyzed in an earlier chapter, *Kiss Me Deadly*. The 1955 film has been characterized as marking the end of *film noir* as well as presaging the rise of neo-*noir*. Some of the connections between the two films are readily apparent. Both are detective films in which the central characters pursue a multiple murderer and both end catastrophically for all involved. Other points of comparison are more intriguing. The closing credits of *Seven*, like the opening ones of *Kiss Me Deadly*, scroll downwards from the top of the frame to its bottom, forcing the viewer to read them from the bottom up, a formal device as unusual in 1995 as it was in 1955, and one that may even be an homage to the 1955 film. Both movies employ multiple strategies in their cinematography, editing, and soundtracks to disorient viewers. Both also conclude on an apocalyptic note, with the sense that the central characters, whether Mike Hammer or Somerset and Mills, have been enfolded from the outset into a grand plan with horrific implications, a plan of whose very existence they had been unaware.

The pre-credit sequence of *Kiss Me Deadly* with its abrupt, unoriented shots of Christina's legs as she flees along a highway in terror, and its post-credit shot of her legs spasming as she is being tortured, with its sounds of her screams continuing even after her legs have become still in death, are only two instances of jarring and abrasive moments in the film. As with the credit sequence, they were highly unusual practices for 1955.

In an entirely different way, the credit sequence of *Seven* shows unoriented images that are confusing to the viewer who does not yet know what they signify. We see black and white autopsy as well as crime scene photographs, color shots of gauze-covered fingers stitching a book together, as well as shots of those fingers blacking out eyes and in other ways disfiguring some of the still photographs. The lettering of the credits appears crudely hand-drawn and unstable. The letters appear to jerk around as if the film itself were coming apart while being projected. In both films, these early instances promise a film whose story will be grim and whose formal techniques will be discomfiting.

However, while both movies employ abrasive and non-traditional strategies, they function within and not outside of mainstream Hollywood cinema, like most of *film noir*. In this they support David Bordwell's argument against claims that *film noir* is a radical alternative to Hollywood style (Bordwell, 1985; see Chapter 3). The narrative confusion in *Kiss Me Deadly* does not depart radically from Hollywood practice – mystery films commonly present the audience with confusing events that are gradually clarified; *Kiss Me Deadly* simply pushes the envelope. The confusion in *Seven* goes more deeply since it takes us the majority of the film to realize that we have been watching the unfolding of John Doe's plan all along, but, again, it functions within the Hollywood paradigm.

The downward-spiraling character trajectory of both films is summarized in *Kiss Me Deadly* by Velda's embittered comment to Mike Hammer, "First, you find a little thread, the little thread leads you to a string, and the string leads you to a rope, and from the rope you hang by the neck." In each film, the detective appears for a time to be succeeding in his pursuit until he finds it all circling back onto him, catastrophically.

Both films also underscore the presence of the accumulated culture of the past in a society on the verge of collapse. It is common for movies to reinforce the widespread notion that high culture is "good for you," that exposure to privileged artifacts of past culture will elevate people's moral and social character. In both of these movies, however, things that had traditionally served as emblems of cultural progress are employed mainly by the villains. In *Kiss Me Deadly*, Dr Soberin patronizingly refers to the Bible and Greek mythology to intimidate hirelings and mock victims. At best, things like Christina's reference to a Victorian poem can serve as a clue to lead Mike to Dr Soberin, but her knowledge is of no help whatsoever to her.

Comparably, in *Seven*, Somerset places great emphasis on literary works in the Christian tradition in his search for John Doe. He illegally traces John Doe's library readings, discovering that most of them depict sin and punishment, like the Bible, Milton's *Paradise Lost*, and Dante's *Divine Comedy*. When Somerset suggests that Mills read them, Mills is furious. He purchases a copy of Dante but, after looking at it briefly, flings it away while contemptuously muttering, "Fucking Dante." He cannot understand how books that are centuries old could have any bearing on the case but, to placate Somerset, he gets CliffsNotes versions of some of the works. Ultimately, they reveal what is on John Doe's mind and provide the rationale for his killings.

These two films were made forty years apart and reflect that time difference. Although both are visually dark, the first was shot in black and white with a 1:66:1 aspect ratio and the second in color with a widescreen 2:35:1 aspect ratio. The first concerns a 1950s tough guy private eye working alone against the underworld; the second concerns municipal police detectives and has nothing to do with gangsters, nuclear anxiety, postwar consumer culture, or *Playboy*-type sexpots. Both firmly reflect the eras in which they were made and yet both share the *film noir* tradition. We will now look at those things which make *Seven* a neo-*noir*.

Seven *and Neo-*Noir

However strongly *Seven* is rooted in *film noir*, no informed viewer could get beyond the opening credits without recognizing it as a neo-*noir*. This involves much more than its 1990s setting, its color and widescreen cinematography, its nudity, casual profanity, and graphic bodily mutilation. One example of this is evidenced simply by the fact that, although Somerset is African American and Mills is white, racial difference has nothing to do with the movie's dynamics. Such a credible, post-racial posture was inconceivable for films made during the *film noir* era. In multiple ways, *Seven*'s narrative and thematic development, cinematography, editing, and soundtrack differ extensively from norms of the studio era. This section explores the film's identity as a neo-*noir* with attention to its formal and thematic strategies, its graphic forensic imagery, its concentration on surveillance and paranoia, its focus on a serial killer, and its millennial anxieties.

Formal devices

Seven's formal practices place it visibly among those of the 1990s filmmaking industry. Lighting has always been important to *film noir*, and the best films of its canonical era employed evocative, often Impressionistic, black and white cinematography by masters like John Alton, Stanley Cortez, Nicholas Musuraca, John F. Seitz, and Ernest Lazlo. The *"noir"* in *film noir* referred as much to its visual textures as to its themes. Its use of chiaroscuro lighting and ominous darkness gave viewers the sense that they were watching more than a "realistic" depiction of story events; they were watching those events unfold in a highly mediated visual environment evocative of the dark forces eruptive in the films. Furthermore, constant experimentation with lighting and camera effects occurred throughout the *film noir* era. *Kiss Me Deadly*, for example, culminated by embodying its greatest evil not in intense darkness but in the screeching, sheer white light that blasts from "the Great Whatsit" (see Plate 29, p. 141). After black and white lost its commercial viability in the 1960s, neo-*noir* filmmakers used stylized color and lighting to depict what Raymond Chandler termed a world gone wrong. *The Long Goodbye* uses washed-out-looking color to depict its desiccated world; *Chinatown* and *Farewell, My Lovely* moved in a different direction by using deep browns, reds, and ambers to give a partially nostalgic feel for the prewar US from which *film noir* emerged. Furthermore, since the 1970s, even the normative status that black and white held during the studio era has changed and the format is now perceived as exotic and non-"realistic," as evidenced in black and white neo-*noirs* like Kenneth Branagh's *Dead Again* (1991) or the Coen Brothers' *The Man Who Wasn't There* (2001).

Much of *Seven* is shot at night or in dark places, but even in exterior daytime scenes the relentless rain and filth of the city make everything grungy. We see poorly lit spaces with heavy grays, dirty blues, and coppery, urine-like yellows. The concluding exterior scenes look sun-bleached, indicating not a fertile, unpolluted countryside but a wasteland. Such visual environments resemble those in horror films and, from the beginning, *film noir* has had many affinities with horror. In both genres, the cinematography generates environmental menace. A major difference between them is that horror employs the supernatural and *film noir* encases its destabilizing forces within the world of the normal. In the 1940s, many of Val Lewton's films, such as *Cat People*, were fascinatingly ambiguous, functioning equally as horror and as *films noirs*. Today, the forbidding, tomb- or prison-like lighting in the recent *Saw* (2004, 2005, 2006, 2007, 2008, 2009, 2010) and *Hostel* (2005, 2007, 2011) films (often called "torture porn") resembles that in some neo-*noirs*. And the boundaries are even further blurred in the blending of *film noir* with science fiction in films like *Blade Runner*, *The Terminator*, and *Minority Report*.

Seven's grunginess is further evident in the apparent physicality of the very film that we are watching. We see scratches on the filmstrip and the lettering in its credits appears hand-scrawled and uneven. The letters do not remain fixed on the screen, as is standard, but spasm periodically in a jerky fashion as if the filmstrip had briefly been trapped in the projector's gate and then lurched free, and at times the entire screen flashes to white. The cutting between shots in the credits seems rough and choppy in ways that would only have been seen in avant-garde or experimental films during the studio era. Some of these strategies align us with the point of view of John Doe, whose hands, during the credits, are meticulously sewing the bindings of his notebooks and pasting materials into them, such as diverse images in both color and black and white as well as his writings. The grungy imagery resembles that widely used in punk rock iconography on posters and album covers to celebrate a ruined world. This perspective also extends beyond that of John Doe to that of the film we are watching. When the police break into John Doe's apartment, they discover his approximately two thousand notebooks of 250 pages each containing his writings, collage-like images, and, shockingly, photographs of Somerset and Mills. John Doe imprints his thoughts and activities onto multiple media, including the actual bodies of his victims and the walls and floors of his murder scenes. When he surrenders to the police, he uses his own body as the medium for his message of self-martyrdom by standing, covered in blood, with his arms outstretched in a crucifixion pose (Plate 43). Somerset devotes himself to exploring both the texts and images of old books in the library as his way of tracking John Doe down and uses a modern photocopier to make Xerox copies of some of that material for Mills. A crisp Xerox of a page from an old volume has a different effect on a reader than the volume itself. Throughout, *Seven* evidences a deep

PLATE 43 *Seven*: John Doe (Kevin Spacey). © 1995 New Line Productions, Inc.

investment both in what it is presenting and in the specific visual and aural texture of the ways in which it is presented.

Graphic forensics

This attention to the physicality of images extends to the film's graphic depiction of forensic material, which points to a second area marking *Seven* as a neo-*noir*. Although *film noir* often dealt with sadistic brutality and gruesome death, the PCA forbade the graphic display of mutilation and gore. The audience might have known that a character had been bludgeoned to death but they would not have seen graphic images of the blood, mutilation, and viscera. There is a difference. All of that changed during the genre's commercial decline. The shower murder scene in *Psycho* was considered terrifyingly explicit in 1960, although it is relatively mild when compared with much of today's cinema. After the PCA was abolished in the late 1960s, graphic violence has become commonplace, particularly in horror but also in neo-*noir*. Mainstream audiences have developed not only a tolerance for but also a fascination with such things, and, in ways unthinkable before the 1970s, a staple of network and cable television has become highly rated series, like *CSI, Crossing Jordan, NCIS,* and others, that explicitly depict crime forensics and autopsies.

Seven begins with forensic photographs in its credit sequence and its crime scenes are particularly repulsive. The first one shows a man's corpse on the floor of a grungy room and spattered blood on the wall. Soon we see the first of John Doe's victims in the "Gluttony" crime scene, which is dingy, filthy, and crawling with maggots. The morbidly obese corpse had been bound to a chair and literally forced to eat until his stomach burst. His face lies in a rotting bowl of spaghetti and Mills discovers a bucket of vomit under the table. We soon see the hideously bloated corpse on an autopsy table. Another victim had been bound to a bed in a filthy apartment and starved for a year, given only enough nourishment to minimally survive, while inexorably wasting away in unspeakable agony. When the police discover him, they are nauseated by the stench in the room and initially think that his immobile, emaciated body is a corpse, only to be shocked when he suddenly coughs. He is marginally alive, his mind is long gone, and he soon dies. All of this is graphically presented, contributing to the film's growing atmosphere of horror and decay.

This representational strategy abruptly changes at the film's conclusion. Where, earlier, it had presented graphic images of the murder scenes, it now withholds such images. Upon surrendering, John Doe promises to fully inform the police about his murders only if Somerset and Mills agree to escort him to a place outside of the city. They reluctantly do so, under heavy guard and accompanied by extensive surveillance, physically by helicopter and electronically by recording devices. They stop at a deserted, nondescript area and wait until a delivery truck arrives to deliver a box that contains Tracy's severed head. As Somerset opens it, John Doe quietly tells Mills that his own deadly sin is envy, particularly of Mills's happy life. He then confesses that he has destroyed that life by raping and murdering Tracy with her unborn child, of which Mills had not known. He knows that this will provoke Mills into a murderous rage. The movie does not depict either the rape and murder scene or the head in the box, and when Mills shoots John Doe it is shown in longshot. At the culmination of a film filled with explicit gore, it shows virtually none but shifts into the distanced, non-graphic, yet horrifying culmination of John Doe's plan.

Upon discovering Tracy's head and realizing that John Doe is telling Mills about it, Somerset yells for him not to shoot John Doe because that will mean that he has won. On John Doe's terms, he has.

Surveillance and paranoia

A third area marking *Seven* as a neo-*noir* lies in its focus on modern surveillance and paranoia. John Doe committed his crimes in such a way as to solicit publicity and pursuit. He is fully aware that the police are searching for him while he is also simultaneously meticulously observing both his victims and his pursuers, creating an hermetic cycle of surveillance. *Seven* presents universal surveillance as a fact of life, which goes hand in hand with paranoia. It acknowledges no place for privacy; anyone can be observed and hence menaced. Aside from its confluence with recent media fascination with the serial killer, the film also develops John Doe as a stalker, and a stalker who is himself being stalked. His apartment is heavily bolted. He is paranoid and his activities generate widespread fear. He is not alone; the police and FBI also conduct constant surveillance.

To again align *Seven* with the origins of *film noir*, the genre has always mapped out the utopian modernist impulse gone wrong on a landscape whose denizens are alienated not only from continuity with nineteenth-century traditions but also from utopian modernist aspirations. It presents modern experience as fragmented, disjointed, and often incoherent. The 1940s produced both the alienated urban landscapes of *film noir* and George Orwell's *Nineteen Eighty-Four*. As we noted in Chapter 2, this novel presented one face of state-sponsored surveillance, eroding the freedoms and compromising the identities of those subject to it. At the same time, however, such surveillance was portrayed in a benign light in the police procedural, with state functionaries seen as striving to uphold liberty and protect the public. By contrast, post-1970 neo-*noirs* that are set in exactly the same era frequently depict the state in a different light; its agents are either corrupt (as in *L.A. Confidential* or *Mulholland Falls*) or ineffective (as in *Seven*). Neo-*noir* also links *noir*'s trope of the decline of the modern with dystopian fiction's trope of the degeneration of the future. Films like *Blade Runner*, *The Terminator*, and *Minority Report* conflate *film noir* and science fiction within a nexus of dystopian modernism and are centrally concerned with abuses of state power that lead to erosions and fragmentations of individual identity.

Seven, while not futuristic, is a procedural. Somerset and Mills are not private detectives but municipal employees. If they retire, die, or leave the case, other police officers will replace them. The movie does not mount a critique of governmental policies or indict the state as corrupt; its critique is more metaphysical, more geared to a sense of human hopelessness within a millennial context.

Surveillance is a central presence in the film, but less as a shocking indicator of state corruption than as a sad and pervasive fact of modern life. Somerset and Mills use surveillance techniques, some of which are illegal, to track John Doe. Somerset surreptitiously purchases records of the books people have borrowed from public libraries from the FBI. In this film it hardly makes sense to see surveillance as bad because it is simply there, everywhere, part of contemporary existence. The anxieties about the loss of individuality and privacy so widespread in the postwar years, while still present, have given way in the neo-*noir* era to a sense of a world which no longer offers any alternative.

Mills is surprised to learn about the pervasion of such surveillance, such as the FBI's records of library withdrawals of the general public, and he has already, on a relatively minor level, been victimized by it. When Somerset visits his and Tracy's new apartment for dinner, the building is frequently shaken by the loud rumbling of a nearby subway. Even the dinner plates rattle on the table. They did not know about this when they rented the place, but the real estate agent did. The agent had monitored the train schedule and only showed the apartment to them for short intervals, at times when the train was not passing. On a more profoundly destructive level, Mills is later shocked to find photographs of himself in John Doe's apartment and, finally, by John Doe's intimate knowledge of his marriage, including his unborn child.

Somerset is not naïve about these things. After the first two murders, he knows that a larger plan is in process and correctly predicts five more murders. He does not want the case to be his last one and requests that Mills be removed from it, his first case, because he is not ready for it. His fearful anxiety is contrasted with Mills's naïve, youthful optimism and bravado. Where Somerset says, "I can't get involved in this," Mills boasts, "I'm all over it." On all levels, Somerset is right in ways that Mills could not comprehend. Somerset simply wants to retire from it all; to get out of the city for good. However, at the end, he tells an officer that he will be around, knowing that on a basic level there is no escape.

Serial killers

A fourth area marking *Seven* as a neo-*noir* lies in its characterization of its serial killer. As with surveillance, the mass media in recent decades have depicted serial killers as everywhere and invisible. The serial killer has become an American cultural obsession, widely portrayed in film and on television police series and obsessively discussed in documentary and news accounts. The stories of historical figures like Jack the Ripper, Ted Bundy, John Wayne Gacy, Aileen Wournos, David Berkowitz, the Zodiac Killer, and Jeffrey Dahmer are endlessly recycled throughout the mass media. This extends to fictional characters, like Hannibal Lecter in *Silence of the Lambs* and its sequels and prequels, like Norman Bates from *Psycho*, and the serial killer in the two film versions of the Jim Thompson novel *The Killer Inside Me* (1976–2010). The popular television series *Criminal Minds*, about the FBI's Behavioral Analysis Unit, is largely devoted to its pursuit of serial killers. This cultural fascination goes hand-in-hand with the popularity of police forensics shows. In fact, the partially sympathetic serial killer in the popular series *Dexter* actually works for a police crime lab.

In his *New York Times* review of the series premiere of *Criminal Minds: Suspect Behavior*, Alessandra Stanley comments upon the pervasion of graphic crime shows on CBS in ways partially applicable to the cultural environment for neo-*noir*, joking that the name of the network should be changed to the Crime Broadcasting System. "The network specializes in series that marry elegant cinematography to spooky setups and grotesque crime scenes. They take a high-minded look at the lowest common denominator, trafficking in people's worst fears of abduction, rape, torture, disfigurement and excruciating death. These are horror stories told through a comforting veil of predictability" (Stanley, 2005).

From Hell (2001) opens with a grandly ambitious declaration which it attributes to Jack the Ripper: "One day man will look back and say that I gave birth to the twentieth century." This fits with recent characterizations of serial killers as figures profoundly representative of deep forces underlying and driving our culture. John Doe fits into that mold, a character with a grand plan that he considers a design for society itself. Where serial killers were once depicted as simply psychotic, they have recently been given the status of mirror images of society itself, apparently "normal" while enacting a grand scheme of destruction. Mirroring what Somerset says of John Doe, a Victorian detective in *From Hell* ominously predicts early on that Jack the Ripper is not finished. He knows a larger, sinister pattern is already in progress. This is peculiar to neo-*noir*. Few villains in *film noir* were developed on such a grand scale or even one indicating that they were successful.

In neo-*noir*, it is not unusual for murderous, mad villains to succeed with their crimes. Although the psychotic Travis Bickle in *Taxi Driver* commits multiple killings at a brothel, his motives are entirely misunderstood by the society that declares him a public hero. Jack the Ripper was never caught and Hannibal Lecter as well as Dexter elude police and FBI pursuit. John Doe dies but feels that he does so victoriously, as a martyr to his cause. In an inversion of traditional film representations of the battle between good and evil, evil often wins. Although good often survives, it does so only to be defeated again and again.

Millennial context

A final context marking *Seven* as a neo-*noir* lies in its investment in the millennial anxieties of the 1990s. John Doe sacrifices his life as well as those of others to his plan, but what motivates him? When Somerset and Mills explore his apartment, they find it filled with Christian iconography. Somerset calls his murders "his sermons to us" about the Seven Deadly Sins. John Doe does not act out of desire for earthly profit; his actions stem from a religious mania, but why would a film about such issues appear when it did?

Seven appeared in 1995 amid widespread anxiety about the then-imminent Millennium. That anxiety drew upon Christian discourse, since the year 2000 marked two millennia from the birth of Jesus Christ, a time at which some predicted the world would end. For over a decade preceding and following the millennial year, many films foregrounded concerns about time running out, and time is a central motif in *Seven*. Somerset has a ticking chronometer in his room and he marks the time until his retirement. But the ticking chronometer also holds a larger significance. The movie marks each of the seven days to Somerset's retirement and ends on his retirement day. Unknown to the viewer, this countdown also follows the time that is running out for Mills, Tracy, and their unborn baby, as well as for John Doe. On the film's seventh day their worlds will end.

From its outset the film radiates an ominous mood of something stirring. Like much of *film noir*, it generates a disturbing sense that hopes for the future are unraveling, that past human accomplishments are dissipating since they have led to this dead end. Like *The Long Goodbye* and *Chinatown*, *Seven* ends on a note of wholesale hopelessness and failure. It gives the impression that this is the way things are – this is the way of the world.

It is all over, even as Somerset and Mills discover the first victim. On the second day a workman removes Somerset's name from his office door, indicating that his detachment has already begun. His captain tells him that he doesn't really think Somerset will retire, that he doesn't think Somerset can give up being a cop since he was destined for this work. Somerset replies that giving up his role as a policeman is the whole idea behind his retirement. He then recounts an incident that happened nearby on the previous evening. A man was attacked while walking his dog. After the attacker had taken the man's wallet and watch and left him helpless on the ground, he stabbed him in both eyes. Somerset says, "I don't understand this place any longer."

Somerset's "I don't understand this place any longer" resembles similar observations made by the retiring lawman played by Tommy Lee Jones at the beginning of the Coen Brothers' *No Country for Old Men* (2007) who feels that the evil surrounding him has metastasized beyond his comprehension and that he can no longer even pretend that he can deal productively with it. On one level, such comments reflect anxieties shared by many older people who feel that their world is passing them by, that the securities upon which they have built their lives are becoming ignored or invalidated. But *Seven*, *No Country for Old Men*, and other recent neo-*noirs* indicate that more is involved, that a new era of evil is emerging. Such films partake of a millennial sensibility, a sense that the world is entering a phase so degenerate that traditional agents of law, stability, and continuity can no longer cope with, or even understand, it. Such films offer no hope for a viable future, only the remote possibility of individual detachment from it all.

Tracy shares Somerset's perspective. She does not share her husband's enthusiasm about moving into the city. Soon after meeting Somerset and intuiting him to be a kindred spirit, she confides her anxieties to him, revealing that she is pregnant and terrified at the prospect of raising a child in this environment (Plate 44). Somerset tells her, "I hate this city," and recalls a relationship he had years earlier. When his lover became pregnant, he experienced fear for the first time in his life, feeling that he couldn't bring a child into this world. He wore his mate down until she agreed to have an abortion. Tracy empathizes deeply but, like Somerset, she is powerless.

Over the past three-quarters of a century, *films noirs* have invoked many of the anxieties in our culture as contexts for their particular visions. For some, those anxieties involved psychological dysfunction, personal failings, uncontrollable sexual desire, or erosions to individuality; for others it was the failure of the American Dream; the menace of Soviet Communism, or corruption within our own government; for still others it was spreading plague, criminal cartels, thermonuclear catastrophe, and threats from other races and cultures. Implicit in these anxieties was the fear of the end of a way of life, or even of the world itself. In canonical *film noir* such fear generally applied to the end of the individual world of the film's protagonist, commonly depicted in the character's death. To recall our discussion in Chapter 6, with some movies, individual death also implied a larger context. In *White Heat*, for example, James Cagney's psychotic gangster blows himself up atop a huge chemical storage tank, creating a spectacular explosion. In the late 1940s, such conflagrations carried with them associations of the newly discovered menace of atomic power and possible global destruction. *Kiss Me Deadly* abruptly ends just as what appears to be a thermonuclear explosion is beginning, leaving the extent of the explosion unknown. This implied the literal end of the world, a widespread anxiety for the nuclear-conscious 1950s. But as the twentieth century drew to a close and the symbolically charged

PLATE 44 *Seven*: Tracy (Gwyneth Paltrow) confessing her fears. © 1995 New Line Productions, Inc.

year 2000 approached, a very old anxiety achieved a new pertinence, that of the biblical Millennium, bringing with it the Apocalypse and the divinely ordained end of the world.

Movies engaging such discourse draw upon many symbolic traditions, one of the most resonant being medieval Christianity which describes both the Millennium and the Apocalypse. The Apocalypse (with which the Millennium is commonly linked) is outlined in the Apocalypse of John. During the past forty years, discourse upon the Apocalypse has become blended with that of contemporary politics. Sean P. Kealy, C. S. Sp., has written:

> Prophesying the end of the world is a common activity of Christian fundamentalist evangelical preachers. Until the 1970s they avoided political thinking and concentrated upon saving "souls" from the slaughter of Armageddon. Then they increasingly began to give Biblical apocalypticism a contemporary political interpretation, envisaging the end as beginning with the "Rapture" or the rescue of all Christians to some place with Jesus "in the air" (2 Cor 12:3; 1 Thess 4:17). Those left behind will endure a period of tribulation for seven years. . . . Then Christ and his army of raptured saints will return to defeat the Antichrist in a battle at Armageddon, north of Jerusalem. After this, . . . a thousand years of peace will follow until the Last Judgment. (Kealy, 1987, p. 16)

While this scenario is only one strain of such discourse, it points to the presence in Christianity of a dense, mythic symbology for a universal and culminating conflict between good and evil. Movies that evoke millennialist anxieties, such as *Independence Day* (1996), *Volcano* (1997), *Seven, Fallen* (1998), *The Butcher Boy, Stigmata* (1999), *The Eighteenth Angel* (1998), *The Minion* (1998), and *End of Days*, among many others, clearly draw upon this mythic tradition, using Christian symbology to configure the approaching doom. This is the tradition from which John Doe emerged.

This obsessive embrace of one's own destruction parallels the retrospective narrational strategies of many *films noirs* as well as the settings of so many of them in doomed and ruined environments.

In *Seven*, Somerset carries this sense of despair with him, feeling that the decline of any world for which he had ever held any hope is already irreversible. He has not entirely given up, but nothing he experiences offers the promise that things will turn out differently. When he delivers his closing line, "I'll be around," it seems to indicate that he will be available to help Mills in his presumed imprisonment, but it also indicates what he has always been – "around," cycling endlessly in a world without hope, more as an impotent witness than as an effective agent of change. The sense of stoical hopelessness and omnipresent menace that his resignation indicates brings us back to the beginnings of *film noir,* to the eerie credit sequence of *Double Indemnity* in which the ominous silhouette of the man on crutches is relentlessly approaching and enveloping us.

AFTERWORD

This study can never be completed, and that fact is part of its appeal. *Film noir* is a moving target, constantly changing, constantly revitalizing, and drawing new perspectives into itself. I have barely touched upon some aspects of the subject and have barely mentioned some important films. The nature and complexity of the topic make that unavoidable. Furthermore, after having explored *film noir* intensively for years, I keep coming upon films, cultural contexts for them, and commentary about them that open up new perspectives. While neo-*noir* is obviously a continually evolving phenomenon, even the canon of *films noirs* of its canonical period is not and has never been fixed. New critical contexts have repeatedly opened up space for movies not previously considered, which in turn necessitates a reevaluation of the entire canon. This can be simultaneously bewildering and energizing. Much of the appeal of studying *film noir* is that it not only involves exploring fascinating and complex films but it also opens up ever-expanding cultural and psychological cross-currents that have informed much of the twentieth and early twenty-first centuries. *Film noir* continues to be rewarding.

Film Noir, First Edition. William Luhr.
© 2012 William Luhr. Published 2012 by Blackwell Publishing Ltd.

REFERENCES

Affron, Charles and Mirella Jona Affron 2009. *Best Years: Going to the Movies, 1945–1946.* New Brunswick, NJ: Rutgers University Press.

Belton, John 1994. *"Film Noir's* Knights of the Road" (first appearing in the Spring 1994 print edition of *Bright Lights,* Issue 12, and later online at *http://www.brightlightsfilm.com/54/ noirknights.htm,* accessed September 6, 2011).

Bennett, Tony and Janet Woollacott 1987. *Bond and Beyond: The Political Career of a Popular Hero.* London: Methuen.

Borde, Raymond and Etienne Chaumeton 2002. *A Panorama of American Film Noir, 1941–1953,* translated by Paul Hammond. San Francisco: City Lights Books (the English-language translation of *Panorama du film noiraméricain 1941–1953,* 1955).

Bordwell, David 1985. *Narration in the Fiction Film.* Madison: University of Wisconsin Press.

Bordwell, David, Janet Staiger, and Kristin Thompson 1985. *The Classical Hollywood Cinema.* New York: Columbia University Press.

Brackett, Leigh 1988. "From *The Big Sleep* to *The Long Goodbye,*" in *The Big Book of Noir,* edited by Ed Gorman, Lee Server, and Martin H. Greenberg. New York: Carroll and Graf, pp. 127–41.

Brokaw, Tom 1998. *The Greatest Generation.* New York: Random House.

Film Noir, First Edition. William Luhr.
© 2012 William Luhr. Published 2012 by Blackwell Publishing Ltd.

Butler, David 2002. *Jazz Noir: Listening to Music from Phantom to Lady to the Last Seduction*. Westport, Conn.: Praeger.

Cawelti, John G. 1985. "*Chinatown* and Generic Transformation in Recent American Films," in *Film Theory and Criticism: Introductory Readings*, third edition, edited by Gerald Mast and Marshall Cohen. New York: Oxford University Press, pp. 503–20.

Chabrol, Claude 1985. "Evolution of the Thriller," in *Cahiers du Cinéma in the 1950s: Neo-Realism, Hollywood, New Wave, Volume One*, edited by Jim Hillier. Cambridge, Mass.: Harvard University Press, pp. 158–64.

Chandler, Raymond 1995. "Introduction to 'The Simple Art of Murder,'" in *Raymond Chandler: Later Novels and Other Writings*. New York: The Library of America, pp. 1016–19.

Chartier, Jean-Pierre 1946. "Les Américains aussi font des films 'noirs,'" *Revue du Cinéma*, 2, pp. 67–70.

Cocks, Jay 1973. "A Curious Spectacle," *Time*, April 9. *http://www.time.com/time/magazine/article/0,9171,903961,00.html*, accessed September 6, 2011.

Cook, David A. 1996. *A History of Narrative Film*, third edition. New York: Norton.

Copjec, Joan (ed.) 1993. *Shades of Noir*. London: Verso.

Crowther, Bosley 1944, Review of *Double Indemnity*. *New York Times*, September 7.

Crowther, Bosley 1946a. Review of *The Blue Dahlia*. *New York Times*, May 9.

Crowther, Bosley 1946b. Review of *The Big Sleep*. *New York Times*, August 24.

Crowther, Bosley 1947. Review of *Out of the Past*. *New York Times*, November 26.

Diawara, Manthia (ed.) 1993a. *Black American Cinema*, New York: Routledge.

Diawara, Manthia 1993b. "*Noir* by *Noirs*: Towards a New Realism in Black Cinema," in *Shades of Noir,* edited by Joan Copjec. London: Verso, pp. 261–78.

Dimendberg, Edward 2004. *Film Noir and the Spaces of Modernity*. Cambridge, Mass.: Harvard University Press.

Durgnat, Raymond 1998. "Paint It Black: The Family Tree of the Film Noir," in *Film Noir Reader*, edited by Alain Silver and James Ursini. New York: Limelight Editions, pp. 37–51 (first appearing in *Cinema*, August 1970).

Eagleton, Terry 2003. *Sweet Violence: The Idea of the Tragic*. Oxford, UK, and Malden, Mass.: Blackwell Publishing.

Ferguson, Otis 1941. Review of *The Maltese Falcon*. *The New Republic*, 20, October.

Frank, Nino 1995. "A New Type of Detective Story," translated by Connor Hartnett, in *The Maltese Falcon: John Huston, Director*, edited by William Luhr. New Brunswick, NJ: Rutgers University Press, pp. 132–5 (first appearing in *L'Écran Français*, 61, August 28, 1946).

Garner, Dwight 1997. "Too Little, Too Noir," review of *L.A. Confidential*, September 17. *http://www.salon.com/sept97/entertainment/la970919.html?CP=5AL&DN=110*, accessed September 6, 2011.

Grant, Barry Keith 2010. *Invasion of the Body Snatchers (BFI Film Classics)*. London: Palgrave Macmillan.

Gross, Miriam (ed.), 1977. *The World of Raymond Chandler*. New York: A and W Publishers.

Grosz, Elizabeth 1994. *Volatile Bodies: Toward a Corporeal Feminism*. Bloomington: Indiana University Press.

Hirsch, Foster 1981. *Film Noir: The Dark Side of the Screen*. New York: A.S. Barnes.

Indridason, Arnaldur 2005. *Jar City*. New York: St Martin's Press.

Kalb, Jonathan 2007. "To Sleep the Big Sleep: Call it Murder, My Sweet." *New York Times* Review of *Necropolis #1&2*, August 9, p. E 2.

Kaplan, Ann E. (ed.) 1998. *Women in Film Noir*, updated edition. London: British Film Institute (first published 1978).

Kealy, Sean P. 1987. *The Apocalypse of John*. Wilmington, Del.: Michael Glazier, 1987.

Kehr, Dave 1008. "Critic's Choice: New DVDs: Fox Film Noir."*New York Times,* September 2, p. E 3.

Klinger, Barbara 1994. *Melodrama and Meaning: History, Culture, and the Films of Douglas Sirk*. Bloomington: Indiana University Press.

Krutnik, Frank 1989. "In a Lonely Street: 1940s Hollywood, Film Noir, and the 'Tough' Thriller." Unpublished Ph.D. diss., University of Kent at Canterbury.

Krutnik, Frank 1991. *In a Lonely Street: Film Noir, Genre, Masculinity*. London: Routledge.

Krutnik, Frank, Steve Neale, Brian Neve, and Peter Stanfield (eds) 2007. *"Un-American" Hollywood: Politics and Film in the Blacklist Era*. New Brunswick, NJ: Rutgers University Press.

Leff, Leonard 2008. "Becoming Clifton Webb: A Queer Star in Mid-Century Hollywood." *Cinema Journal: The Journal of the Society for Cinema and Media Studies*, 47(3), pp. 3–28.

Long Goodbye DVD 2002. "Rip Van Marlowe" in the "Special Features" section of *The Long Goodbye*DVD. MGM Home Entertainment, Inc.

Lott, Eric 1997. "The Whiteness of *Noir*," in *Whiteness: A Critical Reader*, edited by Mike Hill. New York: New York University Press, pp. 81–101.

Luhr, William (ed.) 1991. *The Maltese Falcon: John Huston, Director*. New Brunswick, NJ: Rutgers University Press.

McGilligan, Pat 1001. Interview with Daniel Mainwaring, quoted in *http://www.miskatonic.org/rara-avis/archives/200207/0078.html*, accessed September 6, 2011.

Murphet, Julian 1998. "Film Noir and the Racial Unconscious," *Screen*, 39(1), pp. 22–35.

Naremore, James 2008. *More Than Night: Film Noir in Its Contexts*, updated and expanded edition. Berkeley: University of California Press (first published 1998).

O'Brien, Jeffrey 2006. Review of the DVD collection of Val Lewton's films in *The New York Review of Books*, March 9, p. 32.

Palmer, R. Barton 1996. *Perspectives on Film Noir*. Boston: G.K. Hall & Company.

Pike, David L. 2007. *Metropolis on the Styx: The Underworlds of Modern Urban Culture, 1800–2001*. New York: Cornell University Press.

Place, Janey and Lowell Peterson 1998. "Some Visual Motifs of *Film Noir*," in *Film Noir Reader*, edited by Alain Silver and James Ursini. New York: Limelight Editions, pp. 65–75 (first published in *Film Comment*, January–February 1974).

Porfirio, Robert, Alain Silver, and James Ursini (eds) 2002. *Film Noir Reader 3: Interviews with Filmmakers of the Classic Noir Period*. New York: Limelight Editions.

Rockwell, Norman 1943. *Saturday Evening Post* cover, May 29.

Rogin, Michael 1987. *Ronald Reagan: The Movie and Other Episodes in Political Demonology*. Berkeley: University of California Press.

Schrader, Paul 1998. "Notes on *Film Noir*," in *Film Noir Reader*, edited by Alain Silver and James Ursini. New York: Limelight Editions, pp. 52–63 (first appearing in *Film Comment*, September 1972).

Selby, Spencer 1984. *Dark City: The Film Noir*. Jefferson, NC: McFarland.

Silver, Alain and James Ursini (eds) 1996. *Film Noir Reader*. New York: Limelight Editions.

Silver, Alain and James Ursini (eds) 1999. *Film Noir Reader 2*. New York: Limelight Editions.

Silver, Alain and James Ursini (eds) 2004. *Film Noir Reader 4: The Crucial Films and Themes*. New York: Limelight Editions.

Sobchack, Vivian 1998. "Lounge Time: Post-War Crises and the Chronotope of Film Noir," in *Refiguring American Film Genres: History and Theory*, edited by Nick Browne. Berkeley: University of California Press, pp. 129–70.

Stanley, Alessandra 2011. "On the Scent of Psychopaths: Penetrating the Criminal Mind." *New York Times*, February 16, pp. C1 and C5.

Straayer, Chris 2008. "Transgender Mirrors: Queering Sexual Difference," in *Screening Genders*, edited by Krin Gabbard and William Luhr. New Brunswick, NJ: Rutgers University Press, pp. 123–37.

Studlar, Gaylyn 1988. *In the Realm of Pleasure: Von Sternberg, Dietrich, and the Masochistic Aesthetic*. Urbana: University of Illinois Press.

Telotte, J.P. 1989. *Voices in the Dark: The Narrative Patterns of Film Noir*. Urbana: University of Illinois Press.

Time 1944. Review of *Double Indemnity* (unsigned). *Time*, July 10.

Wager, Jans B. 2005. *Dames in the Driver's Seat: Rereading Film Noir*. Austin: University of Texas Press.

Williams, Tony 1996. "*Phantom Lady*, Cornell Woolrich, and the Masochistic Aesthetic," in *Film Noir Reader*, edited by Alain Silver and James Ursini. New York: Limelight Editions, 1996, pp. 129–144 (first published in *cineACTION 13/14*, Summer 1986).

FURTHER READING

Alton, John 1995. *Painting with Light*. Berkeley: University of California Press.

Casper, Drew 2007, *Postwar Hollywood: 1946–1962*. Malden, Mass.: Blackwell Publishing.

Christopher, Nicholas 1997. *Somewhere in the Night: Film Noir and the American City*. New York: Free Press.

Gabbard, Krin and William Luhr (eds) 2008. *Screening Genders*. New Brunswick, NJ: Rutgers University Press.

Hirsch, Foster 1999. *Detours and Lost Highways: A Map of Neo-Noir*. New York: Limelight Editions.

Jameson, Richard T. 1974. "Son of Noir," *Film Comment*, 10, pp. 30–3.

Kammen, Michael 1991. *Mystic Chords of Memory: The Transformation of Tradition in American Culture*. New York: Knopf.

Lehman, Peter and William Luhr 2008. *Thinking about Movies: Watching, Questioning, Enjoying*, third edition. Malden, Mass.: Blackwell Publishing.

Lifton, Robert Jay 1999. *Destroying the World to Save It: Aum Shinrikyo, Apocalyptic Violence and the New Global Terrorism*. New York: Metropolitan Books.

Luhr, William 1991. *Raymond Chandler and Film*, second edition. Tallahassee: The Florida State University Press (first edition, New York: Frederick Ungar Publishing Company, 1982).

Film Noir, First Edition. William Luhr.

Luhr, William, 2004. "Adapting *Farewell, My Lovely*," in *A Companion to Literature and Film*, edited by Robert Stam and Alessandra Raegno. Oxford, UK and Malden, Mass.: Blackwell Publishing, pp. 278–97.

Luhr, William and Peter Lehman 2006. "*Experiment in Terror*: Dystopian Modernism, the Police Procedural, and the Space of Anxiety," in *Cinema and Modernity*, edited by Murray Pomerance. New Brunswick, NJ: Rutgers University Press, pp. 175–93.

May, Lary 2002. *The Big Tomorrow: Hollywood and the Politics of the American Way*. Chicago and London: University of Chicago Press.

Nevins, Francis M. 1988. *First You Dream, Then You Die*. New York: Mysterious Books.

Phillips, Gene D. 2000. *Creatures of Darkness; Raymond Chandler, Detective Fiction, and Film Noir*. Lexington: University Press of Kentucky.

Polan, Dana 1986. *Power and Paranoia: History, Narrative, and the American Cinema, 1940–1950*. New York: Columbia University Press.

Sharrett, Christopher (ed.) 1999. *Mythologies of Violence in Postmodern Media*. Detroit: Wayne State University Press.

Sklar, Robert 1992. *City Boys: Cagney, Bogart, Garfield*. Princeton: Princeton University Press.

Weiner, Tim 2008. "Remembering Brainwashing: Mind Games," *New York Times, Week in Review*, July 6, pp. 1 and 4.

Wills, Garry 1998. *John Wayne's America: The Politics of Celebrity*. New York: Simon and Schuster.

INDEX

Film Noir, First Edition. William Luhr.
© 2012 William Luhr. Published 2012 by Blackwell Publishing Ltd.

visual style (*continued*)
  use of color techniques, 46–7, 93,
    94–5, 120, 149, 162–3, 173, 176,
    204
voice-over narration, *see* narration
  strategies

Wager, Jans B., 60
war films, 33–4, 86, 90, 157, 169
water wars, 186–7
Watergate era, 154, 186
Wayne, John, 42, 90, 160, 172
Welles, Orson, 26, 41–2, 197
Westerns (films), 43, 52, 67, 71, 86,
  157, 160, 167, 169, 171–2
White Heat (1949), 19, 21, 128, 137,
  212
Who Framed Roger Rabbit? (1988), 186

Why We Fight (films) (1942–5), 5
Wilder, Billy, 9, 23–5
Williams, Tony, 60–1
Wizard of Oz, The (1939), 176
Woman in the Window, The (1944),
  179
women, portrayal of, 21, 30–2, 59–60,
  91, 97–8, 127–8
Woollacott, Janet, 65–6
Woolrich, Cornell, 60, 61
World War II, postwar anxieties, 22,
  32–5, 38, 70, 141–2

xenophobia, *see* exoticism; racism

Yankee Doodle Dandy (1942), 5

Zsigmond, Vilmos, 149, 162